W9-DHI-675

FIGHTING TO BECOME AMERICANS

Fighting

Jews, Gender,

to Become

and the Anxiety of Assimilation

Americans

Riv-Ellen Prell

Beacon Press

Boston

Beacon Press
25 Beacon Street
Boston, Massachusetts 02108-2892
www. beacon.org

Beacon Press books
are published under the auspices of the
Unitarian Universalist Association of Congregations

04 03 02 01 00 99   8 7 6 5 4 3 2 1

This book is printed on recycled acid-free paper that contains at least 20 percent
postconsumer waste and meets the uncoated paper ANSI/NISO specifications for
permanence as revised in 1992.

Text design by Wesley B. Tanner/Passim Editions

Library of Congress Cataloging-in-Publication Data

Prell, Riv-Ellen, 1947-
    Fighting to become Americans : Jews, gender, and the anxiety of assimilation
/ Riv-Ellen Prell.
        p. cm.
    Includes bibliographical references and index.
    ISBN 0-8070-3632-3 (cloth)
    1. Jews–United States–Social life and customs. 2. Jewish women–United
States–Social life and customs. 3. Jews–United States–Identity. 4. Jews–Cultural
assimilation–United States. 5. Sex role–United States. 6. Stereotype (Psychology).
7. United States–Ethnic relations.   I. Title.
E184.36.S65P74   1999
305.892'4073—dc21   98-37369

To Steven, with gratitude and love:
Together we explored this new land
and built a shelter for our lives

Contents

Introduction

For what we shall be interested in examining is how Jews see the dominant society seeing them and how they project their anxiety about this manner of being seen onto other Jews as a means of externalizing their own status anxiety.

Sander L. Gilman, *Jewish Self-Hatred: Anti-Semitism and the Hidden Language of the Jews*

Hotel Angst

In the spring of 1994 more than five hundred single Jewish men and women in their twenties and thirties overflowed two hotel meeting rooms that had been joined to accommodate them for a workshop entitled "Jewish Men and Women: Can We Talk?" The workshop was part of a large, national conference of "Young Leadership," a division of the philanthropic organization, the United Jewish Appeal. Members of the Young Leadership group are committed Jews—some who are primarily interested in community activism and others who combine those concerns with observing Jewish traditions and laws. Conference organizers were astounded by the turnout. They reported that they had never organized a workshop that was in such high demand. The organizational consultant who facilitated the event, Debbie Fried, had offered these workshops throughout the country, and found that the topic always drew large crowds.

On this occasion, as on others, she asked the men and women in attendance to draw on their own experiences in order to understand the conflicts between Jewish women and men. She told the participants to complete the following sentences by verbally filling in the blanks: "A Jewish man is . . . and a Jewish woman is. . . ." Men and women alternately offered brief stereotypical portraits of one another. The Jewish men present shouted out the following descriptions of Jewish women: "calculating, narrow minded, expected husbands to be as successful as their fathers, spoiled, high maintenance, challenging, never on time, not athletic except for aerobics, image-conscious, nagging, demanding and don't respect men." Jewish women, in turn, described Jewish men as "egocentric, materialistic, intimidated by successful women, driven, spoiled, wanting mothers more than companions, looking for perfection, fearing commitment more than death, and driven by power." A few women offered positive descriptions of Jewish men as well, including "good husbands, good lovers, and very loving."[1]

The participants reacted noisily upon hearing descriptions that each gender interpreted as unfair. Yet, when Fried asked how many of the people present wanted to marry someone Jewish, virtually all of them raised their hands. "Do we have a problem here?" she asked, teasing the audience with that question. "Can you really want to marry Jews," she suggested, "if you loathe Jewish women and men so thoroughly?" Fried's workshops were designed to explore this very loathing and why it attached to Jewish men's and women's feelings about one another.[2]

The participants in the workshop might have been surprised to learn that at the beginning of the twentieth century and for the following thirty years, when American Jews virtually never married non-Jews, the Jewish popular press, American Jewish fiction, music, and memoirs provided occasions for Jewish men and women, most often children of immigrants, to describe one another through images remarkably similar to those used in the 1990s. For example, in 1901 a columnist for the *Jewish Daily News* complained on behalf of his sex that Jewish women typically judged a man as "alright, if only he had the money."[3] In 1923, Nathan Zalowitz, writing for the *Jewish Daily Forward*, accused Jewish women of presuming that "nothing except the most expensive theater tickets are good enough" when men take them out.[4] Not surprisingly, the *Forward* ran articles with titles like "Is the Modern Girl a Mercenary?"[5]

Jewish women answered these accusations with several of their own. A letter written to the *Jewish Daily News* in 1899 described Jewish men as willing to marry only for money to advance their own careers. A woman writing to the Yiddish newspaper the *Day* in 1925 accused Jewish men of being "puffy" and treating a Jewish woman as though they were "conferring a favor" on her by their companionship and love. Another summarized Jewish men's arrogant insults to Jewish women, concluding her letter, "As a man creates his own God so does he create a woman in his own image."[6]

Young, single Jews of New York in the first decades of the twentieth century and contemporary young, single Jews throughout the United States are divided by what appears to be a gulf of time and space. Separated by four or five generations, these Jews are most likely members of different classes—the former the working class and the latter the middle, if not upper middle class. They live in the same nation, but the time periods during which they lived are characterized by radically different ideas about how Jews fit into United States culture. These two groups of Jews have different assumptions about family, women, intermarriage, and work. Nevertheless, the striking similarity of images that men and women of both periods use to describe each other suggests startling continuity within dramatic social and cultural change.

For both generations these images see-saw between the vulnerability of intimacy ("egocentric, fear of commitment, smothering, looking for mother, and nagging") and the experience of work and consumption ("calculating, demanding, spoiled, materialistic, driven, high maintenance"). They express fears about who is lovable and desirable as often as they reveal deep anxiety over the longing for success and its consequences. Throughout the century, women are continuously portrayed as wanting too much. The images of men link their self-preoccupation to a hunger for economic success. These stereotypes draw the economic world into the center of private life through attributions that are labeled "Jewish" and assigned to men or women.

Fighting to Become Americans is a book about how gender images have served as a powerful medium through which Jews expressed and reflected their relationship to America. To place these representations of demanding women and driven men under the microscope of cultural analysis brings two important aspects of American Jewish life into focus. First, throughout the century Jews have remained anxious about their place in a reluctantly pluralist nation. Second, gender has served to symbolize Jews' relationships to nation, family, and work because both Americanization and mobility place specific yet different demands on men and women. These expectations were critical to Jews' creation of gender identities that became powerful emblems of their Americanness. Changes in gender images throughout the century, however, tell us less about Jewish women and men than they do about Jewish acculturation. These images displace anxieties about cultural difference and economic mobility onto intimate ties not only between Jewish men and women, but also between Jews who share many other types of relationships (including family relationships) and between Jewish women of different classes.

These stereotypes are neither descriptions of "real" Jews, even if they draw on recognizable experiences, nor are they "accurate, if just slightly exaggerated descriptions." These cultural images are not straightforward depictions of everyday life any more than are rituals, games, or television situation comedies. The images' appeal lies in the very fact of their exaggerations, the larger-than-life quality that enables them to express something compelling about reality. Part of what makes them effective is that they simplify the complexity of real-life relationships, reducing them to single images that are nevertheless familiar. Postwar Jewish life, for example, has been contained in the comic image of an indulgent and demanding Jewish Mother, while the high cost and rewards of acculturation at the turn of the century were symbolized in literature and film as the noble but ineffectual Jewish father. However, these stereotypes are not neutral; as they constitute American Jewish identity at-a-glance, they create injury even when framed as humor.[7]

Studying these images, like any other cultural enterprise, allows us to step through a looking glass into a world not quite like the real one, but very much its product by inversion, distortion, and refraction. To study the image is to understand the desires and longings that created it.

Self-Reflections

I do not see these images from a distance. I do not come to this work disengaged, and I can hardly invoke mirrors, distorting ones in particular, without acknowledging that some of my feelings about what it means to be an American, a Jew, and a woman shape this book. I grew up during the 1950s and early 1960s, when most Jews lived in a fairly closely bounded world with one another at the same time that most yearned to be identical to the white middle class. There was a silence about our difference as Jews from the Protestant majority. We *appeared* to be like the majority. We were not "minorities." We were not barred from the suburbs, except for some "elite" developments. Lack of access to social clubs and exclusion from prestigious colleges remained a constant irritant, but opinion polls suggested that our white Christian neighbors did not dread living near us or marrying us to the degree they did African Americans. We worked to be part of an apparent sameness that by necessity made many of us hyper-conscious of our difference.

For me this lifelong struggle to understand what was different and what was not about being an American Jew became a scholarly pursuit. But it was in the experience of difference that I learned to understand the danger of the illusion of sameness. I felt an unspoken anxiety in my family. "We don't want a Jewish president," my father regularly asserted when I was a child. "Why?" I asked in astonishment. Because, he explained, "If things go wrong then the Jews are blamed." What did that mean? Was this some vague allusion to

"Hitler," the shorthand word of my childhood for what came to be called the Holocaust? Did it explain why some people were safe to know–Jews–and others were not–non-Jews? Our difference was not neutral. It was a source of pride, sometimes embarrassment, but above all an anxious uncertainty about anything beyond what we knew.

In my high school and college years, during the mid-1960s, there was nothing unspoken about the danger of a world that proclaimed that all of its citizens were the same, but differentiated brutally between those who were white and those who were not. The Civil Rights movement made me constantly aware of the privileges of appearing the "same" and the high cost of being a minority in the United States, the absence of opportunities and the loss of rights. I received an education in the illusion of sameness in the classes that taught about racism and Imperialism, in campus activism, and in the nightly news, broadcasting violence directed against the powerless whose difference was the rationale for attack.

But the illusion of sameness had an even more personal resonance. In the 1960s, as racial difference emerged as the source of social movements for liberation, others on the Left required the erasure of all vestiges of "parochial" difference. I understood that in my own life one of the best ways to achieve the neutrality required to become part of that world meant distancing myself from being a Jewish woman. Often ridiculed as excessive in every imaginable way by both Jews and non-Jews, "they" seemed particularly difficult to squeeze into the confines of neutrality.

My research on gender stereotypes demanded that I look into the eyes of Jewish women throughout the century. That gaze wrenched from me my own memories of Jewish women as large, noisy, and domineering, altogether too excessive for my 1960s adolescent sensibilities. I often felt most comfortable defining myself in opposition to them. If Jewish women wanted too much, then I didn't want— whether it was jewelry, clothing, or possessions. If Jewish women were controlling, prudish, overly intense, or nurturing, then I knew that I was a wholly other type of young woman. I tried to construct a self apart from what others—especially male friends, student leaders, and television comics—told me were the always detectable and unmistakably unattractive qualities of Jewish women. Neutrality looked good.

How was it really for Jewish women in Europe and in America? Were we really all like that for one or another good reason: fear for safety, or health, or the boredom of recent affluence combined with a history of poverty? For every piety about virtuous and modest European Jewish women, there are stories in my own family of my powerful, take-charge grandmother Riva that suggest quite the opposite. A pious woman, she lived and raised children for seven years alone in Rumania at the turn of the century while my grandfather earned enough money in Canada to bring the family to join him. She managed a family and money, and suffered the loneliness of separation as a highly competent woman.

Certainly the passage across the Atlantic brought many changes for Jewish women. Beginning in the late nineteenth century, affluent Jewish women modeled themselves on the "womanly" virtues of the American Protestant elite.[8] For middle-class American Jews, women became guardians of home and family, in contrast to East European Jewish women whose mastery of the practical encompassed but was not contained by home. Domesticity became the Jewish American woman's primary domain, and most Jewish women did whatever they could to place themselves and their families in that class. Yet, in my own Baby Boomer, suburban generation, being brainy, politically active, and un-domestic seems so familiar and quintessentially Jewish that I wonder what powerful and ambivalent messages both the fathers and mothers sent to their daughters. Suburban mothers were, after all, the daughters and granddaughters of immigrant women whom studies in the early years of the twentieth century described as "aggressive," concerned with working wages and conditions, eager to get an education, and to argue about literature, politics, and philosophy.[9] The suburban sameness of postwar American Jewish life could not erase Jewish women's cultural and familial memories of loss, oppression, power, and triumphant activism. I was not alone in finding the life of being a Jewish woman, with its dual legacy of success and power *and* domestic dependence, confusing.

It was only in the research for this book, diving into the debates and popular culture of the early decades of this century, that I found ways to understand much of that confusion. It dawned on me just a few months after the death of my mother, Mary Prell, as I read through English-language Jewish newspapers, novels, magazines, and a few sermons from early in the twentieth century that I was glimpsing the world of my mother's childhood. These articles defined what a young Jewish woman should aspire to be, a lady who was well-mannered and oriented toward creating domestic bliss. As the youngest daughter of Rumanian immigrants my mother absorbed those lessons. The gulf between the American world of movies, books, and school and her own childhood in the home of immigrant parents must have seemed immense. Her mother was large when ideal American women were slender, loud when she should have been quiet, an observant Jew who did not fit into the mainstream of American life because of the food she ate and the Sabbath she observed.

My mother's task growing up was to become simultaneously an American and a woman, and her mother could be of little help in either pursuit. Mary Prell was the child of an immigrant in the 1920s, when Americans found differences dangerous and womanhood explosive. Power was the last thing she needed; propriety and normality were her paths. She appeared to learn the lessons of Americanization all too well. Indeed, Mary never acknowledged any uncertainty about her role as moral arbiter of womanhood and all other family matters. In fact, it was her very hyper-certainty, constantly routing us on a collision course, that leads me to suspect her deeper anxiety about what she proclaimed was the right way, the best way, the only way to be a woman. I asserted difference from America through protest and critique; she embraced the sameness that she fought to secure through marriage and mobility.

I now understand that the daily battles with my mother through-out my adolescence–about who I could or could not be, and how to go about growing up–were in large measure a war between her vision of womanhood, which was shaped by the shame of being the daughter of immigrants, and mine, which was shaped by a search for a life unconstrained by those traditions. Yet in high school in West Los Angeles, particularly by my senior year in 1965, these family battles seemed much like the other ones raging around me. They were definitively unraveling the pretense that we Americans, let alone we students at Alexander Hamilton High School, were really all the same. What was happening around me was dispelling the illusion of what American society was about. Each year of my college education and activism was shaped by new ways of understanding the cruel injustices of intranational and global inequities, as well as radical redefinitions of gender and sexuality. Unwittingly, I was ripping away at the foundations of suburban Jewish life.

Those acknowledged differences, a decade in the making, finally gave me a vocabulary to understand what it meant to be a Jew–a granddaughter of poverty, shame, and discrimination, and a daughter of opportunity and privilege–who fought with her mother all the time because of the connections between these generations. Children's loathing for their Jewish parents and Jewish women's and Jewish men's loathing for one another are some of the legacies of Americanization. Jews could not Americanize and join the middle class without forswearing their difference from other Americans in that class. For Jews, this longing to belong was inseparable from escaping a European home that, decades before the Holocaust, had orphaned them through antisemitism.[10] My relatives, like most American Jews, negotiated and compromised. We would be Jews; we would maintain our difference, but not too much. The difference was private, under-ground, tied to occasional synagogue visits, and a little Jewish education, but all of it was kept to a minimum. What was most important was to be among Jews, to marry them, to live around them, to go to them as our doctors and accountants–to people our world with Jews just like us, who didn't want to be different. But then every difference between us, from those of gender and class to generational ones, served in larger-than-life terms as icons of danger. A vulgar Jewish woman could shame us all; a Jewish communist could bring down upon us the wrath of a nation. We watched one another carefully.

My interest in Jewish gender stereotypes is a product of my mother's longing to be a lady, and of mine to be freed from watching and being watched. It allows me to explain that what has for a century appeared to be the anguished conflict between Jewish women and men, and between generations of Jews, is in truth a story about how a dominant American culture has dealt with minorities. American Jews have prospered within that narrative of assimilation and have been damaged by it as well. My own life has been inscribed by that story, but it is the study of American Jewish history as a cultural process shaped by gender and Jews' ascent into the middle class that has allowed me to tell it.

Jewish Gender Stereotypes in Historical Context

The images that preoccupied my teens and twenties were not precisely the same as those of the men and women at the Young Leadership conference, just as ours were different from those of our parents. The distorted looking glass of these stereotypes reflects the images of other generations as well.

These gender stereotypes were nourished by Jewish social and economic processes. Because these conditions change, so do the images. Few Jews today would know what a "Ghetto Girl" is; but most are familiar with the "Jewish American Princess." Paradoxically, the freedom and economic possibilities afforded by America to the descendants of immigrants were the source of the stereotypes with which Jews mapped their anxieties about Americanization and mobility onto the terrain of one another's lives.

The consuming woman and the man who provides for his family became the symbiotic pair that brought one another endless grief.

They were subsequently joined in the 1930s and 1950s by images of demanding and suffocating mothers who enslaved their sons, and in the 1970s by princes and princesses who injured one another either by their impossible demands or their indifference. Immigrant Jews left behind in Europe a world of shared partnership in support of the family. American Jews inherited a world in which to be middle class required a man to produce at work and a woman to consume on behalf of the household that socially located her in the world.[11] This economic relationship remained the norm until the mid-1960s.[12] The desire for things—who was entitled to have and to give them—dominated these gender stereotypes, whether they characterized a pompous younger man in the 1920s, overdressed and in search of a fortune, a Ghetto Girl in 1905, whose gaudy dress and "Oriental" body caused middle-class Jews to cringe in humiliation at what non-Jewish Americans saw, or a Jewish American Princess in the 1980s who reached orgasm while holding her father's credit card.

Each of the chapters of *Fighting to Become Americans* examines a popular gender representation. Together, they trace the development from 1900 to the 1990s of a group of changing images of Jewish men and women. At the same time, the chapters reveal striking continuity in the shape of these gender stereotypes. Key themes of desire, consumption, and the "distorted" body persist over time, revealing Jews' relationship with one another within a dominant culture that made the American Jew the representation of excessive consumption and productivity, which were the central features of the consumer economy.

During the period when immigrants and particularly their children were struggling to climb out of a working-class niche, roughly from the late nineteenth century to the late 1920s, the stereotypes were focused on conflict over resources and controlling, autonomous women. As Jews settled into the middle class and their sons began to enter the professions, over a period lengthened by tragedies from the 1930s to the 1960s, the consuming family became the source of stereotypes of the Jewish Mother/Wife. This figure expressed the anxiety focused on the realignment of power relations within the family as women stayed at home and played greater roles in the synagogue and assured their children a middle-class upbringing. As Jewish opportunities for acculturation expanded and a wider range of occupations opened to both genders, from the late 1960s to the 1990s, the stereotypes reflected power struggles over the control of economic and emotional resources. These struggles coalesced in the image of the Jewish American Princess. The JAP embodied the punishment of middle-class success with her ceaseless demands and her unwillingness to yield sexually.

The stereotypes may be read chronologically, from anxieties over women's independence to their suffocating symbiosis, and they may be read as evidence of Jews' changing relationship to the United States. The early gender stereotypes expressed Jews' anxieties about their "hosts'" acceptance of foreign strangers who might never become Americans. The more recent stereotypes portray Jews less as polluting aliens than as expressions of society's preoccupation with the pleasures and dangers of excessive consumption that distinguish the middle class. In all cases these Jewish stereotypes clearly reflect attitudes of the non-Jewish world that construct the changing meaning of Jewishness.

To be sure, racist and sexist stereotypes have always been part of an American culture that since its founding negotiated hierarchic relationships between ethnic and cultural groups. Scholars of such stereotypes understand them most often to be projections onto the minority of the dominant group's fantasies about its own needs and desires. Laziness, sexual assertiveness, and the pursuit of pleasure, all qualities attributed to America's minorities, are best understood by examining those who make the stereotype rather than those who are stereotyped, and by dissecting relationships of power.[13]

The persistent wrathful images of Jewish women and men, by contrast, are held by intimates, many of whom have shared together the scorn of antisemitism. These intra-ethnic stereotypes still involve relations of power, but there are no clearly defined "others." Their shared Jewishness unites subject and object in ways not normally associated with the racial and ethnic slurs directed from a dominant group to a minority one.[14] While gender stereotypes abound in twentieth-century American life in an ongoing "battle between the sexes"–dizzy dames, distracted fathers, gold-digging women, and feckless lovers to name only a few–Jews regard their own gender stereotypes to be marked by their Jewishness, and not simply comments on generic struggles between American intimates.

The inescapable fact is that Jews, like other minorities, carry a double burden in that they represent to a dominant culture what it reviles, while they also attach those castigations to themselves along the divide of gender. As Americans looked upon Jews as marginal, obsessed with money, uncivil, and unworthy of citizenship, Jewish men and middle-class Jews projected those very accusations onto Jewish women and the working class. Similarly, as Jews negotiated the rapid and difficult move into the middle class and beyond, the burdens of that mobility were represented not in terms of the class, but rather as the demands or obsessions of a spouse and a mother. Undesirable qualities, whether they were "excessively American" or "excessively Jewish," were most often attributed to females. The stereotypes integrated the economic aspects of upward mobility and acculturation experienced by Jews with the ongoing attitudes of the dominant culture toward them. The relationship between Jews' growing access to the wider culture and the increasingly strident images of Jewish women suggest that Jews may well feel that the price of admission to America is a rejection of critical aspects of oneself as a Jew. Projected onto mothers, wives, lovers, and partners are the loathsome and unacceptable qualities of affluence constantly represented as Jewish rather than middle-class.[15]

Jewish gender stereotypes ultimately reveal that Jews displace their fear of being different and their tensions around joining and staying in the middle class onto one another–whether they will find love and what will be expected of them by those who love them.[16]

They are a version of what Sander L. Gilman explored in his study of Jewish self-hatred, "the outsiders' acceptance of the mirage of themselves generated by [the dominant culture]."[17] The fragmentation of identity that results from this acceptance produces the self-hatred. European Jews' identity, Gilman suggested, was created in relationship to the Christian society's casting them as "other." Jews who fled those categories projected them onto "undesirable" Jews from whom they sought distance.

Gilman, particularly because of his focus on Jews' writing about the stigma of Jewishness, is singularly drawn to the experiences of Jewish men in their relationship to a hostile dominant culture.[18] The splitting of identity that he describes, however, is far more powerfully articulated in stereotypes that rely on gender to express difference. The womanness of Jews and the Jewishness of women are the primary focus of these images, and consistently reflect the unacceptable qualities attributed to Jews by various Americans through images circulated among Jews. Therefore, gender stereotypes may be understood as complicating an understanding of "the" Jewish response to a hostile society, a response that reveals an internal differentiation within Jewishness itself. Jewish men and women respond to one another in terms of their differences from the larger culture.

Fighting to Become Americans undertakes to complicate that understanding by arguing that Jews' economic mobility required that they constantly reshape their gender and ethnic identities. Jewish men's and women's stereotypes of one another reveal the outline of those emerging changes throughout the century. The tightly woven patterns linking class, gender, and ethnicity demonstrate that American Jews projected onto one another what frightened them most as they found their way into the Promised Land.

Analyzing American Jewish Culture

Every promised land has its desert. The United States offered great expectations to the more than two million East European immigrant

Jews who arrived there between 1880 and 1924. The scholarship on American Jewish life has, however, focused more on the promise than on its mirages.[19] *Fighting to Become Americans* examines the changing images of Jewish men and women with the intent of integrating several scholarly conversations that retell the story of Jewish American experience in terms of the cultural anxieties that beset Jews as they became Americans. Those anxieties are most effectively illumined by understanding how ethnic groups are imaged and symbolized by both members and outsiders.

There are two trajectories in scholarship that historicizes ethnic representation: one studies the way ethnicity is experienced by the ethnic subject, the other studies the ways a minority is represented by the dominant culture. I examine the intersection of external and internal constructions of ethnicity and argue that gender is key to their connection, because it signifies a difference within sameness—a difference that is displaced from majority/minority onto man/woman, or more globally onto intimates.

Because "identity" and "ethnicity" are so often experienced as unchanging and essential elements of the self, the study of how they in fact do change has created an interesting set of new questions for anthropologists, sociologists, historians, and literary critics. They have sought to understand the processes by which groups "invent" their identities by building on collective memories and experiences.[20] Rather than perceiving an ethnic identity to be uniform and unchanging over time, these scholars believe that members of such groups are engaged in recreating their collective identities, drawing and re-drawing the boundaries of their community and self-definitions. Ethnics discard traditions and invent entirely new ones as expressions of their "timeless" cultures. These processes occur within specific conditions, principally in relationship to a dominant, hegemonic culture whose definitions of "insider" and "alien" affect and shape the practices of any ethnic group. While ethnic and racial groups face different issues and problems, neither type of identity is fixed, and both are politically and culturally constructed. Jews reflected these processes in their representations of one another.

In looking for evidence of "invention," scholars have often turned to rituals, pageants, symbols, and folklore to learn how groups, or factions within groups, literally stage the meanings of being an American Jew, German, or Italian. Contrasting the events of one time period with similar events of another can provide a clear sense of what issues and features in communal identity are prominent and why.[21]

Gender stereotypes, despite their ephemeral qualities, provide cultural expressions of Jewish identity not unlike those provided by rituals or festivals. Stereotypes, too, represent a common ground on which the dominant culture meets expressions of Jewish uniqueness. Their ubiquity in the popular press and culture make them sensitive to the emerging ways Jews frame the meaning of being American and reflect Jews' own shaping of an American Jewish culture. These gender representations are a potent example of the complexity of an ongoing invention of American Jewish ethnicity.

If Jews' self-representations are an important clue to understanding their creation of an American Jewish culture, equally important to understanding the context of that culture is an examination of the ways Jews have been represented by the majority society. Recent scholarship in the developing field of Jewish cultural studies examines cultural materials such as medical textbooks, political cartoons, and philosophical treatises and novels to learn how Jewishness has been constructed in Europe and the United States. Some scholars argue that these images of "the Jew" are integral to the antisemitic ideologies of nationalist cultures and movements.[22] These stereotypes, not surprisingly, have often focused specifically on the gender, body parts, speech, and the "character" of Jews, using concrete images to express the alien nature of Jewishness itself. Such representations offer a powerful perspective on the relationship between a dominant culture and a minority one even within an official policy of liberal tolerance. The extreme specificity of these images reveals the intensity of the stigma attached to an "outsider" group.

Stereotypes are powerful but potentially limiting sources for analysis. They favor the fixed and the visual. A wide variety of behaviors and images can be reduced to a small number of stereotypes that might be cast as eternally true. My intention here is quite the opposite. Even though the images I discuss often share similar attributes, it is impossible to understand their meaning ahistorically. These gender stereotypes are powerful because they are sensitive to cultural and historical changes and because they develop within contexts. Nor are the stereotypes only visual. The Jewish women and men who needed only a few minutes to catalogue nearly fifty stereotypes of each other in the Young Jewish Leadership meeting demonstrated that these images are also a verbal language that is anything but static. In sum, Jewish gender stereotypes are forms of speech and visual images that are actively used and modified by Jews because they are a medium through which Jews constitute and reflect on their lives.[23]

Mapping Gender

These two bodies of cultural studies scholarship—studies of ethnic "invention" and minority "representation"—both examine the historical construction of Jewish identity, one from the outside looking in and one from the inside looking out. Jews may be understood through their changing constructions of themselves or through the ways they are seen by others. But each approach assumes in its analysis a unified Jewish identity. Much of the research on antisemitic constructions of Jewishness, for example, focuses almost exclusively on the Jewish male and on the notion that inadequate masculinity is crucial to an understanding of the Jew in the nation.[24]

The insight that ethnicity changes in relationship to class and occupational mobility, as well as to attitudes and prejudices of a dominant culture, does not, however, address the fact that ethnic groups are also internally divided. They may be differentiated from one another along a fracture as concrete as language, with some members judging others as inferior because of language differences. Groups are also divided by more complex matters such as gender and class, which again can create a hierarchy within the group. The study of all minorities—racial or ethnic—is consistently marked by the difficulty of addressing the differences within the minority, especially gender differences. Unless a study is explicitly feminist or focused on gender or sexuality, racial and ethnic minorities tend to be viewed as single groups in contrast to a dominant culture.. How differences between women and men within a given culture play out in their relationship to the larger society is rarely a matter of discussion.[25]

The study of intra-ethnic differences mirrors the same problems found in the scholarship on Americanization and immigration. With the exception of a few feminists, scholars in these fields have either ignored gender differences or assumed that the male path of assimilation was fully explanatory. The difficulty of grasping internal differentiation within groups that were already distinguished from a dominant culture has limited the analysis of acculturation.[26]

Jewish gender stereotypes are a set of cultural images that are produced precisely at the meeting point of internal and external constructions of Jewishness, and thus they address the problem of how to integrate studies of ethnic groups from within and without. Intercultural stereotypes shape intracultural ones. They are a window on American Jewish experience that is remarkably transparent because of their distortions. The stereotypes reveal the tensions and anxieties that other cultural statements conceal, precisely because they are not simple reflections of dominant cultural attitudes. Especially in the first decades of the twentieth century, these images reflect a wrestling with the process of Americanization by Jews that has often been overlooked in favor of attention to the generational dynamic. The richness of these representations lies in their capacity to combine perspectives even as they simplify reality.[27]

The gender stereotypes held by Jews themselves are particularly powerful, because gender remains one of the most persistent sources of internal differentiation in American Jewish culture. Most other intra-ethnic stereotypes that Jews held had disappeared by the 1960s.

Regional, class, and linguistic differences that so often defined groups of Jews in relationship to one another were assimilated through the "internal melting pot" that all minority groups have experienced in the United States.[28] Religious differences persist among Jews, and with a small religious revival that emerged in the 1980s may even be said to be increasing. However, the number of Jews involved in religious sectarian battles is in fact fairly small given that the majority of American Jews are not members of any synagogue. Jewish gender stereotypes, however, persist. They have changed in response to other aspects of acculturation—upward mobility, education, residential integration—and with a decline in antisemitism. Yet, their continuity in the form of male–female hostility suggests that in the United States gender relationships are affected by Jews' experience as a minority within a dominant culture.

Many of the associations of gender—family, romance, sexuality, desire, and marriage—have become linked to Jews' relationship to America. Tensions between minority men and women, at least symbolically, represent how each gender understands his or her place in the larger society. For Jews, like many other minorities, that relationship is complex and dynamic, simultaneously involving a profound desire to assimilate, to separate oneself from minorities who cannot assimilate, and to maintain the integrity of one's own group. Jewish men and women frequently represent one another with ethnic, gender, and national identities that position one in opposition to the other.

When an American Jewish man asserts that a Jewish woman is "too parochial," "too Jewish," and "less attractive" compared to non-Jewish women, he asserts a myriad of relationships among himself, his own people, and the larger society. Gender images point the way to understanding a whole series of tensions between the minority and dominant culture that are internalized by members of the minority. When an American Jewish man claims that Jewish women are "too demanding," he suggests that being a Jew is rooted in the experience of the economy and the culture, and that gender is a dimension of both. Recognizing the complexity of internal divisions within a group reveals a more subtle picture of the process of acculturation in the larger society. One is not simply in or out of a group, assimilated or merely acculturated. Rather, relations between members of the minority group continue to mirror relations between the minority and majority groups.

Fighting to Become Americans is about the experience of American Jews in the twentieth century. But its framing within scholarly conversations about ethnicity, gender, and class suggests that the myriad ways minorities represent themselves, particularly within their own groups, may well provide a different perspective on acculturation. However these groups march toward, or are barred from, a place at America's table, their stories about and images of one another bear the imprint of that journey. That imprint takes shape within relations between men and women, who are at once separated by their genders and joined by their group's differences from others. What cultural symbol could more perfectly reflect the experience of a minority connected to, but distinct from, a larger society than the images of men and women and other intimates in relationship to one another? When connection within a group bears the sharp edges and scars of a relationship to the larger society, then intimate relations within the minority group are potentially affected and even damaged. Relations of love, sexuality, and attraction are held hostage to the dominant culture. In the twentieth century, Jews became Americans through their use of stereotypes of one another as men and women and intimates as surely as they did through work, education, and the transformation of Judaism, because acts of differentiation were acts of Americanization.

CHAPTER ONE

Ghetto Girls and Jewish Immigrant Desire

Women, women want! Please, please want—
begin to want!

A turn-of-the-century New York
street vendor's cry

Each Sunday throughout most of the 1920s a page of young women's photographs appeared in the socialist working-class newspaper the *Jewish Daily Forward*.[1] "Portrait Studies of Jewish Women" featured black-and-white photographs that had been sent to the *Forward* by the young women's friends. The women's portraits appeared in the paper's weekly art section, which regularly included "Masterpieces by Renowned Artists" and photographs of "types" and "scenes" from life in Jewish communities throughout the world.

The "Portrait Studies of Jewish Women" in the *Forward*'s Sunday section stood as a monument to the success of the daughters of immigrants—young, unmarried Jewish women from throughout the United States—although occasionally photographs appeared from Berlin, Warsaw, and other European capitals. Each portrait is posed, stylish, and on occasion even mildly daring. In 1925, for example, Ray Staroselsky of Philadelphia smiled broadly at the camera, her lips darkened by lipstick. Her long strand of pearls fell over her bare shoulders, meeting a flower at the top of her dress. A single soaped curl rested on the center of her forehead above thick, dark eyebrows. She smiled broadly. Ruth Dienstag of New York posed for a New York photographer with Sylvia Schaefer of Texas, who was probably on a visit. Both of them had wavy short hair; one wore a double strand of pearls. They looked youthful and American. Their photos appeared next to "A Jewish Girl from Rosistz, Vohlin." This European Jewish woman stared out with deep-set eyes, had dark, thick long hair, and

"Portrait Studies of Jewish Women."
Jewish Daily Forward, October 11, 1925 (courtesy of The Forward Association, Inc.)

wore a dress that exposed none of her shoulders or neck.[2] By the end of the 1920s the portraits appeared less frequently, and the women in them were affluent enough occasionally to wear a fur.

With these photographs, the *Forward* proclaimed that young Jewish womanhood—modern, American, and desirable—was worthy of display for others to see. The subjects were "our girls," as the Jewish press proudly proclaimed, not the rich uptown Jews or American Gentiles, but the Yiddish-speaking women often called East Side girls, or by their English-speaking critics, "Ghetto Girls." They were young, unmarried working women, identified only by their name and often their city. They emulated movie stars and debutantes. They posed and paid for photographs and anticipated a good future.

Outside of the photographers' studios these young women worked in factories and stores; by the 1920s perhaps some had advanced to work as stenographers, department store saleswomen, or less often teachers. They were wage earners who supported families and sent money to the Old World to bring relatives to the New World. Many sought education; virtually all longed for marriage. They were cultural pioneers, exploring the terrain of a new urban American life with immigrant parents who could provide few tools for mapping this world. They translated their ambitions in their attention to the styles that they emulated in their photographs. These young women were, for example, often conduits for bringing working women's trend-setting styles to urban, immigrant ghettos. In an anonymous article, "The Autobiography of a Shop Girl," a Gentile described an evening spent with a Jewish friend from work on New York's East Side. Of her friend she wrote, "A shop girl is always sweller in her dress, no matter how poor she may be, than her relatives."[3] She described another friend, Bessie, as "the queen–for she was a saleslady! She gave tone to everything. She dictated fashion to the whole tenement house and everybody in it imitated her and envied her."

An Anxious Image

Journalists reporting on the exotica of the Lower East Side traded in images. The young working women of the ghettos of Chicago, Philadelphia, Boston, and especially New York served as the source of one such image–the Ghetto Girl, who was garish, excessively made up, too interested in her appearance, and too uncultivated to dress smartly. Her vulgarity embarrassed other Jews.[4] Those who disapproved of her created the Jewish gender stereotype of the Ghetto Girl. The young women who lived in urban Jewish ghettos were not the Ghetto Girls–a powerful cultural representation of anxiety engen-

dered by East European Jews, the working class in general, and
women workers in particular. There was no equivalence between the
woman of the ghetto and the Ghetto Girl. She was the nightmare of
excessive Americanization and desire projected by professionals and
middle-class Jews onto young working-class Jewish women.

Neither their male contemporaries, nor the German Jewish young
men and women who came more than a half-century before them,
offered such a powerful and complex image of immigrant American
Jewish life. The "Ghetto Girl," in journalism, philanthropy, social
work, and drama, to mention only a few of the settings where this image was circulated, was a lightning rod for the sentiments and anxieties that beset those undertaking Americanization.

The Ghetto Girl emerged as a hyperbolic stereotype in a milieu created by the mass East European immigration between 1880 and 1924.[5]
About two-and-a half million Jews, largely from the Russian empire,
joined Southern and other East European peoples in a migration that
reshaped the United States. East European Jews followed by several
decades the emigration of 250,000 German Jews, many of whom had
prospered and successfully acculturated in the United States by the
1880s, when the East European exodus began.[6] When large numbers
of East European Jews arrived, all Jews became increasingly stigmatized as "outsiders" and "aliens." American anti-Jewish sentiments no
longer distinguished between German Jews' carefully cultivated status, and "Russian" Jews' lack of it.[7] By 1900, German Jews were de-
spondent over the erection of an ever-increasing number of social barriers that excluded them from their formerly relatively free access to
American life. In an environment of increased discrimination and
multiplying stereotypes whose racism erased intra-Jewish differences, the Ghetto Girl image emerged and crossed over between Jews
and Jews, and Jews and non-Jews.

"Our girls" were transformed into Ghetto Girls when American
Jews felt vulnerable to the condemnation of Americans. Because they
were not in one or another instance Christian, or middle-class, or
well-mannered, their differences made them outsiders, and in turn

they projected those feelings onto the style and dreams of young Jewish working women. All those threatened by the image of the Ghetto Girl were concerned about being barred in one or another form from the nation because they were Jews.

The stereotype followed the course of mass immigration, becoming more common in the 1910s and disappearing by the mid-1920s. As Jewish women left the working class, as Jews changed residences and occupations, and as immigration laws virtually halted the arrival of new East European Jews, the shape of Jewish difference no longer resembled a vulgar working-class woman.

The stereotype was especially complex because so many different classes and communities of Jews and non-Jews expressed a relationship to America through it. Ghetto Girl, for example, implied someone and something entirely different to urban professionals, wealthy Jews, the members of the middle class who had more recently left behind America's urban Jewish ghettos, and to the readers of the *Forward* and other Yiddish newspapers. To Progressive reformers and middle-class Jews who most ardently responded to the stereotype, she embodied vulgarity and unregulated desire. To journalists and readers of the Yiddish press, when she was represented as Ghetto Girl rather than neighbor or relative, she withheld wages from those who needed her because of her love of fashion. What she wore and wanted was the concern, differently articulated, by all those who worried about her.[8] Few of her detractors read the *Forward*. It is impossible to know how they would have regarded the early 1920s portrait gallery's photographs of women intent on being stylish Americans. Would they have seen young beauties, garish imitators, or women driven by a desire for luxuries?

At least one observer of the ghetto, the non-Jewish journalist Hutchins Hapgood, reported no Ghetto Girls in his magazine sketches of ghetto life gathered into a 1902 volume, *The Spirit of the Ghetto*. Like other writers of his time, he too was interested in typologies of Jews, but he had a more complex understanding of the Jews he observed. He was particularly interested in Jewish women. He described the Old World Orthodox wife as "drab and plain in appearance." He noted other types of Jewish women as well. He was particularly impressed by the intensity and intelligence of Russian immigrant Jewish women and their commitment to equality and socialism. Although he noted the "rakish American hat" and "the piquant manner and dress of a Jewess who is beginning to ape American ways," he was not blind to their other qualities. And the excesses that so troubled so many Jews who found nightmarish Jewish women in the ghetto were clearly invisible to Hapgood.[9]

The Ghetto Girl stereotype, as Progressives and particularly middle-class and affluent Jews used the name, is worth investigating, to learn why this specific group of women was so disturbing to other women and men, most often their fellow Jews in the early twentieth century. One cannot overlook, either, the fact that Jewish men who lived in and wrote for the newspapers of the Jewish working class also used a version of the Ghetto Girl stereotype to express their anxiety about their own access to American society.

The vulgar image of the Ghetto Girl was in an accusing mirror that distorted and reflected those who saw "her." Like the fairy tale's bitter queen whose magic mirror told her again and again that someone else was more beautiful, the image of a "vulgar" Jewish woman reminded established Jews that they might forever be found wanting by America's dominant Protestant majority. If any Jew's life whispered vulgarity, excess, or the open pursuit of pleasure, many Jews worried that their non-Jewish neighbors might more aggressively enforce their boundaries between insiders and outsiders. Their success notwithstanding, Jews in this period had reason to believe they would never find a place as insiders in the institutions of privilege dominated by native-born, Protestant Americans. To most writers of the period, immigrants' "race" was carried in the blood and virtually precluded acculturation. "No injection of Americanism will get it out of their system," wrote Peter Roberts in 1920 as he argued that lacking their own nations, Jews and Poles were condemned to a racial solidarity that made them unfit for citizenship.[10]

Jews confronted a far more virulent antisemitism during the period of mass immigration than had previously existed in the United States. German Jews who had prospered and had epitomized cultivated American life found themselves despised and excluded as Jews by former Christian allies in business, philanthropy, and social clubs.

In the late nineteenth and early twentieth centuries, Jewish Americans' anxieties about one another echoed the various accusations of those who sought to restrict immigration from Eastern Europe and to impose barriers on Jews' access to the nation's institutions.[11] A variety of politicians portrayed Jews as the architects of industrialization and finance capitalism, often painting them as greedy opponents of farmers and working men on the one hand, and a threat to the American aristocracy and its "natural right" to leadership, on the other. Every accusation and restriction cast Jewish Americans, whose avarice was visible to the astute observer of Jewish mannerisms and appearances, as polluters of a pristine nation.[12] As German Jews became more visible in the American economy, whether as peddlers or as bankers, slurs and caricatures of Jewish male avarice multiplied.[13]

In the nineteenth century, the Immigration Restriction League sought to close the nation to the "new immigrants" from Southern and Eastern Europe as well as Asia. One of the League's spokesmen, Edward Ross, a pioneer of American sociology, argued that East European "Hebrews" were aggressive, "slippery," and never involved in "basic production," emphasizing their ability to own and display without work. The League succeeded in 1896 in passing through both houses of Congress restrictive legislation that kept illiterates from immigrating. The law was designed to close the United States to Southern and East Europeans, many of whom could not read or write, and Jews who read and wrote Hebrew and Yiddish rather than the language of their country of origin. President Grover Cleveland vetoed the law.[14]

In the 1880s, when East European immigration increased rapidly, American entrepreneurs began to court patrician, old stock Americans and to separate themselves from German Jews. To cement this alliance they established a set of institutions that came to symbolize the American elite—clubs, preparatory schools, resorts, country clubs, and fraternities. Jews were systematically excluded from all of these elite institutions, even ones that they had initially helped to create, such as the Union League in New York City.

This elite formation depended on an ideology of Anglo-Saxon supremacy that was as evident in social club admissions as it was in immigration policies. Affluent Jews saw in the Ghetto Girls' flamboyant styles their deepest anxiety that all Jews lacked refinement. They didn't belong.[15] This antisemitism intensified conflicts between Jews. Not only did middle-class Jews see in their poor and working-class counterparts liabilities to acculturation, Jewish men often accused Jewish women of vulgarity, a term with which the patrician class branded them. One group of Jews' effort to embrace and then hold dear the propriety of bourgeois life was undermined by another group. "Jew" became a frightening phantom that could haunt those Jewish men and women who aspired to or felt well rooted in America's tolerant and liberal middle class. At the turn of the century, German Jewish participants in the Jewish Women's Congress held in Chicago reflected on their relationship to East European Jewish newcomers. In their zeal to aid their "less fortunate sisters" they described the Russian Jew as a "pariah in the midst of his confreres," and "our semi-barbaric Russian immigrants, not susceptible to the keen edge of the civilizers' art."[16]

The Jewish cartoonist Foshko, whose work appeared in the Yiddish *Day*, was interviewed for a 1918 article on Ghetto Girls. He explained that their extravagance in dress was caused by lack of time for shopping and the styles manufacturers created to attract their attention. "Such styles that by their glaring patterns they know will appeal to a taste that is not educated—much in the same way as traders dangle bright beads before the eyes of savages."[17] The article described Foshko, in contrast to other "students" of the East Side, as a person who "feels for the East-side rather than studies it." His feelings nevertheless left him anxious enough to compare young working women to "savages."

Herman J. Mankiewicz expressed this mind-set in 1918 when he reflected on his college experience at Columbia University during the 1910s. He dismissed the charge that college life was antisemitic by explaining that "Jewish" qualities were undesirable in anyone. "We Jews know that to be loud-mouthed, to be aggressive, to be without manners, to be greedy, to be selfish and to be avaricious are not Jewish traits, but we do know that there are many Jews who display these traits . . . and if we are fair-minded we cannot and do not object to the Gentile who is loath to associate with the Jewish owner of them."[18]

Like the Jew at college, the Ghetto Girl symbolized the unattractive opposite of a bourgeois (in this case) woman, who had long served as the model of Jewish integration for urban Jews in Europe and the United States.[19] By contrast, the Ghetto Girl's taste was far too conspicuous; she was betrayed by the cheapness of what she had and wore. She was loud in public and immodest. Her wages financed her own excess, making her autonomous and out of the control of the family. The Ghetto Girl stereotype integrated Jews' anxieties about their differences from Americans with Americans' fears of invasion by non–Anglo-Saxons who violated America's cultural purity.

As dangerous as she was to another class, within their own class young Jewish women were made to represent the illegitimacy of wanting things as well. The very gender dynamic that Jews embraced in order to Americanize suggested that women's desires would be supported by the economic productivity of a husband. Jewish men, therefore, saw in the Ghetto Girl the dangers of "excessive" consumption that would require their own economic efforts. Wanting and having were matters of consequence for men and women as Jews and as participants in the American economy.

The Ghetto Girl came to life as the face of an American Jewish culture changed. The Jewish working class sought mobility and Americanization. That process occurred as the meaning of being an American, and even a legitimate American immigrant, were debated and contested. Jews who had arrived in the nineteenth century and who had been confident about their place in the nation found themselves at its margin. Marginal immigrants, in turn, were fighting their way into an economy that would allow them to have what other Americans had, even as their own status as citizens was put in question.

This volatile mix found expression in the body of the young Jewish woman whose style, appearance, and desires became an alternative stage on which Jews and Christian Americans anxiously debated what it meant to be an American and a Jew. In the period of American Jewish experience often called the "Age of Optimism," because of expanding economic opportunities and the development of an organizational life, this Jewish gender stereotype revealed the extent and complexity of Jewish anxiety as they Americanized.[20]

The Bourgeois Response–Containing Jewish Desire

In 1900, a *New York Tribune* journalist, interested in new immigrants, compared Jewish women on the Lower East Side to those who lived in fashionable upper Manhattan.

> Does Broadway (upper New York) wear a feather? Grand Street (lower East-side) dons two, without loss of time. Are trailing skirts seen in Fifth-ave.? Grand-st. trails its yards with a dignity all its own. Are daring color effects sent over from Paris? The rainbow hides its diminished head before Grand-st. on a Sunday afternoon.
>
> If my lady wears a velvet gown, put together for her in an East Side sweat shop, may not the girl whose tired fingers fashioned it rejoice her soul by astonishing Grand-st. with a copy of it on the next Sunday? My lady's is in velvet, and the East Side girl's is in the cheapest of cloth, but it's the style that counts![21]

By turns sympathetic and ironic, the journalist suggested that East Side young Jewish seamstresses were doomed in their efforts to imitate the wealthy. The pattern failed to provide the good taste. They

The illustration for the article "The Modern Ghetto Girl" suggests that there was no acceptable image of a young immigrant Jewish woman. The Ameri-can Jewish News *published instead a picture of an idealized "Palestine" young woman in their issue dated March 22, 1918.*

substituted excess for style, the inexpensive for the elegant, and hence failed in their pretense.

A journalist for the English-language Jewish press approached the young female perpetrator of excess differently. Unlike the detached, ironic tone of the American writer, she expressed "shame."

> I do not know whether a hardened New Yorker will notice it, but plant a stranger from out-of-town on Avenue A, One Hundred and Sixteenth street to Pitkin avenue, on a Friday and Saturday night, and if he is of a sensitive turn of mind he will be

first astonished and then disgusted at the appearance of the
girls who pass by. If he is a Jew he will also be angered and
hurt, for the girls he sees are all of his own race. It is lovely to
dress in fashion, charming to wear your hair in a graceful little
dip; and a touch of powder and a little familiarity with rouge-
stick does bring out nicely that atmosphere of elegance and co-
quetry so dear to the hearts of girls and so enticing to the minds
of men; but the fashionable dress of the East-side girls shrieks
its cheapness and mimicry of the real thing. . . . Her exaggerated coiffure, with its imitation curls and soaped curves that
stick out at the side of the head like fantastic gargoyles, is an offense to the eye. Her plated gold jewelry with paste stones,
bought from the Grand Street peddlers on pay-day reveals its
cheapness by its very extravagance.

What is the matter with this girl? Is this bad taste acquired?
Is it inherent in her character? Or is it simply a transient mood
of the immigrant? Or perhaps is the East-side girl quite normal
in taste and all this talk just prejudice? These questions I have
heard wrangled and argued so often.[22]

Marion Golde suggested that a Jew's pain was not shared by others who were confronted with a Ghetto or East Side girl. Whether her
taste was the product of an "inherent" weakness, or a stage in Americanization, Jews' "racial" kinship made the Ghetto Girl a problem for
the entire group. The Ghetto Girl failed as an American woman who
should be coquettish but not excessive, and fashionable without being garish. She failed as a Jew because her exaggeration brought pain
to her "race."[23]

Bourgeois Yiddish writers and journalists remarked upon the
styles and excesses of Jewish women as well, advocating for the need
for good taste and restraint for Jewish immigrants. Tashrak, the pen
name of Israel Zevin, a journalist, humorist, and the author of a popular etiquette book for Yiddish-speaking immigrants, also wrote
about women's dress: "It is actually among the poorer classes that
women blindly follow the dictates of fashion. . . . It is awful what poor
taste most Jewish girls have. Consider the garish colors you can see
on a Saturday or a holiday on Jewish streets. If fashion decrees that

women should wear red (this season), does it follow that a woman with red hair and freckles must dress in a color that makes her look like a scarecrow?"[24] Tashrak did not recoil with shame and horror or call upon his race to deal with the problem of fashion. But he singled out young Jewish women for being unable to discern the difference between good taste and fashion in order to embrace the former and ignore the latter.

Not surprisingly, even rabbis commented on the subject. For example, Rabbi Israel Levinthal of Petach Tikvah synagogue in Brooklyn, New York, delivered to his newly middle-class congregants in 1916 a sermon that he titled "Style." He told the story of Dina, Jacob's daughter, who was raped by a prince of the Hivvite people where Jacob's family was visiting (Gen 33: 18–20). Rabbi Levinthal told them that "great Jewish sages" had already noted that Dina's misfortune came "because she went out to copy the fashions of the daughters of the land." He went on to exhort his congregants that "it was style, the fashion that reigned among the daughters of the land that fascinated her. What more needed lesson for our daughters, for our women of to-day. If I had the power I would have read aloud in every Jewish home the portion of the Torah which contains our text and have them placed before every mother's eyes!"[25] The rabbi's biblical text underlined the dangerous path awaiting women interested in style.

Few articles or comments about Ghetto Girls were written simply as colorful descriptions of the new immigrants. In the reformist mood of the time, they normally carried a moral, if not solutions to the "problem." Social workers and settlement house professionals often evoked this image in their work. Lillian Wald, longtime director of New York's Henry Street Settlement House, reflected in her memoirs how she handled the excesses of the Ghetto Girl in the century's first decades. The settlement house movement provided many services, particularly for the children of immigrants. None compared to the process of Americanization to which Wald was devoted. She told "Bessie's story" in order to illustrate her methods for dealing with the troublesome habits of immigrant women. Wald invited Bessie to the "cozy intimacy of my sitting room." She wrote that the young woman immediately guessed that the summons was "on account of my yellow waist" (the shirtwaist was a popular style of blouse produced by garment workers, many of whom were young Jewish women). Wald continued, "It was easy to follow up her introduction by pointing out that pronounced lack of modesty in dressing was one of several signs; that their dancing, their talk, their freedom of manner all combined to render them conspicuous and to cause their friends anxiety."[26]

Wald believed that Bessie could conform to the vision of American womanhood she advocated—modesty, simplicity, and circumspect behavior—only by abandoning the garish waist. When Bessie protested that she couldn't simply throw away an item of clothing that she had recently purchased, Wald offered to buy the waist for what was at the time a large sum, the five dollars that Bessie paid. Wald reported that her offer to buy the waist and burn it because Bessie's dignity was worth more than five dollars was illuminating. Bessie responded to Wald's offer saying, 'That strikes me as something grand. I wouldn't let you do it, but I'll never wear the waist again."[27]

Wald taught new values to immigrants by showing the Bessies of the Lower East Side just how highly she valued good taste.[28] Young women's display of bright and "vulgar" clothes signaled to the middle class and to professional enforcers of middle-class values (social workers and teachers) that their most important lessons went unheeded. Hard work, thrift, and moderation were key to becoming good Americans. Curbing young women's desires was one of the most important foundations for this transformation.[29] In order to be accepted, Jews needed to be better, and Jewish women needed to be more exemplary than other women as they pursued an American life.[30]

Lillian Wald's memoir is indirect about the gravest danger facing Bessie. Social service workers of the period were more anxious about unmarried women's sexual activity than virtually any other vulnerability they faced. An article on Jewish immigrant girls in Chicago by

Viola Paradise, a social worker, writing in 1913 for *Survey*, the first professional social workers' journal, was one of the few that linked immigrant women's consumer and sexual desires to one another overtly. Paradise analyzed the Jewish woman's desire to "look stylish": The danger comes later when the girl realizes that she will never be able to afford as many and as nice clothes as she wants. Then she is in danger of taking a wrong way to get the luxuries which America has taught her to crave."[31] Paradise was concerned that the Ghetto Girl would turn "the wrong way"–toward prostitution–to support her taste for extravagance.[32] Many Progressives believed that "white slavery" or white women's prostitution preyed disproportionately on Jewish women.[33] The middle class was required to guard them vigilantly by monitoring their clothing, behavior, and associations.

The Clara De Hirsch home for working girls, for example, was a late nineteenth-century boarding house and vocational school founded by members of New York's German Jewish elite who worked to socialize their East European young women charges with the middle-class values they espoused. They assiduously tried, and failed, to train these young women for domestic service. Factory work, they feared, would put young women in a mixed-sex environment that might lead them to sexual activity so closely tied to the leisure and pleasures associated with the growing working class of unmarried young men and women.[34]

Reformers' fear of women's prostitution, rather than sexual pleasure, reflected their sense of the dangerous attraction of the trappings of Americanization. Immigrants' experience of America was, at least in part, powerfully tied to the consumer economy and the availability of an unprecedented number of attractive and novel items. In their minds the erotic appeared to serve the wish to consume rather than the other way around.[35] Desire may have put immigrant women at risk, but at the same time it made them Americans. Social workers like Paradise and Wald, and philanthropists like the founders of residences for immigrant women, confronted the problem by attacking desire, which they represented as the tragic flaw of the young Jewish woman. However they may have criticized the corrupt institutions of American life, these reformers never abandoned their conviction that the greatest threat to a young woman's virtue and ability to Americanize was her own desire to consume.

The Jewish Working-Class Response: Holding Tight

Ghetto Girls were not only condemned by Americans and the Jewish bourgeoisie. The *Jewish Daily Forward*, which had so eagerly announced through its portrait gallery the existence of attractive young Jewish women, used its English pages to restrain them. These journalists did not recoil in shame as they commented on the problems of Ghetto Girls. The Yiddish socialist press, rather than engaging in a class war, offered its own version of gender warfare.[36] What troubled male writers was, to use a popular phrase of the day, "what women wanted." Where the Jewish middle class saw vulgarity and acquisitiveness, Jewish working men saw dangerous and excessive desires.

The *Jewish Daily Forward*, for example, frequently dissected young women's pleasures and characterized "their" East Siders as "Trolly Car Girls with Rolls Royce Tastes." Though these women lived in tenements, "their hearts are bent on palaces." They are "gripped by the current mania for speed and pleasure." Leo Robbins's 1923 article only promised "disaster" for these "little girls" who passed up marriage proposals from poor Jewish men to wait for a rich man's offer that would never materialize.[37] Commentators repeatedly suggested that these inflated desires led women to pursue impossible dreams beyond their workplace or home. The illegitimacy of their desires showed in their "bad taste," which one writer suggested "shriek(ed) louder than the whine of the beggars' tatters."[38]

Members of her own community projected onto the Ghetto Girl stereotype their fear that young Jewish women would abandon them. The Lower East Side had no Prince Charmings with wealth to underwrite palaces, fancy cars, and other pleasures. Beneath the ridicule of these young women is an unmistakable anxiety about women not staying behind to share with their peers a life without such possibilities.

The community expressed a second anxiety as well, that working-class daughters' love of pleasure threatened their families if it took away their wages and their affection. "Our girls" became Ghetto Girls when writers and leaders imagined the young women's heartless indifference to their kin. This concern appeared not to be founded in reality, for most immigrant Jewish families were supported by young adult family members.[39] Young women shared their wages with their families. A Bureau of Labor study of wages from 1900 to 1910 indicated that in Jewish families working daughters produced almost 40 percent of the family's total yearly earnings on average. Jewish daughters turned over sometimes as much as 100 percent of their wages, though on average about 89 percent, to their parents, in contrast to Jewish sons, who gave only 70 percent.[40]

East European Jewish women joined an American work force which had begun to integrate women in the early nineteenth century. The entry of native and "new immigrant" women from Northern and Western Europe and Ireland into the labor force caused changes in relations between wives and husbands and between the generations. A similar process occurred within Jewish families when Jewish women went to work. Working-class Jewish men, working primarily in seasonal employment that typified the garment industry, were paid too little to be the sole supports of their families. Unmarried Jewish daughters' wages made a significant contribution to the family's earnings. This left working-class unmarried Jewish women, like other young women workers, relatively free of many forms of traditional authority for five or six years before their marriage, and gave them particular autonomy in spending the wages that they earned.[41]

Ghetto Girls evoked precisely the same anxieties as did American working-class women in the mid-nineteenth century who were also a target for attack. Often forced to work by their fathers' inability to support families, they constituted the first group of autonomous urban women whose freedoms were continually attacked by the same

Jewish women working in a hat factory, before 1920. In the era of the Ghetto Girl, these workers wore fashionable clothes, but show none of the extremes in clothing, jewelry, or hair styles that troubled the middle class.
(Courtesy of the YIVO Institute for Jewish Research, New York)

array of journalists, moralists, and philanthropists who worried over Ghetto Girls. Their sexuality, autonomy, and display were also conflated into a single image of a dangerous and out-of-control woman. However, the anxieties expressed by immigrant Jews in the press were a particular version of the fear of independent women: Jews were frightened that with her alienation from her parents she might withdraw her wages and leave her family.

Writers in the Yiddish press associated young working women's love of fashion with a diversion of wages to buy fine clothes rather than to help their family. Zelda, a regular columnist for the English page of the *Jewish Daily News*, wrote in 1903 about the evils of this behavior: "You, working girls, listen to the voice of one of you–don't endeavor to mimic the pampered pet of material fortune. Those luxuries are beyond the station of a working girl. For the price of one silken rag, your mother, your toiling father and your little sisters and brothers can have better, purer food, warmer and better garments,

"DID I PUT TOO MUCH ON, POP?"

This cartoon, a weekly feature known as "East-Sidelights," appeared in the Jewish Daily Forward's *July 17, 1927, issue. The young woman, dressed as a flapper, asks a janitor if her makeup is too excessive. The cartoonist draws both of his characters— a worker at the bottom of occupations and a "new" woman—unsympathetically.* (Courtesy of The Forward Association, Inc.)

comfortable rooms in a better neighborhood and a dozen other things that they haven't now, and suffer because of the lack of it."[42]

The Jewish immigrant family's economic vulnerability and cultural displacement explain why the Ghetto Girl was a powerful symbol of their fear. Jewish immigrant and second-generation literature, so often devoted to the struggles between sons and their immigrant parents, pointed to the second generation's yearning for consumer items, clothing, and pleasure, which threatened to disrupt the economic basis of the family as well as its ties of connection to one another. The Ghetto Girl personified the danger of a desire that alienated her from her parents as well as the men of her generation. While sons were always moving toward separation from their families, daughters were considered more in the control of their families until their marriages. This patriarchal formulation made unmarried daughters' autonomy more threatening.

Debating the Sources of the Ghetto Girl

The Ghetto Girl stereotype was powerful and widespread enough to generate debates within each battalion of accusers. Journalists for the mainstream press on occasion countered the image with another. One reporter for the *New York Herald Tribune* in 1900, for example, sympathetically reported precisely how a young working woman managed to put together her outfit for her Sunday promenade. He wrote that, "To the uninitiated the costume represented an outlay of $20.00 at least, although she had achieved it at an expense of $3.30, and was able to go abroad without proclaiming her dire poverty at home." He revealed that by denying herself any luxuries, the young seamstress could buy a few items, use scraps given to her by other relatives in the garment industry, and make her fashionable outfit herself.[43] He portrayed her as a model of economy and sacrifice, rather than excess and self-indulgence.

Other journalists in the English-language Jewish press defended rather than condemned the Ghetto Girl. Mrs. Miriam Shomer Zunser, writing for the *American Jewish News,* declared the picture of the Ghetto Girl exaggerated: "Notwithstanding the fact that many excellent folks have already discussed this creature, and have already doomed her to eternal glory or disgrace; (most likely disgrace, if prevalence of opinion counts). The 'Ghetto girl' is in fact like the girls in any other community except that she bears within her heart the sorrow she borrowed from her race."[44]

Sophie Irene Loeb, a journalist for the *Evening World,* explained to a writer for the Jewish press in 1918 that the young Jewish immigrant woman was simply taking an early step in her evolution toward Americanization.

> Naturally, you will find a certain amount of crude-dressing on the East-side, but this is not an inherited trait. Good taste in dressing is acquired like any other of education, and what showiness these girls exhibit is but the elementary stage in the acquirement of this education. . . . Many of the girls come from a miserably paid position in the old country to a well-paid position in New York, and the change may have made them a little reckless. They may have spent too much money with too little judgment, but this failing is transitory and the girls emerge from it with a refinement equaling the best.[45]

These journalists, representing different positions as American-born, educated Jewish immigrants and children of immigrants, dismissed the Ghetto Girl's excesses as misunderstood or an evolutionary step toward full Americanization. Sympathetic and compassionate, they appealed to better information and understanding from those who took offense.

Only a radical feminist activist like Margaret Sanger simply condemned the entire discussion as irrelevant. In one of her pamphlets on women's health that was translated into Yiddish, she criticized social reformers for their attack on young women's pleasures. She argued that they denounced women's clothes as "frivolous" and wasteful because of their own patrician background, and urged the reformers to pay attention to the injustices that they perpetuated, rather than working women's love of clothing.[46]

However, the vast majority of articles in the press about these women condemned them. In an interview with Mrs. Sholom Asch, wife of the famed Yiddish writer, the paper learned that she had inquired of her non-Jewish friends why these "girls" were so extravagant.[47] They attributed it to the girls' lack of education. Mrs. Asch contended rather improbably that these immigrant girls encountered in America "freedom." "No restrictions, no encumbrances, they were perfectly free to do as they pleased, and had plenty of money to spend as they pleased."[48] In this version of immigrant reality, the luxuries and freedoms of young working-class women could only be tamed by the educations they refused to pursue.

The most forceful critic of Ghetto Girls was one of the most well-known Jewish women of her day, the writer Fanny Hurst.[49] In an interview given to the *American Jewish News* for its 1918 article on "The Modern Ghetto Girl," Miss Hurst gave her impression of the East Side girl: "When I go down to the East-side and look upon those pasty, white faces and the hopelessly vulgar, stupid dresses, I am filled with wonder and admiration that these girls with all their vulgarity, should rise to the heights that some of them do and be so great in achievement."[50] The journalist, Marion Golde, asked Hurst to name the cause of "this extravagance in dress and taste." She characterized Fanny Hurst's response as "striking."

> It is due to the vivid, aggressive temperament and imagination of the Jew. The girl walks down Fifth Avenue. She sees a latest model dress or hat, or the latest modes in coiffures, and immediately her aggressive imagination fastens upon these modes. She goes home and models her own style on them, but not possessing the good taste that prompted the original mode, a contorted exaggeration results. It is the reaction to a vivid imagination and temperament that lacks the restraining force of instinctive good taste.[51]

In short, the Ghetto Girl was, as Hurst phrased it "a contorted exaggeration." To her accusers it was the Jewish working woman who created a self that was out of proportion to the norm.

But the real contorted exaggeration was in the work of those who circulated the representation. The frantic, panicked rendering of young Jewish womanhood was created by Jews who felt threatened by non-Jews, men threatened by women, the middle class threatened by working women, native-born Protestant Americans frightened of a nation of immigrants, and participants in a changing economy frightened by their own attraction to consumption and leisure. Each of these groups fought to define community, nation, and class by exclusion. The Ghetto Girl represented what threatened the order of each category.[52]

The various faces of this stereotype suggest nuanced differences in the anxieties to which the Ghetto Girl spoke. The vulgarity that haunted Fannie Hurst, an acculturated Jew, was a different threat than that experienced by the young male readers of the *Forward*'s English page who feared the autonomy of young Jewish working women. Progressives' anxieties that required the control of young women certainly paralleled their other concerns about creating a homogenous American nation. Nativists' obsession with an agrarian America endangered by the city and leisure were threatened by urban working women who controlled their own resources and exercised their own taste.

What unified the Ghetto Girl's faces was her desire. Her accusers who stood across her class and within her culture were joined by nothing other than their condemnation of her excessive and undeserved wants. Her illegitimate desires might make her vulnerable to sexual predators, deprive her family of its needs, reveal her as a cheap imitator of style, or betray her class in her search for a fortune. Although the Ghetto Girl was always portrayed as a working woman, paradoxically her wanting was never connected to her own productivity. She sought either what was wrong, or things to which she was not entitled. Her desire was the meeting ground of anxieties about Americanization, class status, and gender. Her *Jewishness* was the source of her excess and her marginality. The Jew in the woman and the woman in the Jew were condensed into the cultural representation of the Ghetto Girl. The Jew was the alien to the nation, avaricious and aggressive. The woman was marked by her desire, in this setting defined primarily by consumer items of fashion and leisure. Her class was marked by the illegitimacy of that desire, wanting those things to which others, but not she, were entitled.

The Ghetto Girl, like stereotypes of other autonomous women, blurred all of these boundaries. Desire, a sexual impulse, became inseparable from an economic relationship between men and women that enabled consumption. While middle-class women of this period were increasingly defined as consumers, Ghetto Girls were prohibited from these very desires because they were unmarried and not members of the middle class. As marriage regulated sex, so in capitalist societies, it regulated consumption, since marriage legitimated both of them.

East European Jews were newcomers, at best, to both this division of labor and practice of consumption, which most of them fully embraced as they entered the middle class. The Jewish and non-Jewish bourgeoisie were constantly frustrated by the Ghetto Girl's sense of entitlement to the pleasures of freedom and consumption, which eventually stood for all the anxieties provoked by Americanization, antisemites, and the consumer society. The Ghetto Girl's desire for consumption led her sexuality in their minds because of rapid economic changes in a relatively new consumer-driven economy.[53]

The Ghetto Girl allowed Jews, like mad scientists of fiction, to imagine altering one or another identity of their body politic–gender, "race," culture–in order to create an acceptable American without "Jewish" qualities that marked the Jew as different and unacceptable.

Dangerous Mirrors–Ghetto Girls in the Eyes of the Beholder

Jewish qualities were of course those that were feared by Jews who were seeking a secure place in America. Not surprisingly then, the wealthy Jewish women of the late nineteenth century were targets of the same accusations that they so often leveled at new immigrants.

Unflattering antisemitic portraits of affluent Jewish women appeared in the American press in the nineteenth and twentieth centuries. After 1875, the American dominant culture's preoccupation with how Jews dressed, spoke, and amused themselves formed the crucial justification for social discrimination.[54] In 1880, for example, in *Harper's Bazaar*, a light-hearted article was devoted to schoolgirls cheating on their compositions. The girls received their comeuppance for their plagiarism when the friend they had relied on for help gave each of them, unbeknownst to one another, the same essay. Their guilt was revealed when girl after girl read the essay "Women Jews," which began

> Women Jews—By this term we do not mean Jewish women—
> those pretty, black-eyed daughters of Israel, conspicuous chiefly
> for their inordinate fondness for cheap jewelry and proportion-
> ate distaste for swine's flesh. No, it is not of those we would
> speak, but of that class of women, be they olive-skinned descen-
> dants of Abraham or pale-faced American Gentiles, who habitu-
> ally ask and expect a dealer to "fall" a few cents on the stated
> price of every article for purchase.[55]

So conventional were these stereotypes that they were merely the backdrop of the story, and more important, what could be antisemitic about a work that suggested these qualities were detachable from Jewish women? If only behavior could change, antisemites would certainly disappear, at least according to popular magazines of a middle-class America.

Affluent Jewish women's behavior then was constantly criticized in the writing and speeches of Jewish men who were doggedly pursuing acceptance. They strongly condemned women who dressed up and wore jewelry, and they often lamented how such behavior influenced the opinions of Christians.[56] An etiquette note concerning summer resort dress from an 1883 English-language Jewish newspaper, the *Jewish Messenger*, offered a typical, if sarcastic, admonition: "The more richly you dress, the more rightly you can claim to be refined. Hang out a diamond from every finger. Nothing is daintier than to see diamonds flashing amid griddle cakes and syrup."[57]

Jewish women consumed too much, but Jewish men were unnaturally productive, either as a result of their business success or criminality. By their genders they were a matched set of aliens to American life. Before Americans created quotas limiting Jews' access to education, workplaces, and leisure settings, Jewish men served as foils against national values. They personified materialism and acquisitiveness, attributes thought to be the opposite of American virtues.[58] For example, Robert Woods and Albert Kennedy's *Zones of Emergence*, written around 1910, described the Jews of Boston as "born real estate speculators," and "natural traders" whose neighborhoods, by contrast with the Italians, were "crude" and "riotous."[59]

Antisemites saw these mercantilist tendencies underlining their lack of physical ability. Their labor was never the honest work produced through sweat. As early as 1820, for example, a far more benevolent time in Jewish-Christian relations in the United States, the news magazine, *Nile's Weekly Register,* speculated why American Jews were denied civil rights that other men were granted.

> There must be some moral cause to produce this effect. In general, their interests do not appear identified with those of the communities in which they live, though there are some honorable exceptions to this remark. But they will not sit down and labor like other people—they create nothing and are mere consumers. They will not cultivate the earth, nor work at mechanical trades, preferring to live by their wit in dealing, and acting as if they had a home no where. . . . But all this has nothing to do with the rights of men.[60]

In far less empathic terms, and nearly a century later, Theodore Bingham, New York's police commissioner in 1907, suggested that the city's Jewish population accounted for half of its criminals, a fact he attributed to their lack of physical fitness for "hard labor."[61] Then in the 1920s, at the height of anti-immigration hysteria, a popular novelist suggested that the fact that Jews "live by their wits alone" made them one of the most "undesirable" races to crowd into America's cities.[62]

Productive without working, consumers rather than laborers, traders by "racial instinct" and hence obsessed with bargaining, Jewish men in a more tolerant nineteenth-century America as well as an increasingly intolerant nation of the early twentieth century appeared to share a striking number of traits with Ghetto Girls. Jewish men and women's behavior, however, was differentiated by gender as well as social class. Therefore, activities related to both of these categories—clothing, manners, and appearances—were subject to constant monitoring by one another.

Jewish women's "behavior" was policed by Jewish men to remove its telltale stains, and Jewish women commented on one another's actions for the same reason. Jewish women enforced their conformity to Anglo-Protestant bourgeois ideals in their own English-language Jewish press, which was a crucial organ for maintaining Jewish identity within an upwardly mobile Jewish population committed to rapid Americanization.[63] Women's pages typically juxtaposed advice about style, fashion, and beauty with lessons in Jewish womanhood and the responsibilities of Jewish women to maintain Judaism. These pages were devoted to articles on the improvement of firmly established middle-class Jews of both German and East European descent more often than to ones that prescribed how to reform Ghetto Girls. These columns nevertheless bristled with anxiety.

For example, in 1918 Julia Weber's column "Woman and Her Home" in the *American Jewish News* was devoted to the question, "Have You a Pleasing Voice?" Weber told of standing at a railroad station where a Jewish girl greeted her companions "each boisterously and in a loud voice, arousing criticism all about her." She recounts that her companion said about "this type of Jewish girl,"

> She knew how to buy good clothes and how to wear them, but this type of girl, with such a manner and voice, will never be accepted in good society, no matter how many redeeming qualities she may have. While there are thousands of splendid Jewish girls who are ladies in every sense of the word, yet there are others who, like this girl, help bring severe criticism upon all Jewish girls. Her voice is either loud and harsh or shrill. She does not realize that this stamps her as uncultured and vulgar.[64]

Her "friend" could claim expertise because she was a "professional reader," an actress who recited on social occasions. Her solution was the following.

> A girl should speak in low and well modulated tones and for the benefit of her listeners only. She should be careful not to speak in the throat or she will swallow her words. If she talks through her nose in that shrill tone she produces the same disagreeable sound as is produced by speaking with the nostrils pinched together. . . . She should speak so that every word is heard yet is modulated with a view to a pleasing, clear and forceful expression of thought and feeling. Just a simple exercise on the vowels a-e-i-o-u will produce excellent results.[65]

Sandwiched between advice about how to equip a bathroom, the value of fish in the diet, and an explanation of the symbolism of the *Mezuzah*, the "Woman and Her Home" column revealed that good taste in clothing was insufficient proof of the acceptability of a Jewish woman. She was betrayed by her voice, her nasal tones, and her volume, all of which were telltale signs of coarseness that kept her from "good society," in other words, from acceptability to the non-Jewish world.[66]

The parallel between this article and one in the Yiddish press directed to the children of immigrants is striking.

> Have you ever been on a street-car when the theatre-goers are homeward bound? Have you ever been in a restaurant when the workers are at their noon-day meal? If so, you have surely been struck by the loud talking and laughing of some girl. You, no doubt, immediately called her unrefined and vulgar. Would you want another to class you the same way simply because you forget to control your voice?
>
> And you and I have a double responsibility as Jewish girls. Not only we as individuals are judged, but indeed the whole nation is judged by each of us. If you are known as unrefined in your small circle, and I undignified in mine, why then is it said: "the Jews are loud and unrefined." So remember girls how much depends on you and me.[67]

Yiddish writers who established etiquette for immigrants offered the same advice. Tashrak wrote that no matter how well dressed a woman was, a "shrieking laugh" gave away the fact that she was "no lady" (a *proste yente*–a common gossip).[68] Jews' well-being across classes depended on containing the vulgar wants and behaviors of Jewish women.

Other commentators repeatedly returned to the Jewish woman's body as the key to her problem. The cartoonist Foshko, by contrasting the styles of Fifth Avenue and East Side women, suggests that taste runs well beyond education to the core problem for the Ghetto Girl.

> You may say that such crazes in fashion are worn by the Fifth Avenue girl and that they become her, but there is this difference. The Fifth Avenue girl lives in an atmosphere of her own– a rich atmosphere with leisure and luxury. Her body has acquired the mold of her life. The girl on the East-side also lives in an atmosphere of her own and her life has fashioned her body in harmony with it. What would therefore become the Fifth Avenue girl looks out of place on the East Side girl. Realize that the make-up of a girl on Clinton Street who works at a machine cannot be the same as the make-up of a girl from Fifth Avenue![69]

As Ghetto Girls were less often featured in the press because Jews were in the ghettos in far smaller number, her phantom qualities persisted and required careful monitoring, most often by other women. An anonymous writer for the *Day* in 1930 suggested that Jewish women's bodies were a special burden to them in their efforts to dress well for work. She asserted that Jewish women were not extravagant when they purchased clothing and stockings because "the average working girl in New York City has got to look smart and trim if she wants to keep her job." This requirement is not a hardship for the "Gentile girl who usually has small features, light eyes, and a slim figure. This girl will look neat and pleasing in almost any dress she puts on, and her hats, even if in some popular and rather extreme mode, will not make her conspicuous. Jewish women, on the other hand must be careful in the clothing they wear because they are easily 'typed' as flamboyant and 'conspicuous.'"

She continued:

> Many Jewish girls are of the oriental type of physique. This may be very beautiful in its proper setting, but in an Occidental, Gentile country a really graceful curved nose is regarded as a "hooked nose," the vivid coloring: black eyes, full mouth, black hair, appears "common" and "loud," the full well-developed figure is "blowsy" or "fat." To dress herself in accord with the ideals of Americans, the Jewish girl must offset these intimations of vulgarity by making it her rule to wear the simplest clothes possible. But alas, as we all know by this time, the simplest clothes are the most expensive![70]

An Oriental body was not a Jewish woman's only problem. A 1929 article in the Yiddish newspaper, the *Day*'s English section warned that the Jewish woman's "style" might lead her to lose her job. The writer recounted her story of a Jewish girl who "obtained an excellent position in the office of an ad man." The "Jewish girl" was unusually clever, but nevertheless, her boss had to fire her. She wore "low necked afternoon dresses of beaded silk," "high heeled satin shoes," and excessive makeup. "It was cheaper for him to get a less brilliant worker than to destroy the carefully built up impressiveness of his reception room."[71] Terry Selber, writing for the same newspaper in 1926, commented on a similar problem and quoted a non-Jewish expert who explained that Jewish women's "intensity manifests itself in their clothes."[72]

Affluent Jewish women were haunted by the same phantom of excessive desire. As journalists lectured the aspiring middle-class Jewish woman, so too did they write to constrain the successful Jew. Another "Woman and Her Home" column in 1918 exhorted its fashionable readers to learn "that good dressing does not mean exaggeration; that the exhibition of a veritable shop of jewels cannot hide untidy hair and an over-painted face, . . . that impeccable tidiness of nails, hair, teeth, and shoes are more desirable than a five hundred dollar fur cape and a pair of diamond earrings."[73] These gender stereotypes conspired to suggest that something was wrong with Jewish women.

The Special Burden of Jewish Women

Ruth Schwartz Cowan writes that in this period throughout America the tone of most American women's magazines was one of guilt. "Readers of the better quality women's magazines are portrayed as feeling guilt a good lot of the time, and when they are not guilty they are embarrassed (about clogged drains and dirty children). In the years after World War I, American women were made to feel guilty about sending their children to school in scuffed shoes."[73]

Women's columns in both the Yiddish and the English-language Jewish press did offer, like the dominant culture's women's press, a constant stream of advice about proper food, homes, etiquette, decorum, and families. But the improvement of Jewish women by means of the transformation of their every feature went farther than that. The woman in the Jew, whether working-class or middle-class, constituted a barrier to access to the dominant culture.

The very body of the Jewish woman became a cultural terrain subject to Americanization. And Americanization was a process that extended well beyond the world of immigrants. The vulgar Jewish woman/Ghetto Girl violated the nation. She challenged a Protestant American commitment to restraint, to the separation of classes, and the regulation of sexuality. Therefore Jews policed one another, watched, condemned, and constrained their own use of display in their ongoing effort to find a niche for themselves in America.[75] Clothing, jewelry, hairstyles, shoes—no element of decoration was too small to worry over as a sign of vulgarity or acceptability.

Explanations for why Jews' failed to be orderly and restrained varied. A wide range of commentators and newspapers insisted that there was something stubbornly crass about Jewish women that kept disrupting and overriding their efforts to become acceptable to the larger society. American Jewish women's failures appeared more connected to their bodies than the causes of guilt that plagued the American women described by Ruth Schwartz Cowan. Jewish women's most personal features—voice, style, comportment—seemed constantly to be on the verge of developing into social stigma.

Not Me–Not Them

The more Americanized that Jewish women became, whether they sought "ostentatious" or well-tailored clothing, the more likely they were to betray their Jewishness. Desire doomed them because it could not erase what was stubbornly and persistently "wrong" with them: that they were outsiders and Jews.[76]

At precisely that same historical moment, beginning in the late nineteenth century, every cleavage among Jews living in America became a focus of attack. Affluent Jewish men maintained a ceaseless assault on Jewish women's perceived consumer excesses. Wealthy German Jews, suddenly cast as dangers to America, turned on East European Jewish women and men, attacking their vulgarity. Jewish men ridiculed Jewish women. Rich Jews attacked poor ones. The more established Jews condemned Jews who had more recently emigrated. Jews were at once too American in their dress and too Jewish in their demeanor, in either case fundamentally wrong. Each group of Jews differentiated by social class, gender, region of origin, and religious practice, and condemned one another's bodies and styles to demonstrate their own respectability in a world that questioned their suitability for the middle class and citizenship in the nation. The tasks of acculturation, involving either rapid or gradual change, turned Jews against one another. The most powerful boundary marker for Jews appeared less in the positive assertion "I am an American," than in "I am not a Russian Jew, not a worker, not a Jewish woman."[77]

Americanization required men and women to distance themselves from undesirable former selves. Immigrants tried, sometimes desperately, to Americanize by changing their language and their appearance. The process seemed to require them to differentiate themselves from some other group or gender of Jews. To distance oneself from a vulgar, noisy Jewish woman was another way to assert one's status as an American.

Their very ability to become Americans required Jews to make minute distinctions in an antisemitic world. Jews' apparent ability to assimilate to the white Christian world around them only heightened the sense that difference was dangerous.[78] Because, like other Americans, young Jewish women could buy what they wanted with the money they earned, what they purchased was constantly condemned as lacking in taste. A writer for a Yiddish daily commented in 1902 how much the "shop girl" resembled the rich. "The very latest style of hat, or cloak, or gown is just as likely to be worn on Grand street as on Fifth avenue. The great middle class does not put on the newest styles until they have been thoroughly exploited by Madam Millionaire of Fifth avenue and Miss Operator of Essex street."[79] From the point of view of the Jews of the Lower East Side, the shop girl was as attuned to style as were the wealthy. To the Jews of the "great middle class," this behavior, by contrast, had to be constantly controlled to protect against embarrassing imitation. Their place in that class remained vulnerable despite their economic standing.

The need for ever-increasing precision to keep some people out and some people in the mainstream because of their manners and style rather than their ability to consume placed Jews in conflict with each other, and placed both Jewish women and men and the Jewish working class and middle class in particular struggle.

The Swell

Women provided a particularly powerful source of intra-ethnic representation, so much so that it transected class; vulgar women worked within and across class among Jews as internalized forms of antisemitism. Men did, however, briefly serve as a far less elaborated intra-ethnic stereotype parallel to the Ghetto Girl in the Yiddish press. Men's lives were rarely a matter of concern to the bourgeois, English-language Jewish press, which was singularly focused on women.

The contrast between the male and female images is instructive. While critics blamed women's excessive consumption on their false values and moral weaknesses, young Jewish men were held up to scorn because they were insufficient providers. Their desires were underwritten by the labor of others—either through credit or a wealthy father-in-law. In the century's first years the *Jewish Daily News*'s English-language columnist, the Observer, used East Side men's excessive purchases of clothing to critique them and the credit system. The Observer called such men "swells." In a column mockingly titled "A Model Man," he wrote,

> Look at the moderate incomes of these young men, and then look at their extravagance in clothing, eating, and giving themselves amusement. How can men wear thirty-five dollar suits of clothes, and fourteen dollar Panama hats, and seven dollar "pumps" when they don't earn more than twelve or fifteen dollars per week?
>
> This problem is easily solved, when you remember that they don't pay for most of what they wear or eat. True each of these unwilling contributors is fooled but once, possibly twice, but there it ends. (But) as long as there is more than one tailor where credit may be obtained so long will these men be seen wearing the finest of clothes.[80]

In a later column he described a seashore resort on Long Island that wealthy German Jews frequented where the pretender East Side men used the fine clothes that they purchased on credit to attempt to attract a wealthy young heiress. The Observer wrote that a Swell without money "was a serious joke."[81]

More than twenty years later, Leo Robbins lampooned the Swell in the English page of the Yiddish newspaper the *Jewish Daily Forward* as a "PHG," "which stood for "Papa Has Gelt" (Yiddish for money). The PHG pursues young women and "worships her papa's bank account." A charlatan and a failure, "the PHG is really a PIG."[82]

It was only in the American press that men were accused of vulgarity in a way that is reminiscent of the Ghetto Girl. A 1900 article on East Side fashion, in the American newspaper, the *New York Tribune,* dealt with the subject of good taste. In the section "Nothing Is not Up to Date," the author suggested that men's only choices in fashion were "in the matter of collars, neckties and socks (where) their fancy can display itself." These items define a set of men's types— "sports," "hot sports," and "stiffs."[83] The writer joked, "The point is to combine on the small space allowed as many colors as possible. Purple and lavender, green and red, dark and light blue make contrasts which, as the wearers say, are 'not to be beat.' Is it funny, or is it pathetic? One is at loss to decide, and compromises by a smile and sigh."[84]

Jewish immigrant men were also portrayed as lacking refinement, and their rare occasions of being fashionable were falsely achieved through dishonesty born of their lack of productivity. Such behavior was laughable or immoral, depending on the point of view of the writer. These men's Americanization was, at best, a thin veneer over an inadequate manhood. The ideal American Jewish man, as outlined in the same pages that condemned the Swell, idealized professionals and praised the working man whose capacity to learn English, dress well, and participate in clubs and balls all indicated their success as Americans, which the journalists believed reflected well on all Jews. By contrast, the Swell, like the Ghetto Girl, was attracted to what America offered, but his failure to provide for himself and others rendered him dangerous to others.[85]

These stereotypes might share the excessive desires of the undeserving newcomer to America, but there were crucial differences between them. If Jewish men worked hard and became productive, the press seemed to suggest, they might legitimately have good clothing and even wealthy fathers-in-law. Women, however, needed not to want. Their desire was insatiable and they lacked a legitimate path to it. The middle-class German Jewish women were proof of that. At least within the context of the Jewish ethnic press, little attention appeared to be paid to the Jewish male body, despite considerable attention to it in classic antisemitic literature.

The Ghetto Girl, by contrast with the Swell and in relationship to the vulgar Jewish woman, revealed the ways in which America beckoned and pushed away, forcing any single group of outsiders to fight among themselves as they Americanized. The Ghetto Girl represented those internal struggles. This moment of mirroring simply reflected the fact that one Jew's Americanization was the other's nightmare.

The period in which the Ghetto Girl served as a potent stereotype for Jews coincided with American citizens' struggles to become an urban and pluralistic society, their ambivalence about capitalism and industrialization, and their anxieties about changing roles of women and the family. Not only did Americanizing Jews share many of these anxieties, they served as symbols of them for a nation that at its most tolerant remained hostile to Jews' desires to maintain a unique cultural identity.

The Ghetto Girl provided a cultural meeting ground of American fears, if not open antisemitism, and American Jews' own evolving sense of their identities as participants in the nation's middle class. For the dominant culture bourgeois norms allowed them to draw the boundaries of society to exclude outsiders by color. If Jews were harder to categorize, then their unsuitability was established by other measures embodied in the stereotype that placed them beyond white, genteel society.

At the same time, Jews who yearned for Americanization, and with that the middle class, disciplined themselves by rejecting characteristics that were "Jewish" and "female" that might betray their difference. The socialist, working-class Jewish press was far less likely to evoke the stereotype. Nevertheless, the importance of mobility to

Jewish workers made the specter of desire out of control a frightening one. For young Jewish women and men who wanted a life in the American middle class, the need to shape and contain consumer desire made the Ghetto Girl a representation of scorn and fear in their community as well.

Whatever differences divided Jews, the shame, pain, embarrassment, and rage created by the stereotyped image of an autonomous and desiring Jewish woman were the product of America's reluctance to allow those marked as "different" to join the nation on their own terms. The Ghetto Girl's qualities—vulgarity, excess, and desire—figured into intra-ethnic gender stereotypes for the remainder of the twentieth century because Jews' difference from the nation continued to find expression in an anxious place at the margin, represented primarily as an unattractive Jewish woman. Her capacity to embody what was frightening and desirable about America—consumption, freedom, economic dependence through marriage, and display—cast her in this problematic role as an icon of Americanization.

CHAPTER TWO

Marriage Making Americans

> The American Jewish woman, even the
> immigrant woman, is still obscure and
> mysterious in our literature. She is the
> princess under a magic spell to whom we
> have not yet gotten close. We are familiar
> with the shop girl. . . . We also have an idea
> of the "green" Jewish woman, of her life in
> the first years of her immigration. But we
> know very little of her after she is no longer
> "green," but has become an "American lady.
> . . . " We know even less about her daughter
> who was already born and raised here and
> who, after her marriage, creates her home
> and family life entirely according to the
> American Pattern.
>
> Mordechai Dantsis, "The American Jewish
> Woman" (in Yiddish), in the *Jewish Woman's
> Home Journal*, October 1923

Fanny Edelman, an immigrant from Galacia, recounted in her 1961 autobiography that marriage was her primary motivation to leave Europe. She recalled her terror at her father's tyrannical control over each of her older sisters' marriages. As a poor salesman, her father had no dowry to offer, so he overcame this liability by finding during his travels orphans and other unfortunates who were from "good families," who were descendants of scholars, or who held high status occupations. He brought the men home and presented them as bridegrooms for his daughters, showing no regard whatsoever for the young women's preferences or feelings. Edelman wrote: "I used to dream of running away from our little town and from my severe father and coming to the free world called America. I used to dream that in America I could fall in love and marry without being forced to live with a man my father had selected for me."[1] She gained her father's approval to leave home simply because she convinced him that a ship's fare would liberate him from the burden of marrying off another daughter without a dowry.

But her fantasies did not stop there. Confronted with difficult family and economic problems in the United States, sleep came to her nightly only when she could imagine a lover *and* a fortune in the New World. "At night I used to cry. But I did not cry for long. I would imagine that a handsome young man was falling madly in love with me, and that I was going around dolled up in expensive dresses, and covered from head to toe with diamonds. In that way I fell asleep with a smile on my face."[2] Freedom, choice, love, marriage, and luxury were all of a piece with America in Fanny's mind. More often than not, marriage in the United States facilitated Fanny's and millions of other young Jewish immigrants' escape from their parents' Old World ideas and their foreign neighborhoods to what they hoped was an unambiguously American life. Fanny was not alone in her fantasies. Marriage loomed large in the lives of young urban men and women who poured into America's cities from Europe as well as from rural areas, in search of work, freedom, and new lives.

For Jews, the Fanny Edelmans and their American-born sisters were not simply individuals who hoped for a good life. They caught the imagination of writers, journalists, and social workers who understood that these young women's' fantasies about love and marriage were as much reveries about American life as they were about love. Marriage was closely tied to Americanization, and a powerful stereotype of it was the eager Young Jewish Woman in Search of Marriage. She was a favorite subject of popular culture throughout the century's first decades because she captured the hopes of Americanization as well as its folly and pain. To explore this stereotype is to understand how the private lives of Americanizing Jews–their love, marriage, and domesticity–became essential strategies in their upward mobility, acculturation, and resistance against assimilation.

The Ghetto Girl condensed the many anxieties Jews experienced as they Americanized. An American marriage was a critical step in the process of Americanization. Marriage created a new household through freely chosen love that simultaneously rejected traditional Jewish authority relations and espoused the nation's values of freedom, equality, and pleasure. Paradoxically, however, Jews also resisted Americanization through marriage, by overwhelmingly rejecting non-Jews as spouses.

The Young Jewish Woman in Search of Marriage seemed, at least initially, a more legitimate image of young Jewish womanhood than the Ghetto Girl. Marriage itself promised to contain her desires and to connect her to the Jewish people through her marriage to a Jewish husband.[5] She represented the desire for mobility and its material expressions, but unlike the Ghetto Girl with her meager financial independence, the Young Woman evoked another type of anxiety because of her dependence on her husband's wages. Marriage created new families on whose behalf financially dependent wives purchased an ever-growing array of consumer items. The intimate link of Americanization and marriage through the young Jewish woman created a stereotype that allowed gender to become coterminous with mobility. Twentieth-century marriage paradoxically became the setting for couples both to reproduce Jews and to produce an American lifestyle.

The marriage of immigrants and their children was a matter of cultural importance far beyond particular ethnic groups. As American Jewish culture was caught up with images of the Young Woman in Search of Marriage, the dominant American culture was similarly focused on marriage as an image of "amalgamation," a common word of the era for the fusion of different peoples into one nation. Marriage, particularly in the 1920s, was offered in theater, film, literature, and the press as a means for the children of immigrants to Americanize by cutting themselves off from their unique, Old World cultures. Rather than marriage serving to solidify intra-ethnic bonds, in the popular imagination it was the most direct route to destroying what Theodore Roosevelt and others contemptuously called "hyphenated-

Americans," those who tried to forge dual identities in the United States. The idealized marriages that brought the descendants of Europeans together solidified their relationships as white people. Interracial marriage was never implied by this pursuit of amalgamation. Americanization required forgetting the past in order to join a racially divided nation imagined for the future.

In this chapter I examine the meaning of marriage and romance for the period of immigration and initial acculturation, from the late nineteenth century to about 1930, and provide a context for the discussion in chapter 3 of the stereotypes of the young Jewish woman in search of love and matrimony and her male counterpart.

The Meaning of American Romantic Love for Jewish Immigrants

Marriage was an important theme in immigrant Jewish literature. Few writers portrayed it from the point of view of a young immigrant woman as effectively as Anzia Yezierska.[4] "The Miracle" is the story of Sara Reisel, who left Savel, Poland, for America in search of love. Zlata, one of the townspeople of Savel, received from his daughter Hannah Heyeh a letter that sealed Sara Reisel's fate. Zlata read the letter to the town: "America is a lover's land. In America millionaires fall in love with the poorest girls. Matchmakers are out of style, and a girl can get herself married to a man without the worries for a dowry." Hannah Heyeh then reported her most astonishing news. "I, Hannah Heyeh, will marry myself to Solomon Cohen, the boss from the shirtwaist factory, where all day I was working sewing on buttons. If you could only see how the man is melting away his heart for me! He kisses me after each step I walk. The only wish from his heart is to make me a lady. Think only, he is buying me a piano! I should learn piano lessons as if I were a millionaire!"[5]

This news convinced Sara Reisel that her life in Poland had no purpose; she had to go to America, where Hannah Heyeh, a young woman Sara Reisel judged less attractive than herself, had her fate radically altered. America afforded the possibility of marriage to a loving, attentive man who offered leisure and the high culture of piano lessons. Indeed, Sara Reisel's prospects as a dowry-less daughter of a teacher were horrifying to her–unattractive, humble men without hope for a better life were all that awaited her. Her only chance to raise money for boat passage rested with her parents, whose sole valuable possessions were silver candlesticks and a Torah. Sara Reisel and her brother convinced them to do the unthinkable–to sell those things so essential to their Jewish lives. They reluctantly consented to give their daughter her one chance to find love, marry, and achieve prosperity.[6]

Hannah Heyeh's letter is reminiscent of the letters written by real-life immigrants, as well as other fictional characters, which inspired recipients to try their luck at pursuing different fates in the New World. Those letters typically reported new immigrants' wealth, possessions, fine clothing, and extraordinary opportunities. In the New World a Jewish woman had reason to believe that marriage would make her an agent of her own fate. Marriage promised to be the arena of her transformation, in the way that the prospect of making a fortune captured the fantasies of the young Jewish man of equally little status or fortune.

Another Yezierska character, Gedalyeh Mindel, wrote to his family in the story "How I Found America." "My sun is beginning to shine in America," he told them. "I am becoming a person–a business man."[7] Hannah Heyeh's letter, in contrast, promised love and marriage as the source of her status. Her husband would provide pianos and other measures of being "someone." To her family and neighbors in Savel, this love created physical comfort, ease, and a new identity. While the relationship described in Yezierska's story was not coldly calculating, focusing only on economic advantage, it was also not romantically indifferent to personal comfort. The miracle of New World marriage was that it involved both.

Many immigrant women yearned for an education, and some found the United States attractive because of its free public education, without antisemitic quotas. A marriage of one's choice, however, appeared to have been the common dream of most Americanizing women.[8] In America, on her own, a Jewish immigrant woman escaped the system of arranged marriage. She did not have to accept her father's choice of a mate, depend on his raising money for a dowry, or accept a status system that rendered her desirable or undesirable. One immigrant woman interviewed remarked, "In this country all my generation married for love."[9]

By way of contrast, Miriam Shomer Zunzer's 1939 memoir of her family's life in Minsk, Russia, succinctly described traditional notions of European Jewish marriage—though these were already under attack in the late nineteenth century.[10]

> At the time there was no other way than through the medium of a match maker or marriage broker by which a girl of the Jewish middle class might obtain a husband. No one ever thought of such a thing as love. In the sense that we understand it today, love was a conception quite foreign to Jewish life. To be sure a husband loved his wife and a wife her husband, but that was after the two were married. And even then they were not supposed to love one another for physical reasons. Jewish sons and daughters married according to the laws of Moses and the wishes of their parents, so that the will of God might be done and the nation of Israel increase and multiply.[11]

In fact, romantic love was an ideal already embraced by Jewish progressives in nineteenth-century Europe.[12] Yiddish theater in the 1870s featured plots that condemned arranged marriages.[13] Zunzer's family biography included stories about her own father's romantic letters to her mother during the period of their engagement in the latter part of the century. The very act of writing letters between the parties of an arranged marriage was unknown in the town of Pinsk, Russia, where the bride, Zunzer's mother, lived. The exchange and contents of the letters were affected by the secular ideas of European poets and thinkers. The letters were hardly an intimate exchange between the intended spouses: the bride's father read them aloud to the townsfolk who were both startled and impressed.[14]

Once Jewish immigrants came to the United States, attitudes toward love were very much a matter of public discussion in the lives of both immigrants and their children.[15] No longer the purview of Jewish intellectuals and Progressives, immigrants and native-born Jews encountered transformed expectations and opportunities for love, courtship, and marriage in every quarter. As one immigrant wrote, "But on coming to America an even greater hero . . . caught me in his tendrils. The hero was: Rabbi Amour, the God of Love."[16] Wage-earning young women's financial independence played a major role in their increased interest in learning about their marriage choices and exploring the world of love as well.[17]

For example, the "Bintel Brief" (Bundle of Letters) in the *Jewish Daily Forward* allowed readers to ask and receive advice from one another.[18] In 1906, "Unhappy Stranger" wrote about her parents' pressure on her to marry a cousin in America, while her true love whom she "released" when forced to move to the United States awaited her return to him in Europe.[19] She wrote, "But my love for the European lover is too strong, for me to decide to fulfill my parents' wish. The only people to whom I shall listen, are the dear readers of your paper. I hope that I shall find good advice in your Bintel Brief."[20] Five readers responded with unanimity. They urged her to choose love, a new life and family, and to disappoint her parents, despite the cost. Mrs. Barnett from Somerville, Massachusetts wrote that "she ought only to fulfill her heart's desire. Who can enter her heart and weigh or gauge the measure or strength of her love for her cousin or for the European? Let her ask herself and await a reply from her feelings. She will then see whether her duty to her parents, to the cousin or her true love tips the scale."[21] Becky Frumkin described her choice of a husband against her parents wishes: "And although it was necessary to travel 5 thousand miles in order that my love triumph, I plodded through this great distance, and I feel to-day, that I live and prosper. Therefore I advise you. . . . Do not listen to your parents' arguments and do as you please."[22]

The readers of the *Jewish Daily Forward* did not easily forswear family obligations, a central concern to immigrants, but matters of love inevitably created new rules. Even if love sent the immigrant back to the Old World, as was the case of "Unhappy," pursuing it was very much a matter for the New World.[23]

This central theme of the "Bintel Brief" correspondence—that matters of the heart were inseparable from the process of becoming American—was echoed in the English-language pages of the Yiddish press as well.[24] This section of the paper, specifically directed to the young adult children of its readers, affirmed the "love match" in many different columns. Both men and women columnists in the *Jewish Daily News* declared a marriage without love "immoral."[25]

Nevertheless, the agent of European Jewish arranged marriages, the matchmaker (*shadchen*), did not disappear from American life. He continued to function in the United States in the first decades of the century, although his role was a source of considerable controversy and debate. He was both condemned and praised in the Jewish press. His epitaph was written and rescinded year after year, and decade after decade. However, there is no question that when his services were used in the New World, they often supported a set of values consistent with life in the United States, for example, creating matches based on wealth rather than traditional status.

By 1900, articles on marriage brokers in both the New York and Jewish press indicated that their declining popularity was making it difficult for them to make a living. Those interviewed railed against the freedom of Jewish youth and their preoccupation with love.[26] As one disgruntled shadchen complained, "They learned how to start their own love affairs from the Americans, and it is one of the worst things they have picked up. . . . The love in which they learned to put so much faith dribbles out in trips to Coney Island and walks around the park before marriage."[27]

Immigrants and their children encountered ideas of romantic love through the popular culture that surrounded them. Writer Kate Simon described the contrast between the romantic love portrayed in the Yiddish press and in the American cinema.

> It was in the kitchen that we learned to understand Yiddish from my father's accounts of union news read from the socialist paper, the *Freiheit*. My mother read from the *Jewish Daily Forward* the heartbreaking stories gathered in the "Bintel Brief" that wept of abandoned wives, of "greene Cousins," sprightly immigrant girls who were hanky-pankying with the eldest sons of households, set to marry rich girls and become famous doctors.
>
> (But) the brightest, most informative school was the movies. We learned how tennis was played and golf, what a swimming pool was and what to wear if you ever got to drive a car. We learned how tables were set, "How do you do? Pleased to meet you." We learned how regal mothers were and how stately fathers, and of course we learned about Love, a very foreign country like maybe China or Connecticut. From what I could see, and I searched, there was no love on the block nor even its fairy-tale end, marriage. We had only Being Married, and that included the kids, a big crowded barrel with a family name stamped on it. Of course, there was Being Married in the movies, but except for the terrible cruel people in rags and scowls, it was as silky as Love.[28]

Young American Jews were not limited to watching movies to encounter the meaning of romance. At the turn of the century a new urban culture further altered marriage and the family. City streets were alive with young men and women in pairs and groups drinking sodas in new shops, attending movies, meeting at dance-halls, and walking in parks. Sweethearts were interested in one another's attractiveness, and marriage promised the continuation of pleasure, leisure, and "ultimate happiness."[29] Americanization implied romantic love for Jews as surely as it required the use of English. For these

Jews little else competed with love and marriage as the quintessential experience of becoming a "real" American.

Marrying In and Marrying Out

As alluring as American culture obviously was, Jews maintained their identity as Jews—in large part, until the 1960s, by primarily marrying one another.[30] Other ethnic groups in the United States in-married until about 1910, even in the multiethnic city of New York.[31] Evidence suggests that ethnic groups in some cities continued to marry others from their own groups through the 1930s.[32] However, after this period, and among the children of immigrants in particular, many ethnics began to marry men and women of their generation from other ethnic groups. Out-marriage was consistently affected by a person's generational distance from immigration. As a result, the older immigrants from northern Europe intermarried to a far greater extent than new immigrants, and the children of new immigrants intermarried more than their parents.

Julius Drachsler's major study of New York marriage for the years 1908–1912 demonstrated just that. About 10 percent of the foreign-born in New York married people from outside of their own group. About 30 percent (32 percent for the men and 30 percent for the women) of the second-generation native-born did so.[33] From these figures Drachsler predicted that Americans were moving toward "amalgamation," and that intermarriage suggested a breakdown in ethnic group solidarity.[34] A subsequent reanalysis of Drachsler's data allowed a more precise understanding of marriage patterns. First-generation immigrants married one another. Second-generation, American-born were also wed to one another. Immigrants who arrived in the United States at about the same period of time also preferred one another.

Jews proved to be an exception to the rule of intergroup marriage. Although second-generation Jews in New York City did intermarry at a much higher rate than the first generation, their absolute numbers were very small. Less than .5 percent of first-generation Jews of New York intermarried. Not even 3.5 percent of second-generation Jews intermarried. Jews from different nations did intermarry, but they married other Jews. By the early twentieth century, they established an identity as Jews that overrode their differences in countries of origins. By 1912, the second generation had established Jewishness as a common transnational identity that cut across Central and East European identities in twentieth-century United States.

Jewish immigration to the United States was fairly evenly divided between men and women; this was not the case for other European groups.[35] For example, between 1900 and 1910 both the Irish and Italians emigrated with one sex disproportionate to the other. Heavily skewed sex ratios, even among immigrants, usually resulted in people marrying outside their own group. Where different generations competed for the same mates, marrying someone from a different ethnicity was more common than remaining single.[36] Even when the sex ratio became more balanced because of increased immigration, out-marriage persisted among other groups. Jews, however, were tied to one another through strong and overlapping bonds of group loyalty. They shared common neighborhoods, occupations, language, and, for many, religious practices. That young Jewish adults would marry other Jews was the clear expectation of families, peers, and the community of the time.[37]

Out-marriage, nevertheless, was a competing norm of American life. Paradoxically, young Jews thought of their marriages in ways that were strikingly similar to the very ideals of intermarriage. Romantic love, loyalty to the nation, the opportunity for mobility, and the pleasures of beginning an American family were evoked by those who idealized interethnic marriage as well as by those, like Fanny Edelman, who dreamed of Jewish marriage. Romance and Americanization were baked together into a single wedding cake. The nation of "Americans" and the nation of American Jews understood their futures to be the product of the marriage of a younger generation with new ideas and new expectations, and with high hopes for economic success. The similarities between the American and Jewish American "cakes" created both anxiety and attractions.[38]

The American Nation as Intermarried Lovers

The popular culture of the 1900s to 1920s surrounded Americans with images of interethnic marriage.[39] Marriage was a potent symbol and a "foundational fiction" that defined the marriage of "strangers" as the ideal means for achieving a new American nation.[40] By the 1920s, films, plays, novels, and magazines portrayed white ethnics— including Italians, Irish, and Jews—marrying one another with great regularity.

The literal marriage of different cultures served as the ideal trope for the New World, built as it was on relations of consenting individuals who created a new society alienated from the bonds of tradition and kinship that they had left behind.[41] In portrayals of the frustrated love of "Indian princesses" and young European-Americans fleeing their parents in nineteenth-century melodramas, in Israel Zangwill's 1908 play *The Melting Pot,* and in interethnic marriages in films and novels in the 1920s, a variety of writers envisioned America as a New World produced from the literal unions of strangers.[42]

In Zangwill's play, for example, the rebellious daughter of a Russian nobleman who was the perpetrator of the early twentieth-century Kishniev pogrom found true redeeming love with the impoverished son and sole survivor of a family of her father's victims in New York.[43] Both children turned away from the Old World of their parents, with its stifling demands and useless prejudices, to anticipate creating their own family and vision of America. The United States was personified by the union of youthful opposites whose future, like the future of the nation, rested on a rejection of the past, whether it was Tsarist oppressors or traditional Jews.[44] Zangwill, a British Jew, was an important public figure in the United States; nevertheless many Jews were ambivalent about his message and his own intermarriage.

Three years before *The Melting Pot* went on stage, the organized Jewish community, its rabbis, journalists, and other professionals were in fact given a very public opportunity to express their attitudes toward intermarriage in America. In 1905 an immigrant Jewish woman, Rose Harriet Pastor, a writer for the *Jewish Daily News*, married J. G. Phelps Stokes, a Protestant Yale graduate and a member of upper-class society who was involved in New York's settlement-house movement. The marriage was a sensation in the mainstream press, among young factory women, and in the popular culture.[45]

The Jewish community's response was condemnation. The *Jewish Daily Forward* attacked the match and reminded readers that the *Jewish Daily News* had not countenanced such matches before Pastor, one of their own writers, had announced her engagement to a non-Jew. Adding insult to injury, the marriage was celebrated in the Episcopalian church, fueling the perception among Jews that every intermarriage led to the erasure of Jewish life.[46] A friend of Pastor's at the wedding reported that Rose "put on a cross as an indication of her broad tolerance."[47] Jewish fears that intermarriage would destroy the Jewish people seemed to be realized in this romantic match of opposites that resulted in a Jewish woman becoming part of an alien Christian world.

The image of the melting pot itself was much disputed by Jews. An editorial in the Chicago Yiddish *Daily Jewish Courier*, entitled "The Fire Beneath the Melting Pot" rejected the cultural message of American assimilation.

> In his *The Melting Pot*, Zangwill compares America to a large crucible into which are cast the sons and daughters of all nations and tongues to be melted and to emerge as Americans—an entirely new type. Beneath the great American melting pot (during war) the fire is much stronger and the flames leap higher and more powerfully than in times of peace. The flames of the World War make the human contents of the melting pot whirl swifter. But the result of the process is exactly the antithesis of that which Zangwill has depicted in his *Melting Pot*. They are not fused into one piece; on the contrary, the various nationalities come forth detached, hardened, and at distinct variance with each other—each nationality manifesting in its own

way its love for America. Only the war could have established the fact that living in the same country does not mold the various nationalities into one nation.[48]

The intermarriage of outsiders may have been a conceit of popular culture, but it did not flourish at a moment when the integration of America's races, classes, or children of immigrants was afoot. The century's early decades were a period, as noted in chapter 1, when barriers were erected to keep Jews and other "marginals" out. A racial hierarchy was firmly in place and groups were segregated residentially. The nation itself was swept up with a xenophobia that cut off immigration. The Progressive era, with its promise of liberal reconstruction of the nation, race, gender, and ethnicity, continued to define a hierarchy of citizenships.[49] The fantasy of melting pot marriages simply underlined the fact that "difference" was as unacceptable in the popular culture of the nation as it was to the lawmakers in Washington, D.C.

Americanizing Jews did not intermarry in great numbers, but marriage, nevertheless, continued to provide the promise of the "modern" American family. To create a new household and family was part of becoming attractive Americans with an outlook focused on pleasure and consumption. The marriage depicted in American popular culture may have been very attractive to young Jews who chose to reject its overt message—intermarriage—in favor of a secondary message that marriage was the route to Americanization. Conversely, that message also produced anxiety, because if one lacked sufficient means and abilities to become a contemporary American household, one's place in the nation was clearly at risk.

Melting-pot marriages were ubiquitous in music, film, and theater. Irish-Jewish intermarriage, for example, was a staple of ragtime composers.[50] Early Hollywood films also regularly featured ethnic intermarriages.[51] Immigrant women writers saw in the plot of a marriage between a native-born white male and an ethnic woman the realization of her hope for freedom from her family and Americanization.[52] Immigrants looked in upon an America created by the marriages of

their children to the children of former strangers and cultural enemies.

From 1922 to 1927, Jewish–Irish Catholic romances appeared in
seventeen films, despite the rarity of such marriages at the time.[53]
Hollywood used this theme to emphasize the importance of leaving
behind "ethnic prejudice" in order to create new American families.[54]
The Cohens and the Kellys, for example, paired hapless Old World fathers whose initial enmity was overcome by the marriage of their
children, Nannie Cohen and Terry Kelly. The film was so popular that
over the next seven years it spun off sequels set in Paris, Africa, Scot-
land, and Atlantic City.[55] The Americanization envisioned by uniting
the Irish and the Jews resulted in the erasure of differences. Its humor relied as much on vaudeville ethnic stereotyped fathers whose
foreignness made them funny as on the appeal of the young couple's
youth and promise.[56]

The most striking quality of the original Cohens and Kellys film is
the young lovers' attractiveness in contrast to their families.[57] Their
mothers were large and unfashionable. Their fathers were awkward,
aggressive, and foreign. Their younger brothers were constantly
scrapping and disheveled. But Nannie Cohen was slender, fashionable, and beautiful, and Terry Kelly was large, handsome, and powerful. The film's many conflicts were resolved by the two families' return to their old neighborhood and the prejudiced fathers finding
common ground. The film assured its viewers that the birth of a
grandchild, following the secret marriage of Nannie and Terry, would
lead to the creation of a new American family free of prejudice and
with promise for a better life.

This cycle of films was directly indebted to the 1922 production of
Ann Nichols's play, *Abie's Irish Rose.* The critics panned it, but it
played for more than two thousand performances. Nichols wrote the
play, a novelization, and then sold the rights for two different movie
versions and a radio serial. Jesse L. Lasky released it as a 1928 Paramount film, paying the highest price recorded for screen rights–a half
million dollars against 50 percent of the profits.[58] *Abie's Irish Rose* was

The Jewish Cohens and the Irish Kellys face off in their apartment building in The Cohens and the Kellys, *a 1926 film made by Universal. Only the marriage of their two older children will unite these families.*
(Courtesy of the Museum of Modern Art Film Stills Archive, New York)

one of the ten most popular plays produced in 1922. It offered its au-
diences a vision of American love which disregarded ethnic differences.

The Most Popular Narrative

Abie's Irish Rose was especially interesting as a popular American
narrative because, other than ethnicity, the protagonists' social characteristics were identical. Their simultaneous similarity and difference emphasized the arbitrariness and insignificance of what appeared to the older generation to be a cultural divide. Abie and
Rose-Mary were each the child of financially successful immigrant
fathers who raised them alone after their mothers' deaths. Solomon

Rose-Mary the Irish Catholic bride is comforted on her wedding day by Mrs.
Cohen, a friend of the Levy family. This classic work about melting-pot mar-
riage, Abie's Irish Rose, made as a film by Paramount in 1928, portrays Mrs.
Cohen as good-hearted despite her ostentatious and tasteless style of excessive
display.
(Courtesy of the Museum of Modern Art Film Stills Archive, New York)

Levy and Patrick Murphy personified a softened version of the stage
Jew and Irishman of vaudeville.

Abie, a brave soldier, and Rose-Mary, an entertainer and nurse,
met in France during World War I. Abie and Rose-Mary pursued their
attraction for one another aware of their fathers' "irrational preju-

dices" toward the other's religions and backgrounds. Both their fathers shared one wish–to see their children wed to "their own kind."
Abie and Rose-Mary's love for one another, however, stood in the way
of the fulfillment of their fathers' dreams.

Ann Nichols began Abie and Rose-Mary's story in France, where
they met during the war and became secretly engaged at its close.
They returned to the United States and their fathers, believing that
they could find a way to persuade the older generation of the importance of their match. They reunited in New York and secretly married, still hoping to convince their fathers of the possibility of their
marriage. However, Rose-Mary's and Abie's fathers disavowed them
when they learned of their marriage. The couple nevertheless improbably enjoyed the continuing love and support of their priest and
rabbi, who heartily endorsed their union. The rabbi's and the priest's
acceptance of Abie and Rose-Mary's marriage translated onto the domestic front what they learned at the battle-front: that differences
were petty when faced with overpowering experiences of death and
love. One God and one nation overshadowed what had previously appeared to be significant differences. America's future lay in the marriage of differences, not Old World obsessions with prejudice. Love
transcended what origins divided.

Abie and Rose-Mary established their own home, and in the novel
Abie pursued his true interest in music after his father disowned him
and he left their joint business. Rose-Mary ruled over their domestic
bliss without complaint at their hardships. Like the Cohens' and
Kellys' younger generation, Abie and Rose-Mary were the film's only
attractive characters.[59] Their good looks signaled to the viewer that
they were destined for a good life. Their restraint, good taste in clothing and simple home furnishings all contrasted with the vulgarity
and excess of both the immigrant Jewish and Irish characters. They
were true to their dreams, and freed themselves from their Old World
fathers' prejudices.[60]

The Old World was vulgar, but not necessarily unloving. A family friend of Mr. Levy, Mrs. Cohen, supported Abie and Rose-Mary

Abie and Rose-Mary's wedding conducted by a rabbi is the second of the three they will have presided over by clergy of America's three faiths–Protestantism, Judaism, and Catholicism–in the 1928 film Abie's Irish Rose. *None will satisfy their fathers, who cannot reconcile their children marrying outside of their faiths until the births of their grandchildren.*
(Courtesy of the Museum of Modern Art Film Stills Archive, New York)

throughout their ordeal, while at the same time she served as comic relief for the audience. In addition to her annoying preoccupation with her illnesses and body, she embodied excess and was constantly portrayed as overpowering in demeanor and clothing. Her lack of good taste served as the perfect foil to Rose-Mary, who was slender, restrained, and reserved. There was no question which of these women belonged to the New World and which must be superseded.

This play and film set the precedent for casting New World marriage as unions of hope, attractiveness, and economic freedom. Just as Mr. Levy and Mr. Murphy were reunited following the birth of their grandchildren, so all of the other films suggested that in the end differences between white Americans could be set aside.[61]

American popular culture and drama thus exploited marriage as a theme to formulate national ideals. These expressive forms also replicated the harsh realities of an American homogeneous culture that was increasingly intolerant of differences.[62] If the melting pot existed, it was in the cultural imagination of the 1920s. Endogamous marriage and romance served as symbols to Jewish immigrants and their children of what intermarriage represented in the mass culture: the beginning of a new type of middle-class family–rational, attractive, hopeful, and independent.

Marriage in the Popular American Jewish Narrative

Jews marrying Jews, however, never led to harmonious cultural images. New World marriage produced anxiety and uncertainty about whether it could deliver its promises of class mobility and Americanization. While parts of the popular Jewish press affirmed the importance of marriage, others saw American marriage, even between Jews, as a symbol of freedom out of control. Precisely because Jews believed that love and desire hastened the process of Americanization, romance and relations between the sexes served as an unparalleled vehicle for commenting upon life in America.

The uncomplicated plots of early twentieth-century films and dramas provided resolution for all conflicts. By contrast, Jewish venues such as advice columns, cultural commentary, and fiction represented marriage as a source of struggle between men and women. Issues of social-class mobility and gender conflict found constant expression in Jews' own stories about Americanized marriages, and during the century's first decades occupied even more cultural space than concern for intermarriage. In these writings Americanization was repeatedly represented as Jewish women and men pursuing romance, freedom, and (for women in particular) the material trappings of America.

Abraham Cahan, writer and editor of the *Jewish Daily Forward*, and one of the most powerful immigrant voices to reflect on Americanization, devoted much of his journalism and fiction to love and marriage. His persistent pursuit of the theme of love in his writing reveals just how dramatically he believed the New World transformed relations between Jewish men and women. Immigration upended European Jewish conceptions of marriage, the family, and Judaism itself. Cahan was obviously fascinated by the need to understand these new "scripts" that cast the pursuit of intimate relations in the United States as uniquely American. In short, the right to pursue love symbolized for him, as it did for many other writers, the cultural transformations brought about by immigration.[63] Jews, however, used this metaphor to different ends than did many of the artists, politicians, and journalists of the larger society.

For example, Cahan's story "God Is Everywhere!"–written in 1902 for the *New York Commercial Advertiser*–juxtaposed New World love with Old World Judaism.[64] Annie, a young immigrant woman, fell in love with Joe, a Galician Jew who loved another woman. In her desperation to win Joe's love, Annie took her aunt's advice to visit a saintly rabbi in New York. Her aunt contended that this Polish hasid and miracle worker had a soul so pure that "the Most High attends to his prayer."[65] Americanized Annie protested, "But what can he do for me, auntie? Prayers won't help me. They won't melt Joe's heart. Do you think they will? If my face didn't, prayers won't."[66] In desperation Annie secretly searched out the saint in order to change her lover's heart. When she explained her mission to the rabbi-saint, who averted his eyes from her face to preserve his modesty, he first inquired about Joe's observance of Judaism. She explained that it was "about average" and added, "But why should I be more religious than all the other girls?" Annie urged, "This is not Galacia, rabbi. This is America. People are educated here. They wear neckties and go to the theatre."[67]

The rabbi described Annie as an American—lacking respect, impatient, angry, and a blasphemer. Cahan economically represented Annie's crude Americanization through her pursuit of love. No wonder that the saint continually reflected on his own fall and cursed the day when he set foot on American soil. At the same time, Cahan's rabbi took pity on Annie and advised her that he would pray for her peace and piety, but only if she stayed away from Joe for six months, during which time, the reader learns, Annie found and married another man.

Cahan's great novel, *The Rise of David Levinsky*,[68] offered a more devastating view of Americanization and love. Levinsky's success as an American manufacturer was purchased at the price of love. His extraordinary rise from penury to financial success by dint of his wits and hard work undermined his ability to find the love of a woman he could marry, and the novel ended with him successful and alone, his longing for a young socialist woman and an Old World out of his reach. He used money to buy sex and intimacy, but real love alluded him.

Whether in the having or the longing for it, love served Cahan as a powerful symbol of Americanization because it revealed the reordering of the most fundamental principles of European Jewish life. Levinsky's mother had planned for him to be a scholar. In the New World he abandoned traditional learning, and despite his low status in the Old World as an orphan, he was able to amass a fortune. He was rewarded for violating the Sabbath, and for eschewing commitment to family and moral purity. What mattered most "there," mattered least "here." Levinsky's success was clearly portrayed at the cost of his ability to give or receive love. If love and romance symbolized the New World, Levinsky's lack of both suggested that he was caught between worlds, able to succeed without completing his transformation. Capitalism had replaced traditional Judaism, but gave him no basis for private life. He could not forge a link with a woman of his own generation, and longed wistfully for a world to which he would never return.[69]

However, love was not solely the matter of fiction. Between 1917 and 1920, a satire column of the Yiddish weekly *Der Amerikaner* (*The American*) used with great consistency the relations between husbands and wives to poke fun at Americanization and its challenges to traditional authority and European Jewish life.[70] The columnist allows us to understand how immigrant Jews reconstructed the interest in love and romance that dominated American popular culture. He created a criticism of assimilation and acculturation through his satire of romance and Americanization. His readers inhabited a world of traditional Jewish observances along with their attractions to the contemporary society of their times. Images from the Bible were powerful for them, and part of their cultural vocabulary.

In 1917, the first column appeared in the form of a contemporary women's commentary on the Weekly Portion of the Bible, entitled "The Up-to-date Tsen U Rene."[71] The author, a Lamed Baysnik, was a nom de plume for Leybe Baseyn or Leon Elbe, who immigrated to America in 1905 from Minsk, Russia, where he was born in 1879. His father was a *hazan* and he was yeshiva educated. He was involved in a variety of socialist politics in the United States and worked with the National Radical Schools in Minsk. He was a writer and editor in the Yiddish press until his death in 1928.[72]

Elbe used his column, sometimes written in a rabbi's voice and sometimes in a woman's, sometimes presented as biblical commentary and at other times as prayers and spiritual literature, to ridicule Americanization through the medium of conflicts between men and women.[73] The columns portrayed Americanization as the pursuit of immigrant men and women for freedom, material objects, and personal power. If his satire poked fun at these men and women, it was to reveal that Americanization was best represented in their foibles, and in their relationships to one another.

Elbe signed his columns "a Lamed Baysnik." His name is a word-play on the name Lamed Vavnik, which literally means "thirty-six." The Lamed Vavnik are the thirty-six righteous people in every generation on whose account rabbinic commentary held that the world exists. A Lamed Baysnik (from the Yiddish word *bais,* meaning "house") implied a man whose righteousness was the product of his knowledge about the household. Playing on the popularity of magazines and newspaper sections on "woman and home," the author presented "homely" interpretations of the Bible that promised to draw out the meanings of the text that satirized women's and men's domestic lives. The writer introduced his column by describing American men and women to his Yiddish immigrant readers in terms of their "puffs."

The first column, on June 8, 1917, was titled "Go and Seek: A Translation of the Pentateuch": "A Modern Women's Yiddish Bible for girls and women with puffs and hats, for rich and average, bad looking and good looking, tall and short; and also puffed up men will find here a taste of sense, plenty to laugh at, and lots of other things. All who read it should become strong and healthy."[74] Women wore their puffs in the form of fashion, and men demonstrated their puffs through pride and pretension. Marriage in America, like Americanization itself, created a connection between a consuming woman obsessed with puffs, and men puffed up with money and success.

For most of the first year the satire column took the form of biblical commentary for women. Exegesis followed a line of biblical text. The biblical phrase or section appeared in Hebrew, and the Tsena U' Rena (Go and Seek) commentary was written in Yiddish. His first column began with the phrase taken from the weekly Torah portion, "Beha'alotekha" ("When you light the lamps") (Num 8:1–12:16) "Miriam and Aaron speak about Moses" (Num 12:1) in which they slander their brother's non-Israelite wife. Miriam is struck with leprosy as a punishment. Elbe commented on the passage in Yiddish in the form of an invented rabbi's–Reb Leybele–question and answer.

> Miriam and Aaron talk angrily about Moses. Reb Leybele asks
> why does it say "and she spoke," since Aaron also spoke. The
> justification is that a woman always can speak for two. She's an
> expert in talking and therefore the posuk (phrase) honored her
> and put the "speaking" into the feminine form because speak-
> ing and gossiping are female work. . . . Reb Leybele continues to
> ask why does Miriam come before Aaron (in the word order of
> the phrase)? The justification is–ladies first. From that we see
> ladies first is from the Torah.[75]

Not only did Elbe ridicule women with the classical Jewish view
that they speak excessively, he also added the principle of "ladies
first," which newcomers to America took to be a quintessential example of the power inversions of the New World that gave women status and respect over men. Indeed, "ladies first" was used as a comic
proof-text, demonstrating that in addition to their "natural" desire to
dominate, women learned that in America they deserved special
treatment.

The Lamed Baysnik was, however, even-handed, turning his pen
on men in the next paragraph.

> It's a mitzva (religious requirement) that women should dress
> up nicely for their husbands so that men should not have
> thoughts about other women. The up-to-date version says styl-
> ish women don't dress up for their own husbands, but for other
> men because they know that if other men like their appearance
> their own husbands will like them too. There are men who will
> not give the slightest bit of attention to their wife until they real-
> ize that others give attention to them. Only then will they be-
> come jealous.[76]

In this passage he portrayed men as vain and interested in display
to underline their Americanization and their superiority. Women
were thus forced to draw the attention of men other than their husbands. The Lamed Baysnik suggested that male and female puffery
were the products of a new set of social circumstances that rendered
husbands fickle and wives dominating.

Der Amerikaner, in sum, noted American values and ridiculed them for its Yiddish-speaking audience. Its editors and readers, though firmly committed to American life—its science, art, and literature—nevertheless found changes in relationships between men and women an apt symbol for the anxieties and difficulties of American life. Later that year, for instance, a Lamed Baysnik commented on the weekly portion Pinchas (Num 25:10–30:1). He not only braided together women's desire for power, love, and Americanization, but included women's suffrage as well. He began with his own comment on the "burning issue" of marriage. His biblical text concerned the Daughters of Zelophehad: "They stood before Moses, Elezar the priest, the chieftains, and the whole assembly, at the entrance of the Tent of Meeting, and they said, 'Our father died in the Wilderness. Let not our father's name be lost to his clan just because he had no son. Give us a holding among our father's kinsmen.'" (Num 27:1–4) The Lamed Baysnik embellished the story so that the Daughters of Zelophehad learned that they could not have land and must marry. The daughters rebelled because they lacked a dowry. His column proceeded: "Nowadays, who will marry poor girls? You yourself know that a boy doesn't go crazy over a poor girl because he would rather take an ugly rich one. But you know that you have to buy a rich one. As our mother Eve said kaniti ish, 'I bought a man.' [but more usually translated "I found/have given birth to a son/man"] And with what will we buy men if we don't have any property." He continued, "(this is) a constitutional issue because the constitution is against giving equal parcels to men and women." However, he added: "But since you complain that your father died a poor man and didn't leave a dowry for you, I'll ask God about it. God agrees to a parcel of land just as though they had been men. You see dear sisters that the Daughters of Zelophe were the first fighters in the women's rights movement. Their victory was the first for women's rights."[77]

This commentary reflects simultaneously on contemporary issues of marriage, suffrage, and women's power. Men did not love women without property; suffrage addressed the identical issues. The

Daughters of Zelophehad were cast as both New York "East-Side girls," struggling to be found desirable without money, and as biblical suffragettes. Women were in conflict with men over relations of love and power, even though God, in opposition to the Constitution, supported women's rights. The reader found in this satiric biblical commentary a Jewish vocabulary for commenting on power relations between men and women newly negotiating American society with its current interest in women's rights.

The popular music of this period also reflected the inversions and power relations associated with women's transformed status. *Magazine of Songs* (*Lider Magazine*) was a semiannual Yiddish publication of popular songs that spanned the most prosperous years of Yiddish theater, from about 1897 to 1911. It printed Yiddish parodies and adaptations of popular English-language American songs.[78] *Lider Magazine* included its share of songs about "ladies," referring to America as the land of "Leydiz Foyrst [ladies first]." The status implied by the term *lady* was particularly appealing to women who were no longer forced into arranged marriages or without resources and autonomy. Popular songs such as "Rosie, You Are My Posie," became in Yiddish "Sadie, You're a Lady" and "The Gal from Yankee Land" could declare in Yiddish that "my countryman (landsman) is Uncle Sam."[79] The music expressed many of the sentiments of *Der Amerikaner*'s satire, which revealed that the promise of American love and marriage was also a struggle over the power to control, to define, and to display oneself.

Der Amerikaner, like all of the Jewish press—both Yiddish and English-language—was fully absorbed with marriage and women's roles. Just as American magazines reflected a cultural preoccupation, if not obsession, with marriage and family during the century's early decades, so too did the Jewish press. Jewish writers feared divorce as fully as did other Americans. Similarly, companionate marriage, which was committed to the equality of the sexes, was as important to immigrant and native-born Jews as it was to other Americans. Just as the nationalist ideology of the melting pot was imagined to be realized through marriage, so were changes in Americans' lives symbolized in new forms of marriage and women's independence. Advocates of the new marriage envisioned a different foundation for society strikingly like that of "melting pot" marriages–choices and freedom unfettered by institutions or ideas from the past.

The feminist-generated debates about marriage underlined the fact that choice and freedom were only one set of issues relevant to the new marriage.[80] To feminists, economic freedom and dependence were also issues of great importance. The expectations that Jewish Americans discovered as they entered American society held for virtually all Americans who embraced the middle class.

Marriage meant that women would, by contrast with those in East Europe, leave the public sphere by giving up jobs and returning home to create a proper domestic world. Marriage placed men and women in a set of economic relationships eagerly anticipated by the Jewish immigrants and their children. Rose Cohen remembered asking her father, "Does everybody in America live like this? Go to work early, come home late, eat and go to sleep? Will I have to do that too? Always?" He responded, smiling, "No, you will get married."[81]

Companionate marriage and love implied a very specific set of social relationships built on men as providers and women as consumers and managers. Ethnic and native-born Americans shared not only this division of labor, but the promise of a better life tied to a marriage of equals. Underlying each of these debates–companionate marriage, feminism and marriage, and melting pot marriage–was the significance of marriage as a key institution that would establish a new democratic, middle-class America in which men supported women who created homes and families for the twentieth century. And within each debate about marriage, particularly in the late 1920s, was a persistent theme of the unceasing embattlement of men and women over wanting and producing. Although marital discord was rarely discussed in marriage manuals of the time, the rise of divorce rates nationwide led to constant speculation about what was wrong with women, what was wrong with young men and women, and what was wrong with the society of the times. The new emphasis on women's rights and freedom exacerbated that sense of growing incompatibility between the sexes.

Writing for the English pages of the *Jewish Daily Forward,* Lawrence Lipton made just this observation about immigrant popular culture when he noted that America was "a new Eden for immigrant Jewish women." Lipton argued that women were gaining increasing power in the United States, as reflected in Yiddish songs about women's freedom and stock Yiddish theater plots concerning wives who run off with their "star boarder." Immigrant men were on notice, he claimed, that women would not be controlled by men. The source of their power ultimately derived from their ability to choose a marriage partner and to insist on their right to spend money and consume. Lipton wrote that "the young immigrant girl was already in many cases 'a good European' when she came here. She had already, to a great extent, emancipated herself from parental tyranny and contract marriage. Her notions of *liebe* [Yiddish for love] were not far from American notions of love."[82] In America, Lipton claimed, Jewish women were free to marry, free to buy, and free to pursue a marriage to a man who would earn well. Many European Jewish women came eager to assume American values that ensured those freedoms. In short, women were transformed from "*yiddene* (a petty, talkative woman) into the lady." Ladies, Lipton claimed, used marriage to assert their autonomy.

In all of the examples, from "The Bintel Brief," to Cahan's and Yezierska's fiction, to the puncturing satire of *Der Amerikaner* and Lawrence Lipton, to dominant cultural debates about companionate marriage and melting-pot marriages, Jews found powerful images of Americanization in love. Love created opportunities through freely chosen marriage that undermined the authority structure of traditional Judaism by giving women and youth control over their own lives. That power, its promises and disappointments, made marriage the compelling trope of its time. Americanization through marriage and romantic love offered immigrants' sons and daughters a crucial alternative to their parents' world, one they were eager, even desperate, to leave behind in order to become Americans.

The American popular culture that created a nation out of the marriage of opposites was turned on its head by Jewish immigrants and their children. In both cases love created new possibilities for new families in a new twentieth-century nation. Even as Jews sought an American Jewish life, they found themselves beset by the same conflicts that haunted most early twentieth-century Americans who looked to marriage as a source of a new division of labor, pleasure, and romance. Marriage as the setting for realizing desire for aspiring middle-class Jews created conflicts between men and women that helped to produce an elaborate stereotype of a young Jewish woman set on success, in search of marriage, and vulnerable to a wide range of accusations about her desires from her peers, her family, and social services agents.

The Young Jewish Woman in Search of Marriage could serve as both an emblem of the folly of Americanization and the hope for an American Jewish identity, because during this period marriage was a magnet for competing ideas about who might be an American citizen. Jews in general and Jewish women in particular meditated on their place in America through the institution of marriage as it had been in Europe and might be in the United States. Marriage would continue to serve Jews as a powerful symbol of that relationship for the remainder of the century, because it entangled economic relationships, the reproduction of the family, and private identity within the nation.

CHAPTER THREE

Consuming Love:
Marriage and Middle-Class Aspirations

I am speaking the truth when I say that many a man has remained a bachelor or married some wealthy girl just because the girl of his choice refused to share the ups and downs of married life with him.

Letter from Blackstone, a lawyer, to the *Jewish Daily News*, July 9, 1989

It is best for a man to feel the burden of married life in order that he be fired with ambition. . . . People often forget that were it not for the extravagances of women some men would never work hard and make a success in the business world.

Letter from Gladys, to the *Jewish Daily Forward*, March 3, 1923

In 1900, a popular anonymous journalist for the *Jewish Daily News*, the most widely read Yiddish newspaper of that year, described in his column an evening spent with the "ghetto's dozen most clever girls, none of them being of wealthy parentage." The Observer, the name under which he wrote, valued the opinion of these intelligent and Americanized daughters of New York Jewish immigrants. He queried the young women on the subject of marriage and married life. The Observer, like other journalists in the Jewish press, wrote a story that was likely to encourage a lively debate. He chose a popular theme: what young American-born and Americanized immigrant Jewish women hoped for their lives and expected in a marriage. The reasons that Jewish men, afraid of women's high material expectations, felt they could not marry had been the source of just such a heated discussion in the Observer's column the year prior, and the debate continued well into the century's first decade. On this occasion the Observer wrote that the young women informed him that "the unanimous opinion of that intelligent group of girls was that none would marry a man whom they dearly loved if he earned twelve dollars a week." He added, "One girl went so far as to say that she would never marry unless she had 'five rooms and a bath.'"[1] These young women asserted a simple truth. For them, marriage was the route to their dreams of love and a better life. They were not small dreams.

Fifty percent of New York's Jews in 1900, for example, lived in the Lower East Side, an inhumanely congested area. They were housed in tenements that had little light, let alone a private bath.[2] A study conducted by the United States government from 1907 to 1910 learned that Russian Jews paid more for housing that they shared with more people, quite often seven household members, than any other immigrant group living in the nation's seven poorest districts.[3] In 1902 a building boom in the ghetto produced larger and more attractive apartments, including some with private baths. They were designed only with the most privileged in mind.[4]

If a wedding was their route to "five rooms and a bath," then what these young women sought in marriage was quite simply membership in the American middle class, assuredly not the one from which they came. They dreamed of an "American" life that included many comforts advertised in the press and visible in the offices where they worked or the schools they attended. They linked those pleasures to loving sweethearts and husbands whose successful accomplishments made them compatible with their own efforts at becoming an American—English language skills, an appreciation of the arts and ideas, and knowledge of American styles and tastes.

The Observer responded to these aspirations harshly. Because, he reasoned, few men could afford "five rooms and a bath," a woman with these expectations would "be doomed to become a woman suffragist [which he equated with a spinster] or else take less than five when she marries."[5] He explained that the unmarried women of the ghetto had to lower their expectations. They might have to do their own cleaning, work at a business with their husbands, or "slave" in some way. He promised, however, that the future would bring them greater wealth and prestige.

> The girl marries some "twelve dollar man." She is satisfied with less than "five rooms and a bath," and perhaps she does her own washing and ironing too. The years go by and we find the erstwhile simple and unsophisticated girl the president of some Jewish charitable auxiliary; her husband is proudly one of the directors of the institution, and the housework—why that's being attended to by two or three or even more servants.[6]

The "ghetto's dozen most clever girls," presumably real subjects of a conversation, in this article nevertheless served as the embodiment of one of the most popular stereotypes of their day, the Young Jewish Woman in Search of Marriage. She appeared in the Jewish ethnic press, in plays, music, and in humor through the 1930s. This stereotype was, as suggested in chapter 2, in one sense a variation on the Ghetto Girl. She sought marriage rather than autonomy, worked in an office or department store rather than the sweat shop, and was more interested in domestic items of home and the pleasures of the theater than with the flamboyant clothes and decorations of the working woman. She was more likely native-born. Like the Ghetto Girl, however, this stereotypical Jewish woman was judged dangerous to Jewish men, and by extension to the Jewish people. Her desires were also represented as insatiable, leading her to drive away men of her class who might not measure up, or to yoke a man to ceaseless work to satisfy her wants.

In chapter 2 I suggested that marriage was a powerful symbol for both the American nation and the Jewish minority, carrying different significance for each. The acculturation imagined was "amalgamating" for the nation and supporting ethnic solidarity for Jews. Not only did marriage provide that model for Jews, it also offered a counter-image of an Americanization that created pretension and foolish values.

However, the Young Jewish Woman in Search of Marriage held more complex significance within the Jewish community, where she was not only a symbol of Americanization gone awry, but she also seemed to complicate and even undermine the very path to Americanization. This stereotype reveals the intragenerational struggle between unmarried Jewish women and men created by a middle-class economy that placed their desires in conflict. It reflected, then, the struggle between nation and outsider, assimilationists and Jewish particularists, and between unmarried Jewish women and men who saw in marriage simultaneously a vulnerable search for love and the avenue to mobility and Americanization.

The Woman in Search of Marriage, like the Ghetto Girl, had her male counterpart. The stereotypical successful, unmarried Jewish man took instead of giving. Rather than loving freely, he sought a dowry or other financial compensation to marry. He was "conceited," indifferent to young women from the working-class origins that he was poised to leave. In some versions, he was either unwilling to spend money on dates, or dated with no intention of marriage. His indifference to Jewish working women made him dangerous to the Jewish people because, as many social service experts of the time claimed, he was threatening to leave in his wake a tribe of "old maids."

In these same venues the Jewish Woman in Search of Marriage and her male counterpart shared another quality. They were often portrayed as profoundly vulnerable, afraid of being undesirable and unable to find love or marriage. Their vulnerability was the product of their class, which doomed them to being alone. Working-class men and those bound for the middle class shared a fear of demanding women. Working-class women worried that for lack of a dowry they would not find love with a man like themselves, someone interested in the promises of American life. These linked images of women and men–their excessive desire and fear of isolation–gave powerful expression to the anxieties inherent in Jews' aspirations for the middle class.

The children of Jewish immigrants were committed to creating identities in which their Jewishness, their membership in the middle class, and their Americanness were closely braided together. Anxiety, often expressed as the fear of not finding love or finding a love whose demands were impossible to meet, continued to invade their certainty about their place in that class. The braid remained secure only if one found love in order to marry. Therefore, the stereotypes suggest that anxiety about marriage and love was in effect the product of anxiety about Americanization and mobility. The demands of Americanization ensnared the love that promised to be "free." Even before the turn of the century, therefore, New World love and marriage, shiny bracelets of hope and promise, threatened to become treacherous fetters blocking young Jews' reach to Americanize. Their anxiety about excessive desire and unattractiveness because of their parents', or their own, lack of resources mirrored their fears that the middle class was unattainable.

The Demands of the Middle Class

Jews' aspirations for Americanization often took concrete form: membership in the middle class with all of its comforts. Jewish intellectuals, journalists, and workers wrote not only about democracy, religious freedom, and working conditions, but about better housing, wages, and clothing. Jews' ability to join the middle class and enjoy its benefits was testimony to their suitability for American life.

At the same time, many Jewish observers attributed "crass" Americanization to a preoccupation with clothing, money, or conspicuous consumption. As the *American Hebrew* suggested in 1917, the "citizening of the foreign born girl" must separate her from her own foreign world. Otherwise, "out of touch with real American standards, she adopts . . . the pathetic symbols of the only standards she seeks—the whitened nose and the high-heeled slipper."[7] Other condemning voices blamed the "modern" Jewish wife who created a home that had contemporary furnishings but was "spiritually empty."[8] These attacks on materialism and fashion chastised both Jewish women and men for their indifference to the proper attitudes toward their roles as citizens and Jews within America. Their acculturation required them to stay on the right side of a fine line drawn between success, which was praiseworthy, and immodesty, which was not.

East European Jews entered an American economy that had developed a distinguishable middle class with its own consciousness and activities around the mid-nineteenth century, including distinctive residences, clothing styles, and furniture.[9]

The middle-class mother and wife, in the late nineteenth and early twentieth centuries, reigned over the domestic domain as "angel of the house," managing her children and household. Her husband carved out a public life in a workplace where he relied on new, rational business skills to amass sufficient money to support the expanding needs of the middle-class, single-wage, household.[10] The middle-class American family of the turn of the century devoted great resources to consumption.[11] Women played a pivotal role in that culture as consumers. Immigrant women, with middle-class aspirations, learned to Americanize by learning to consume, financed by a husband who embraced the American work ethic.

By the late nineteenth century, a crucial aspect of women's management of the household involved their buying an ever-increasing array of items for the home and every member of the family. Before 1890, parents personally produced what children ate, wore, or played with. In the next twenty years, throughout the period of mass immigration, baby clothing alone became one of the largest national industries, powered, of course, by immigrant labor.[12]

Children's new needs simply reflected every other aspect of the changing nature of the American economy and culture. Beginning in the 1890s, the culture of consumer capitalism, created by American corporate business in cooperation with a significant number of American institutions–from museums to educational institutions to churches–defined a world of expanding wants and newly defined needs. As historian William Leach argued, the fundamental lesson in Americanization for immigrants was to adjust to the "elemental feature of American capitalist culture–the cult of the new," which undermined attachments to the past, and offered a greater number of affordable consumer items that democratized desire.[13] The period of mass immigration was one of rising wages, but even more of increasing consumption.

A study published in 1911 of industrial workers in the United States noted that because of their occupations immigrant workers earned lower wages than native-born workers. But, the study suggested, the position of immigrants "as measured by the command of material comforts" began at once to be "relatively American in standard." A Jewish immigrant interviewed by a social scientist reflected that immediate sense of change. "The people in the same house where I. L. (the immigrant's cousin) lived, were ordinary workers. They lived better here than in the old country, were satisfied and encouraged me that everything will be all right once I start working. They emphasized a little too often the point about working."[14] Consumption, to some extent, equalized Americans. Immigrants ate and dressed better in the United States than in Europe because even low American wages purchased relatively more goods than had been available in the Old World.[15] America appeared to be as accessible as its attractive objects.

Insatiable Desires: Men Just Can't Get Ahead

Like her vulgar "sister," the Ghetto Girl, the stereotypical Young Jewish Woman in Search of Marriage was defined by nothing so clearly as her desires, the very essence of American life in the century's first decades. She was dangerous to young Jewish men who were burdened by what she wanted, rather than to bourgeois and more acculturated Jews, or kin. Her desire was their undoing because their failure to provide for women's wants demonstrated that they had not yet become Americans.

Jews were by no means the only Americans whose sexual and marital battles were fought on the fields of consumer goods and frustrated dreams of success. But, whatever tensions were faced by middle-class men and women in the nation at large, as evident in popular magazines and novels, Jews were convinced that Jewish women wanted more from men than their non-Jewish counterparts.[16] They made a condition of social class–the male provider supporting his family as a consuming unit–a matter of cultural identity precisely because maintaining Jewishness and entering the middle class were both tied to marriage for them. The demands of the middle class that required all men to support their wives were transformed into the demands of Jewish women with whom desire was associated.

These images and issues were played out within the American Jewish world's most popular venue, the Jewish press. Within the Yiddish press, the most common site for these issues was its English pages, which were directed to young adult readers. In the articles and stories featured in the press the burdensome expectations of the Young Jewish Woman in Search of Marriage were a regular subject for three decades, whether the newspaper was conservative, socialist, or Zionist.

From 1899 to 1906, for example, the *Jewish Daily News'* Observer, and the thousands of letters he claimed to receive from throughout the United States, debated whether women's demands made it impossible for men to marry for love. The Observer columnist called the debate "the burning question," and initially attributed its heat to working-class Jewish women's failure to find husbands. He asserted that their problem resulted from ambitious young Jewish men who looked to a marriage dowry to underwrite their need to establish both a career and a "comfortable" American life. Over time, however, the working-class women became the source of their own problems. As he lamented in 1901, "Is there a more serious proposition than this (marriage) for a man to face? Yet, let him lack enough of the national medium of exchange, commonly known as 'the dough,' and the chances are mighty good that he will be looked upon as 'alright, if only he had more money.'"[17] The Observer proclaimed Jewish women to be overly concerned not only with men's assets, but with their occupations. In 1902 he described a woman, one with "a thirst for higher education," who refused to talk with men "who have not a 'handle' to

their names." The handles included "A.B., M.D., Ph.D., or LL.B."–signs
of professional work and high status. Though extreme, the Observer
believed that this woman obviously represented something typical
about young working-class Jewish women that worried him. They
wanted to marry men of position to assure their own place in the
American middle class–one that promised comfort and prestige.

Unmarried and married Jewish women were constantly contrasted to selfless European Jewish Mothers of old. Although some
writers claimed that Jewish women were unfairly accused of excessive wants, the newspapers' constant repetitions of the accusations
gave them an aura of reality. By the 1920s the English pages of the
Jewish Daily Forward ran articles with titles such as "What's the Matter with the Modern Girl?" (1923), "When Dreams Don't Come True"
(1926), and "Daughters Are a Nuisance" (1926). The *Day*, a moderate and Zionist newspaper whose English pages appeared in the mid-
1920s, rehearsed the identical problems with articles and readers' letters about women's expectations and men's indifference to their
needs, leading to difficulty in finding love or a mate for marriage.

In 1923, for example, one of the first articles carried by the new
English page of the working-class *Forward* featured the headline,
"What is the matter with Our Jewish Girls?" Nathanial Zalowitz, who
wrote about men and women throughout the 1920s, recounted a
bachelor friend's attitudes toward Jewish women. He presented his
friend as somewhat extreme, but concluded that his statements "contain a grain of truth." The bachelor friend, Sam, complained about the
Jewish girl's demands for luxury.[18]

> Have you tried to take the average Jewish girl on the second
> balcony? And if you have, did she accept your invitation a sec-
> ond time? Always it must be the Orchestra or the front row on
> the first balcony. . . . Whenever two Jewish girls go to the the-
> ater by themselves they buy gallery seats; but when a man
> takes them out, it is presumed that nothing except the most ex-
> pensive tickets are good enough. Is there any particular reason
> why the Jewish young man must pay $5.60 for two tickets when
> $2.20 should suffice?[19]

Sam, the bachelor, introduced a novel distinction in his diatribe. He compared Jewish and Gentile girls, something which had not occurred in the press prior to 1920.

> The average Gentile girl who sits in the orchestra is [with] a well-to-do business-man or professional; when Sadie goes out with her Milton [who earns forty dollars a week] she must rub elbows with Mrs. de Puymter.
>
> The other day I asked a Jewish girl who was born and bred on Division Street what she considered the minimum weekly wage or salary she could marry. "I guess I could manage to get along on $100.00 a week" was her answer. Of course there's no fear that her [boyfriend makes] on average more than half the sum. The important thing is that she dreams of marrying a rich man. Nothing less than $700 for a bedroom suite, and $800 for a dining room suite will make her happy. She wants a $70 apartment on the Grand Concourse. She would like an automobile, at least a Buick you know.
>
> Thousands of married Gentile women work. In most restaurants the waitresses are married. The downtown offices are full of young brides who feel that now-a-days the burden of supporting a home is too great to be born entirely by the man. They don't consider it a disgrace to help keep the home. But a Jewish girl who has to go to work after her wedding looks upon herself as the unhappiest creature on earth.[20]

In May, 1925 Leon Kornbluth wrote that Jewish boys hesitated to take out Jewish girls because "the price of a girl's good time must be footed by the boy." He claimed that working women were earning more than ever and didn't need an escort "unless there is a prospect of good times." Dates therefore required burdensome extravagance which exploited men.[21]

In 1926, the *Day* featured an anonymous article entitled "I Married a Poor Girl," which articulated men's apparent nightmare of bottomless desire. The author of the article, a dentist, avoided a matchmaker and his promises of marriage into a wealthy family because he feared that their daughter would expect luxuries. He chose instead Rita, "a poor girl," who turned down every extravagance while they

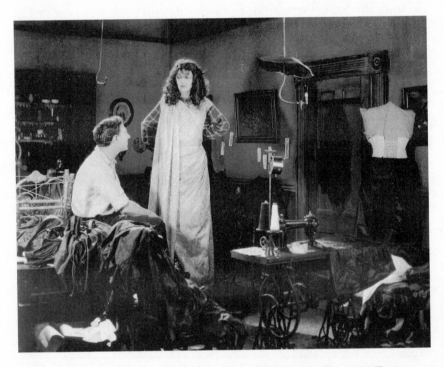

From the 1925 film adaptation of Anzia Yezerskia's novel, Salome of the Tenements *(Famous Players). In this scene Sonia is being fitted for the gown that will satisfy her "hunger for beauty" and will launch her into a marriage to a wealthy man.*
(Courtesy of the Museum of Modern Art Film Stills Archive, New York)

dated. The dentist's marriage proposal included his request that Rita sacrifice alongside him as he established himself, and "she readily agreed." But upon marriage Rita was transformed. She demanded a car, a chauffeur, maids, expensive tickets to cultural events and other luxuries. "Dentist" wrote that he was in debt and desperate and wondered what went wrong.[22]

The press was by no means the sole venue for these concerns. In commenting on a standard plot of popular Yiddish theater, journalist Lawrence Lipton wrote that young immigrant Jewish women became Americans by learning that economic mobility and affluence were what mattered most. Play after play, he asserted, cast a young immigrant woman who yearned for a "black eyed boy with mountainous hair who wrote poetry and quoted Gorki in Russian," only to realize that who she truly wanted was an "Amerikaner boychick [American boy] with a steady job." Despite tearful partings from her penniless boyfriend she chose to become engaged to a business-man.[23] She became an American by exercising her right to choose a mate, and her choice was not for poetry, but to have her needs and wants subsidized by his work.

Anzia Yezierska's immigrant novels often portrayed the young, Americanized Jewish woman driven by her desires for beauty, con-sumer items, and comforts. These longings were personified by So-nia, the protagonist of *Salome of the Tenements,* who appealed to a dress designer to give her a gown for free. She said, "There are peo-ple who will sympathize with a girl starving for bread, but only an artist like you can sympathize with a girl starving for beautiful clothes. And only you can know that the hunger for bread is not half as maddening as the hunger for beautiful clothes."[24] Sonia did get her dress and with it (and other items purchased on credit) the opportu-nity to meet, fall in love with, and marry a wealthy non-Jewish so-cialite active in the Settlement Movement. It turned out to be a rela-tionship doomed to failure.

These Jewish Women in Search of Marriage, in the press or liter-ature, are marked by two desires: to marry and to own. The wants of women may have varied by the political orientation of the newspa-per–home furnishings and opera tickets versus servants or chauf-feurs–but desire that could only be satisfied through marriage re-mained constant. The stereotypes asserted that Jewish women were nothing so much as an unrelenting drain on men's limited resources.

Rejecting Representations

The lively debates created by readers in the Jewish press throughout the century's first decades make clear that Jewish women rejected the stereotypes that were attached to them. They never saw their needs as inappropriate and claimed that the accusations were works of Jew-ish men's exaggeration. In their denial they provided their own story

about Jewish family life, expectations they had to meet, and their difficulties with Jewish men.

For example, one set of women's responses usually insisted that
Jewish men constantly exaggerated female wants. "Maid," a reader
who frequently corresponded with and was published in the *Jewish
Daily News'* Observer column, for example, rejected the claims of
many letters engendered by the comments of the "Ghetto's most
clever girls," that Jewish women wanted too much. She simply noted
that the man "who earns but twelve dollars a week" is probably a
young man, and not "on the same intellectual plane" as women she
called "American girls." Their greater degree of education would
make such a man ill-suited to any one of them, "like a bull in a china
shop." However, she wrote that if such a man were "intelligent" and
"desirable," simply lacking in fortune, then

> All other things being equal, I don't see why a woman, if she be
> a woman in the truest sense, would not be willing to "slave" as
> you call it, and do whatever she feels for herself called upon, to
> keep the common pot a-boiling. Surely, it is a modest enough
> want for such a girl as you illustrated. Five rooms and a bath
> can be had up in Harlem for about $20, and I think a $20 to $25
> man could afford it; and then the dear girl would have her
> hands full keeping her little flat in shape; for surely she does
> not go so far to say that she will not marry—even the man she
> dearly loves—unless she can have a servant.[25]

As Maid portrayed the unmarried Jewish women of her time, she
described them as hoping for domestic "bliss," modeled on middle-
class notions of women as homemakers. She assured the reader that
to want an American-style marriage, in which a woman "stayed
home," was hardly as excessive as wanting a servant. Her very evocation of Harlem identified her with Jews eager to leave the ghetto for
a new neighborhood and a better life.[26]

Other correspondents to the press were more openly hostile to
Jewish men and their accusations. By the 1920s these women frequently attacked Jewish men's characters. Nearly three decades fol-

lowing Maid's letter, H. B. of New York City wrote to the *Day* that "Jewish men, young and old," had developed the habit of "casting aspersions on the opposite sex. . . . I have read letters from doctors, lawyers, and others, wherein almost every sin was laid at the Jewish girl's door. 'She is mercenary and extravagant' says the man who showers presents on a shikse [non-Jewish woman]. When a man has no backbone, cannot earn a livelihood, or stand on his own feet, it is the fault of the Jewish girl." She concluded, "As a man creates his own God so does he create a woman in his own image."[27] She proclaimed that Jewish men's anxieties, self-doubts, and weak character led them to "blame" Jewish women, and countered that Jewish women were vulnerable to the demands of the society and of the men that they hoped would love them.

The custom of the marriage dowry heightened the anxiety of these daughters of the working class. Although no systematic study has been made of the use of dowries and marriage brokers by American Jews, the topic was constantly debated across the Yiddish press, and avidly in the English pages. The nemesis of romantic love, economic exchange between families was alive and well among the children of Jewish immigrants.

Men understood their need for a dowry to grow directly out of women's desires. Women understood men's demands for dowries to grow directly out of their obsession with economic success, which they planned to subsidize through marriages to the daughters of the wealthy. Both men and women felt that their own needs were entirely normal. Men claimed that they were expected to produce more than was reasonable or possible; women felt that their own efforts to become desirable were irrelevant in a marriage market in which they had no capital.

For over two decades Jewish women defended themselves against charges of excessive consumption by asserting that men were simply masking their own demands for dowries, and it was the men even more than the custom they blamed.[28] In 1899, "Your admirer" wrote that men were more than willing to settle down to marriage when they spied "Her." The desirable woman's qualities were "the heaviest weight of golden dollars embroidered in her sweeping train." Then East Side young men will happily lay "siege to her heart and hand (as well as her bank account.) They will not delay one moment."[29] Nearly thirty years later, a middle-western Jewish woman wrote to the *Day* to complain about men's insistence on dowries, and attributed that wish to their lack of drive.

> There are many Jewish bachelors because they feel that it is just too bad that times have changed and a dowry is not the custom any more. Any man who is selfish enough to want to marry a girl believing that he cannot earn a living for two, and depending on the girl's parents to set him up in business had better stay single. . . . Most girls are willing to marry a man of moderate means providing that he shows that he loves her and can give her a home after a sort. They are willing to go 50–50, BUT PARASITES NEED NOT APPLY.[30]

Another writer contrasted Jewish and non-Jewish men: "I have never encountered in my Gentile friends that cold-blooded calculation of some Jewish young men as to the exact value his wife will bring him either financially, or in what he may gain from her social background."[31] These women not only condemned the men's values, but feared that they would be overlooked in favor of "the crude, unlettered daughter of the parvenu (who) basks in the sunshine of wealth."[32]

One woman responded directly to the charge of women's excessive desires by weighing the different demands of Jewish women and men: "Who is it that demands the 'dot' [dowry] if not the Jewish young man? Where will you find a physician who hasn't a price tag on him? Sadie and Katie want orchestra seats, [mentioned critically by Sam, the bachelor in a *Forward* article] but Abie and Sammy want $25,000. Of the two, the girl is less money mad."[33]

The dowry issue only intensified young Jewish women's concerns as they felt called upon to reject stereotypical attributes of excessive desire. They lacked resources and were made to appear demanding

as well. Indeed, a certain desperation marked the tone of many letters from Jewish women. The ones who wrote to the Observer described their limited options if they could not marry. "Jewess" suggested that the only hope for an "intelligent girl" was to "prefer
poverty in a home where confidence and respect were the household
goods, to a union with a conceited money bag or an educated crank."[34]
"Maid," in another letter, asserted that a Jewish woman was presented as "either an old maid or the wife who makes life miserable."[35]

The Middle-Class Partnership as War

Accusations and countercharges underlay the anxieties that beset
young Jewish women and men—love, Americanization, and the fear
of disappointment were inextricably linked. Women's own dreams of
the middle class, while shared with Jewish men, were nevertheless
portrayed by the men who wrote to and for the press as insatiable and
nightmarish demands.

   These children of the immigrant Jewish working class fought one
another on the battlefield of middle-class hopes. At the period in
which Jews emigrated to the United States from Europe, mobility and
life in the middle class demanded that a man provide for a woman
who consumed for and on behalf of her family. Young Jewish men
and women fashioned their representations of one another from the
cultural and economic roles that epitomized the American middle
class. American models to be admired became Jewish sources of disappointment and frustration—the onerous demands of Jewish women
and the unyielding responses of Jewish men.

   The vulgar Ghetto Girl reflected Jews' vulnerability as outsiders
to a nation that was reluctant to imagine them taking their place
within its mainstream. The excessive desires of a Young Jewish
Woman in Search of Marriage reflected another anxiety of young
Jews. A marriage that created an American life demanded great resources. The children of immigrants with limited resources were
hard-pressed to glide easily into that class that signified successful
Americanization. A Jewish working-class woman who "ensnared"

and then "drove" a husband to produce more and more was a gender stereotype that served as a veritable model of America's twentieth-century economy. Something was compelling men to work relentlessly to be able buy all that was necessary to become fully part of the culture and nation, and it was never enough. That anxiety cut across classes, but its demands on the children of immigrants were particularly oppressive. To fail to succeed at work or marriage was to leave them outside the promise and hopes of America.

The great middle-class "partnership" of the male provider and domestic woman was not simply an abstract ideal to which Jews pledged allegiance in their efforts to Americanize. It had powerful implications for the American economy in general and the working lives of women in particular. Evidence of Jewish working women's aspirations for the middle class through the 1920s was as obvious in their hopes for marriage as in the occupations they pursued. The American economy of the period, however, controlled how women realized those hopes.

Working Women Barred from the Middle Class

The stereotype of young Jewish womanhood condensed two qualities that were not necessarily related: she was in search of marriage, and her wants were insatiable. However, the economy of the early twentieth century was organized in such a way that it forged the links between middle-class desire and marriage because women had virtually no other opportunity to reach that class outside of their choice of marriage partner.

Traditional European Jewish marriage was not the source of Jewish women's anticipation that they would leave the work force at marriage; Americanization was.[36] During the century's first decades 75 percent of women wage earners were single, supporting themselves and contributing to their families.[37] If a man aspired to improved circumstances he knew that he must create a business, or acquire "handles" for his name through education leading to a profession. Jewish women, like virtually all working women with similar aspirations, looked to marriage. No wonder that Jews referred to marriage in both Yiddish and English as a "fate."

A short story published in the St. Louis English-language Jewish newspaper *Modern View* near the end of the 1920s illustrated this point. The story, "Leisure Seekers," portrayed two "working girls," Pearl and Goldie, who sewed pieces of heavy coats in a factory. They saved all year long in order to take a summer vacation in the mountains outside of New York City at one of the many "resorts" designed for single men and women.

> Deep in their hearts lurked a tiny hope that out in the country they might meet their fate. The only men they met were the men working in the shop. Pearl and Goldie had seen enough of the misery in the poor workingman's home to make them determined to remain gray haired old maids rather than to marry a poor man. This resolution was not reached impulsively, for the fear of being a gray haired old maid is one of the horrible fears that cause much anxiety to young girl toilers.[38]

In 1927, the same year of the *Modern View* story, labor leader Rose Cohen reported that the first union organizer she met used women's anxiety about marriage as a powerful tool to mobilize working women to action. He told them,

> Girls. I know your thoughts. You expect to get married! Not so quick! Even the man who works in a shop himself does not want to marry a white-faced dull-eyed girl who for years has been working fourteen hours a day. He realises that you left your strength in the shop. You know what he does most often? He sends to Russia for a girl he once knew, one who has never seen the inside of a shop.[39]

Single Jewish women had marriage on their minds, and hence it became a critical tool in organizing women workers.

The vast majority of married women did not participate in paid labor. Only about 15 percent were in the paid workforce in 1910. By 1930, 29 percent of the female paid workforce was married women. The number of married women who labored had about doubled since 1890. Married Jewish women, like the vast majority of all married women, accepted a cultural norm that dictated that women worked primarily out of economic necessity.[40] The growing numbers of employed married women reflected the nation's economic crisis.

Indeed, for families aspiring to join the middle class, keeping women out of the workforce was an important sign of their status. Marie Jastrow recounts her father's response to her mother's secretly taking employment to stave off starvation following the 1907 depression.

> Then in some way—I cannot recall how—Mama's secret bakery job came to my father's attention.
> Papa was angry, but his anger gave way to hurt resentment. It was not the job itself, he said, although that was bad enough. Outside work was completely out of bounds for a lady, and he was surprised that mama had so soon forgotten who she was. . . . "Do as you wish," Papa said in a hurt tone, "but understand that when you hire yourself out, I am shamed."[41]

Men's dominance in the workforce became the source of expectations about their wages and occupations as well. The early twentieth-century American economy was built on the expectation of a "family wage" earned by men. The male wage earner increasingly became the "natural" state of masculinity in the United States, and the failure to realize that state threatened to make women into men and men into women.[42]

Unmarried women were exploited through a cheap wage, ostensibly because they lacked dependents. The inequity between what men and women earned speaks eloquently to the limitations on women's opportunities for economic independence. Their wages from 1921 to 1930, for example, remained substantially below those of male workers. As wages rose for men throughout the decade, all women's wages stayed virtually flat, varying on average between

$15.00 per week at the lowest in 1930 and $16.00 per week at the highest in the mid-1920s. By contrast, on average, unskilled males earned $20.00 a week at their low point in 1930, but earned as high as $23.00 per week in 1929. The highest average weekly wage for skilled male workers was $33.00 per week.[43]

In 1912 a government commission established $8.00 a week as the subsistence level for women in Boston, for example. In 1913 a study of over five hundred female office workers revealed that 59 percent of the clerks, 43 percent of the stenographers, and 13 percent of the bookkeepers, common occupations for daughters of Jewish immigrants, earned less than that. Men doing similar work at the time earned about 50 percent more.[44] Clerical work consistently paid more than sales work, and the gap widened over time. Factory work, particularly with unionization, paid far higher wages, but was considered less desirable.[45] Office and sales work were the occupations of unmarried women for the vast majority of the female work force after World War I. By the late 1920s, when Jewish women began to teach in New York, teachers' salaries were considered middle class, but by the 1930s employment opportunities decreased and teacher training programs disappeared.

Whether in the office, factory, or school women held jobs that virtually never led to promotions. A woman's first job was most likely to be the one that she kept. In contrast to men who moved through occupational ranks, managers assumed that women's work was temporary, so the entire system of an office, department store, or school ensured that women would have no reason to expect otherwise.[46] The workplace was a dead end for the overwhelming number of women, native-born or immigrant, who imagined a middle-class life.

How Work Served as Women's Route to the Middle Class

Jewish women, nevertheless, depended on work as an important classroom for training in Americanization, just not through their wages. They chose occupations that indicated their class aspirations. The *Jewish Daily Forward*'s Lawrence Lipton wrote about this process on the English page.

> The immigrant girl was a working girl. She worked in a sweat shop. But she had dreams of higher things. There was then, as now, a carefully graded hierarchy of jobs.
>
> Many a factory job paid better wages than a shop job and most shop jobs paid better than store or office jobs. What gave [them] their relatively high place in the hierarchy of employment was the higher degree of Americanization that they required. Dress, accents, American mannerisms, one's circle of friends–these, more than the amount of wages, were the criteria of social preferment.[47]

More prestigious work taught women about life in the middle class and introduced them to men who were already a part of it. Rose Schneiderman, one of the most significant women leaders of American labor, was constantly pressured by her immigrant mother to leave the factory for a department store job as her most likely route to a better life. Schneiderman refused because of the family's needs for higher wages.[48]

Women could work among Americanized people and around beautiful luxuries in department stores only if they mastered English and behaved like "real" Americans. At the same time women's employment in department stores indicated that their fathers were earning higher factory wages and were somewhat less dependent on their daughters' wages. Just as more children of Jewish immigrants stayed in school longer by the 1920s, so single Jewish women's ability to take jobs that may have paid slightly less than factory work indicated that young women chose Americanization over earning extra money.

The business office was also a prestigious address. Jewish women were sufficiently employed as stenographers by the 1920s, for example, that one of the first contests sponsored by the new English page of the *Jewish Daily Forward* sought essays on "the job of being a ste-

TABLE 3.1

Percentages of Women Employed by Year (Number in Sample) in Most Common
Women's Occupations among Jews and Italians in Cities of More Than 100,000
Population, 1910 and 1920

	Year	Native Yiddish	2d Generation Yiddish	Italian	Native-Born of Native-Born
Factory	1910	68% (298)	33% (30)	70% (162)	32% (1800)
Operatives	1920	45% (61)	12% (13)	42% (79)	16% (601)
Saleswomen	1910	8% (37)	26% (26)	2% (5)	9% (519)
	1920	12% (16)	13% (14)	2% (4)	8% (314)
Clerical	1910	5% (21)	25% (25)	0	12% (695)
Workers	1920	30% (41)	66% (71)	30% (57)	46% (1755)

nographer." The 1925 announcement read: "We are certain that Jewish girls working as stenographers in the various offices of the city constantly meet situations both gay and grave that will make interesting reading."[49]

The 1900 and 1920 (see Table 3.1) censuses support the anecdotal information about Jewish women's aspirations for white-collar occupations.[50] Since Jews were highly urbanized, Yiddish-speaking women's occupations in cities are a good index of how the most Americanized of Jewish immigrants who came as young children earned their wages. The 1920 census also counted their daughters as "Second Generation Yiddish Speakers," and provided information about their occupations. Many of both groups were likely readers of the English pages of the Yiddish press, and certainly shared their readers' aspirations.[51]

The two censuses suggest that Yiddish-speaking immigrant women were most likely to work in factories, and a small minority of them held higher status jobs. The native-born daughters of Yiddish-speaking immigrants clearly held more prestigious occupations, although the largest number in 1910 remained in factories. By 1920 the majority were employed in offices.[52]

By 1910, Italian daughters who came to the United States at about the same time as Yiddish-speaking women showed considerably less mobility. The census also indicated that Jewish families were more likely to keep their young children in school than either the native-born or the children of immigrants.[53] Nevertheless, Yiddish-speaking immigrant women and their daughters lagged behind in middle-class occupations such as teaching.[54]

Economy and Marriage

Economic opportunities unfolded for the sons of the Jewish working class quite differently than for its daughters because of the advantages of their gender. Yet, these men's hopes for the future seemed consistently clouded by anxiety as well. In 1900, for example, the Observer proclaimed that behind a broad sweep of contemporary problems lurked one common issue. Young Jews wanted more, and their desire for comfort drove men and women apart.

> To those of us who live in the Ghetto and are part of it, the question presents itself at almost every turn. First, there is the "money" question: then the "shatchen" [marriage broker] question: then the "advanced woman" question [suffrage], and the "old maid" and "bachelor" questions; the social clubs even remind us of the questions and the shops and the factories and offices, with their numerous unmarried female employees. In other words, the same social conditions which compel girls and women to work for a living, prevent men from marrying as early as formerly.[55]

The Observer suggested that marriage was a hostage of the demands of those who aspired to the middle class. Men needed resources to succeed, and marriage threatened to distract those funds. Women needed marriage to stop working and join the middle class. Their needs were thus often in conflict, and provided rich soil for the growth of stereotypes. Professionalization, the remarkable transformation of Jewish men's work, from lives as skilled laborers to white-collar businessmen to positions dependent on higher education, occurred in a few decades.

In 1905, in New York City, for example, in the midst of the Burning Question debate, 15 percent of the heads of Russian Jewish households held white-collar occupations, in contrast to the 5 percent who held these jobs in 1880. Similarly, 50 percent of the Jewish immigrant men in 1880 were skilled laborers, but only 35 percent held those jobs in 1905.[56] In 1908, another study of Jewish men's occupations indicated that of those holding white-collar positions, 37 percent were first-generation and 60 percent were of the second.[57] Immigrants and their sons were both moving toward the middle class, with sons in the lead.

However, though they were accorded high status throughout the early decades of the century, professionals did not constitute the majority of white-collar occupations. During these years, Jews succeeded in business. Only in the 1930s did Jews use education as their primary route to success.[58] The other routes to the middle class for Jewish men included real estate, manufacturing, sales, and insurance.

Many of these occupations required capital. Apartments were attractive to New York Jews, for example, because they preferred to invest their money in business rather than in their homes. By the 1930s Jews owned the majority of factories in New York City and a similar percentage of wholesale and retail establishments.[59]

The cachet of professionalization continued to grip Jews, encouraging successful businessmen to educate their sons for medicine and law. That opportunity was certainly unique for immigrants. In contrast to Europe, professions lacked a distinctive tradition in the United States. With the urbanization and industrialization of America at the turn of the century, entering the professions depended upon advanced training and specialization, and afforded a form of status that rewarded achievement and loyalty to a specific group. Jewish immigrants benefited from this limited meritocracy that was available to white men.[60]

Steven Thernstrom's study of occupational mobility in Boston between 1880 and 1970, for example, demonstrated that three out of four sons of Russian Jewish immigrants entered middle-class occupations by the 1920s. Like their fathers, they tended to be independent businessmen, but they also entered white-collar employment. They outranked all other second-generation groups in professional, clerical, and sales categories.[61] Thomas Kessner found similar mobility patterns for Jews in New York during the same period.[62]

Over two generations and fifty years, Jewish men entered and brought their families into the middle class. However, their mobility depended on careful management of whatever funds were available to them. Jews did not arrive in the United States with cash or other resources measured at ports of entry. They managed what they secured toward specific ends. Men, then, participated in the middle class through saving, investing, and working, the roles available to them. But women entered the middle class primarily as consumers, knowing how to spend and manage resources to maximize the family's position as owners of necessary and desirable things. While neither women nor men can be reduced to these economic roles, the *Observer* pointed to the economy as the source of young Jews' problems, because it so often put them in conflict. Popular Jewish stereotypes of young men and women allowed them to project onto one another the anxieties and frustrations associated with mobility for those who were so new to its demands.

The Elixir for Rage

Jewish women's rejection of the "insatiable" stereotype led to their own accusations that Jewish men were arrogant and indifferent. Working-class Jewish women's limited opportunities led them to focus their attention on men of broader opportunities. Jewish men who were likely to stay in the working class as well as men bound for professions portrayed themselves as cast aside or beset upon by these women. Representation and counter-representation, in the press and elsewhere, took on the shape of a dance that was a dizzying round of accusing and feeling accused, seeking and fearing rejection, and pulling away and looking back.

Therefore love and all that it implied–dating, romance, and marriage–had a frightening side; not to find love and marriage took the dancer out of the dance. A loveless marriage was the stuff of melodrama, but a marriage without an economic future provided the tragic plots of many tales of popular fiction and personal letters that appeared in the Yiddish press, both its English and Yiddish sections. The hopes and promises of an expanding economy and the accessibility of consumer items were crucial to the "Age of Optimism" for immigrants through 1930. Young Jews' futures were jeopardized by both excessive spending and insufficient earnings, dangers assigned to women and men in the press and popular culture.

In matters of love and matrimony, the heightened reality of Jewish gender stereotypes began to wear human faces. From the turn of the century to the early 1930s, working-class readers regularly expressed fears of being found unattractive, unmarriageable, and without hope for the future. And both sexes expressed these anxieties through gender representations–Jewish women who wanted too much and Jewish men who either couldn't measure up to American life or who were unattainable because of their harsh indifference to the women of their class and community.

This period of American Jewish life certainly gave rise to a variety of perspectives about the shape of Jewish experience in the New World. Americanization competed with Socialism, Zionism, Anarchism, and communism. Jews debated about which language they and their children should speak in the twentieth century–Hebrew, Yiddish, or English. Debates over Judaism and secularism within that linguistic struggle took up other conflicts about the shape of ritual and the language of prayer, to name only two. The diversity of the Jewish press alone in this period makes clear that Jewish life in America was anything but unified or a matter of consensus.

Nevertheless, even within this diversity the pull of economic success was exceptionally powerful. Americanization, and with it money as the indisputable source of prestige, had the upper hand, because it was the dominant perspective of the middle class in the United States. But it was also compelling precisely because, as a minority, Jews had long experienced barriers to their success in Europe, particularly access to occupations, university training, and land-holding. There were many political movements that rejected those signs of prestige, but there is no denying their tidal-wave force in creating expectations for the majority of Jews.

In their letters to the press Jewish men and women walked on stage in their New World roles reflected in their signatures as "businessman" or "lawyer," in the case of men. What remains most striking, however, about these statements about love and its disappointments was Jewish men's and women's shared sense of vulnerability in being attacked for what was so clearly expected. At this time of great cultural change the costumes of American aspirations fit loosely, and the opportunity for exposure was high. Both Jewish women and men appeared by turns demanding, arrogant, confused, and anguished over what was expected of them, what they felt entitled to, and what was possible.

Jewish women feared that they might not marry, and the English-language Jewish press began to take up the concern as well. For example, Julia Weber, who wrote for the New York-based daily *American Jewish News* asked, "Will Jewish women be able to marry?" She wrote that there was an "Anomalous Tribe" of girls of foreign-born parents. They work as "stenographers, typewriters, bookkeepers, executives, and skilled help in the trades in all our large cities." Weber praised the women for their ability to "handle the English language well," their appreciation of music and "the best books." But Weber feared that these women would not have what they most wanted—"a man who stands high in the business world and with those in the professions." Her $18.00 to $25.00 weekly salary was not attractive to that class of men who were in search of wealthier women, and the men of her own class "fear her demands."[63]

A night school in New York City, before 1920.
(Courtesy of YIVO Institute for Jewish Research, New York)

Celia Silbert, writing for the *American Jewish Chronicle,* another English-language Jewish paper, expressed similar concerns in a 1916 article on "Regents' girls," Jewish working women who sought "advancement" by studying the New York State academic curriculum in night school. The women interviewed discussed their ambitions for better, more regular jobs than the garment industry provided, and for better pay. One woman described the pleasure of school because of the opportunity to "meet boys and girls." She hoped, in fact, that she might meet a boy there to marry. Silbert concluded, "Regents' men admire these girls and a number marry them, but more have neither the admiration for their personality nor sympathy for their endeavors and aims. These Regents' men, while taking pride in their own ambitions, underrate and undervalue the same trait in the Regents' girl."[64]

If Jewish men interested in a better life found women of their own class undesirable, the same process seemed to work in reverse. Jean Jaffe, writing for the Yiddish newspaper the *Day,* noted that the mobility that moved American-born Jewish women from the factory to business, created the "imminent danger" of a woman refusing to marry "one of her own class." An "executive of a women's labor organization" explained to the paper that the problem of women refusing to marry in their class "has grown acute, and as yet no means of solving it have been found."[65]

Working-class Jewish men's fears of that very undesirability found expression in the Yiddish press. The *Forward* received a poignant letter from an anonymous writer in 1906 who described his tragic love that would never find fulfillment because of his occupation. "And I opened my heart to her and told her all I felt, but she laughed at me and told me that if I were an operator [a person who works on a sewing machine in a factory] she would like me but she wants to have a doctor for a husband." Anonymous explained that years had passed since that sad day, and despite the fact that the woman remained unmarried, she still would not consent to marry him.[66]

That same year Yoel Herman wrote that his girlfriend, about to receive his formal proposal of marriage, rejected him because "I dealt in rags. This nearly knocked her over (literally, struck her as with a bullet)." Herman asked if his work was shameful.[67]

In 1923 F. R. wrote to a columnist for the English-language page of a short-lived Yiddish women's magazine, the *Jewish Women's Home Journal,* asking, "Why is it that the Jewish girls prefer the company of the Gentiles to that of their own men?" The "boys are always willing, but the trouble seems to be with the other parties"[68]

These anxieties found their way into the popular music of the period as well. In 1911, a song featured by the American Quartet on the Victor label, "Marry a Yiddisher Boy," included the lyrics: "Why don't you marry me Sadie? I'm a nice Yiddisher boy. I've a good job–in a buttonhole factory, so why do you want to mix up with a goy?[non-Jewish man]"[69]

The English-language *American Hebrew*'s story, "The Pretender: A Moving Tale of How a Modern Girl Shattered Her Own Cherished Dream," laid the blame for men's and women's disappointment in love at the feet of women. The 1929 story recounts a brief courtship between Belle Siegel and a visiting salesman, Harry Samuels. Belle's insistence on borrowing clothes and coats to wear, and demanding that her mother use other people's fancy tablecloths to impress the young man led her suitor to abandon his dream of marriage, leaving New York without offering her a proposal. As Belle wept into her pillow "wondering why she had failed," Harry mused, "'Well, Harry Samuels, you're going back alone,' he said drawing a disappointed breath. 'Even if you did find a girl you liked and wanted to marry. But four coats, five dresses in four days. And lace tablecloths. No Harry Samuels, you can't afford such a girl.'"[70]

Not only did some men, particularly working men, fear that they were undesirable to marry, but they were even more often accused of failing to provide pleasure in dating. Immigrant working women were sensitive to the fact that their foreign boyfriends did not understand dating and "treating," but the American-born were also under siege. Even in the middle class *Day*, men's willingness to spend money on pleasure was a regular matter for discussion. "Small Town" wrote an article for the newspaper complaining, "I Can't Get Used to Jewish Men":

> A Gentile man's solicitude for a woman's comfort, his charming courtesies, and efforts to please and interest her, makes her feel like the Queen of Sheba. When it comes to entertainments, whatever we may think of the custom which requires a man to pay a woman's expenses at least the Gentile more nearly accepts the thing simply as a convention. He entertains a girl in simple comradeship, and not with the puffy spirit of spending his good money. Even a proposal of marriage is given by a Jew in the sense of conferring a favor.[71]

As the decade drew to a close, N. Zimmerman wrote a conciliatory article on the whole problem of the "stingy" Jewish boyfriend.

She noted that a "Jewish Mother" saw her son as a "spendthrift" given to extravagances, but his girlfriend had a more "mendacious tale." She argued that women contrast him,

> to his complete undoing, with Anglo-Saxon employers or mo-
> tion-picture lovers, who tempt with Rolls-Royces and gilded
> night-clubs; artichokes; and orchids even when there isn't a
> wedding; and never sit back of the seventh row even at Mr.
> Ziegfeld's most sold-out successes. This may be a rather ex-
> treme list of expectation and probably most girls are more mod-
> est in their demands.[72]

The writer urged young men to become a little more "reckless," knowing that "romantic girls are impressed by the movies." At the same time she explained that Jewish men are "merely sane and cautious "and that their generosity is hidden until marriage when they are "anxious to invest in permanent happiness."[73]

Americanization, then, placed the children of the working class in conflict for limited resources. Each sought an American dream that assigned them contradictory paths to their goals. Immigrant men and their sons became Americans by taking on the role of providers. They may have wanted luxury, but they were required to support others and to save. Their roles cast one another as tormentors and saviors, sharing a dance in which they might not find partners.

Jewish women and men did eventually marry. Stereotypes of conceited men and the insatiable Young Jewish Woman in Search of Marriage were not accurate descriptions of Jews who were ultimately unable to find love with one another. Those who came to the United States as young children, and the children of immigrants, differed from their parents only in that they married later than European-born adults. There is no way to learn whether the young women working in factories, the department store clerks, or the stenographers married the Americanized men of their dreams, or how many dowries helped finance upward mobility. All that surveys and censuses can tell us is whether or not they married. The evidence there is unambiguous. By age twenty-nine, 88 percent of Yiddish-speaking immigrant women were married, and by age fifty-five, 99 percent of Yiddish-speaking immigrant women were married. In the second generation, 85 percent of Yiddish-speaking women were married by ages 30–34.[74] The marriages were overwhelmingly to other Jews.

Later age at marriage has characterized Jewish women since at least 1920. The average female age at marriage increased from 19 to 23 years by World War II.[75] By comparison with other ethnic groups in the United States, it is also clear that Jewish women and men put off marriage, whether by choice or by necessity we do not know. The 1910 census demonstrated that by age twenty-nine, while 77 percent of the children of the native-born were married, 74 percent of second-generation Italian were married, and only 59 percent of the second generation of Yiddish speakers had spouses. The percentage of Jews married by age thirty-four rose dramatically.[76] The 1920 census demonstrated increasing age at marriage for Jewish men as well. Second-generation Jewish men married later than the first generation did.[77] The fact that men and women married later is a sign of middle-class aspirations, because it allows spouses to prolong education and train for better paying work before there is a family to support. Late marriage might have contributed to the anxiety over whether young Jews would marry, particularly in combination with radically new forms of dating behavior and romance.

The economy did not ultimately discourage Jews from marrying, and the culture did not keep them from marrying one another. However, both the economy and the culture's fingerprints are on the anxious gender representations that cast young Jewish women and men as vulnerable to one another's rejections.

The Dilemmas of Americanization

Jews' commitment to marriage among themselves did not stop their invidious comparisons to others through whom they imagined a different, if not easier future. The "Anglo-Saxon boss," the "gentile girl who happily works after marriage," the "Viking Lord" and the "gentile girl who wants to have fun"[78] all became images of American life against which their Jewish counterparts failed to measure up. While Jewish women and men were perfectly willing to express their own desires for a better life, when those wishes became burdensome they quickly became associated with the opposite sex.

The constant mirroring of demanding women and withholding men, so much like the reflections of Ghetto Girls in the eyes of acculturating Jewish women, projected onto other Jews the urgent wish to Americanize. The struggles of these Jewish men and women were by no means unique. In the nineteenth century, women pursued men, who feared their own economic instability as a result of marriage. American women's magazines from the turn of the century through the 1920s dealt consistently with themes of marriage and financial expectations. Readers of Jewish newspapers might have been surprised to learn that in 1911 *Cosmopolitan* featured an article on "Marriage: A Question of Cash." The journalist admonished American female readers to abandon their demands on their husbands. She reported that a lawyer told her, "The American business man often reached the breaking point at fifty and dropped into his grave prematurely. At least half of the grief stricken widows whose affairs come under my supervision might have kept the husbands they mourn for, in life and health, until the golden wedding day, if their wants had been simpler."[79]

The working class was as caught up with these struggles as was the middle class. Working-class leaders argued that the basis for working men's demands for a "living wage" was their desires, which were rooted in their manhood and citizenship. Women's desires, however, were quite a different matter. Labor advocates typically treated them as "unreasonable," "insatiable," and leading to lives of "shame." Jews, like all workers of this period, debated over the meaning of desire and found women's illegitimate.[80] Clearly these expectations were created by an economy that demanded that men alone subsidize a middle-class life, and required that women with few alternatives for child care abandon the workplace.[81]

Jews, nevertheless, experienced this struggle as a *Jewish* problem. They debated it in their newspapers, wrote letters by the thousands about it, not asking for advice but declaring their vulnerabilities and anger over their treatment by Jews of the opposite sex. Both men and women racialized aspects of Jewish character. They cast women's intensity, men's and women's ambitions, and their aspirations for the future as aspects of Jewish character related to a history of oppression.[82] They saw their dreams and hopes endangered by potential husbands and wives who would not love them, or who "forced" them into marriages that subsidized new lifestyles. Believing that this problem was Jewish, and in their minds unchangeable by the nature of its inherited–even biological–quality only exacerbated their vulnerabilities.

Nothing may be more revealing about these articles, letters, and debates than where they appeared in the press. The *Jewish Daily Forward*'s English pages featured the articles discussed here next to ones on whether men and women should change their names to less "Jewish sounding ones" in order to get jobs and promotions.[83] With one exception the *Forward* and its readers counseled against attempting to pass as a Gentile for economic gain. The same pages that invited discussions of marriage from authors like Bertrand Russell also advised its readers about possible occupations for Jews in sales, technology, and teaching.[84] The *Forward* also sponsored contests asking its readers to write about what it meant to be a Jew and an American. For example, in 1930 the press asked writers to respond to the following: "Precisely what does Jewishness signify to the mass of college students in this country? What exactly do they understand by Americanism? Have they succeeded in synthesizing the two elements? Is their Jewishness primarily religious? Or Racial? or Cultural? Or merely anti-goyishness [non-Jewish]?"[85] Earlier contests asked about "The Meaning of Life," "The Ideal Vacation," and "The Business of Being a Wife."[86] Virtually all of the published letters focused on how life in America affected these matters.

Like the *Forward*, the *Day* in the 1920s framed all of its articles about love and conflict in the context of Americanization. Articles on relationships consistently appeared on the bottom half of the page. Above the center of the English page appeared articles on Zionism, but also contests which asked about how to be an American and a Jew, whether the European-born or the American-born was better suited for life in America, the responsibilities of a college graduate, and, like the *Forward*, how to lose your accent and teach children to speak better English.[87]

Whether to alter one's last name in order to assimilate, what were desirable occupations, and whether or not Jewish women were parasites were in the eyes of readers variations on a single theme. Marriage, romance, and dating were powerful entryways to the dominant culture by which Jews pioneered their own American lives, but the juxtaposition of topics suggests that the links went far deeper. Intimate relationships were the vehicle for expressing the anxieties that inevitably beset the men and women who were attempting to join a society that made them constantly aware of their difference. Disappointments about being found unattractive or undesirable were not unlike troublesome accents and cumbersome names that made it possible to be easily excluded from America's opportunities. Stating that love was elusive because of the constant demands to produce more had an analog in a society whose promises appeared to rest on demands for unceasing personal transformations of looks, sounds, and activities. Jews' "Age of Optimism" coincided with the nation's own age of anxiety. Americans and their leaders were anxious about integrating different cultures and races in new urban settings. At the same time, the world of advertising was making Americans anxious about their lives in order to urge them to buy and want more.

The primary readers of these pages were young men and women, probably most of whom were American-born, and many of whom were as yet unmarried. Their struggles with Americanization differed from the heroic efforts of the foreign-born. They appeared more readily to fit into American society, but their letters and the articles written for them belie the notion that being born in the United States would solve Jews' problems. To the contrary, it seemed to exacerbate them. Their fears matched their hopes. Their increasing access both to mobility and acculturation seemed to increase their vulnerability. They had far more opportunities than their parents, and this enlarged their vistas. Living at a time of heightened antisemitism and growing hysteria over immigration, these young men and women learned that their desires were dangerous to one another.

T. Jackson Lears, a historian writing about this period for middle-class Americans of the dominant culture, characterized it as a time of "fragmented" selves. These Americans suffered from a "clear lack of focus," and often turned to experts and consumer items as sources of self-definition. Immigrants and their children believed in the solidity of that illusory world because it was the gateway to Americanization and the middle class.[88] It exacted many costs from Jews, forcing them constantly to weigh the promise of an American future against the memories and history that set them apart from that class. The least solid portion of Jews' identity seemed to be their confidence in their ability to love, to be found attractive, and to form confidently American families. As the Ghetto Girl had allowed Jews to project their anxieties about their place in America on one another, so the fear of being undesirable allowed Jews to project their anxieties onto an opposite sex who was forever wanting, excessive, or unable to produce. The ultimate symbol of the New World–love–embodied the harsh disciplines of Americanization, mobility, and the consumer society, bringing men and women of many classes and cultures in conflict.

The Young Jewish Woman in Search of Marriage personified the strategies for Americanization that were available to young Jews. Resisting and embracing the nation and the middle class through marriage, they were inexorably driven to gender roles that were calculated to make enemies of intimates.

CHAPTER FOUR

Fading Feuds:

The Eerie Silence of the War Years

> If I didn't worry about this family who would? On the calendar it's a different place, but here without a dollar you don't look the world in the eye. Talk from now to the next year—this is life in America.
>
> Bessie Berger, the mother, in Clifford Odets's *Awake and Sing*, 1935

> I'm not blaming you Mom. But boys and girls can get ahead like that Mom. We don't want life printed on dollar bills, Mom!
>
> Ralph Berger, the son, in *Awake and Sing*

For nearly the first three decades of the twentieth century, those immigrants and their children who were on the road to Americanization reflected on their relations with one another. The energy, intensity, and persistence of those debates, whether they were played out in the press or in popular music, appeared to anchor the process one went through to join the American middle class. Then, the debates suddenly went silent.

Beginning in the mid-1930s, the spaces in the English-language Jewish newspapers that in previous decades had been devoted to family, home, and women's sections were filled with articles on other topics. The venues that had allowed gender to serve as a powerful medium for expressing Americanization simply no longer fulfilled that function. Nor did the more successfully acculturated Jews express their anxieties about the nation by examining and criticizing the lives of those Jews who were more recently Americanized.

The uneasy silence that replaced the lively conflicts over the meaning of American life for Jewish men and women of both the immigrant and native generations defined American Jewish life from 1935 to 1945. This period, not surprisingly, roughly overlapped the years of World War II in Europe and then the United States, and for American Jews was thoroughly dominated by their growing horror over the fate of European Jews. The ongoing process of building an American Jewish life during this time was shaped not only by the terrifying events in Europe, but by antisemitism in the United States clearly brought on by the Depression, by the debates over America's entry into a European war, and by the war itself.[1] For example, during the 1940s from 15 to 24 percent of the American population surveyed defined Jews as a "menace to America." When the United States was at war with Germany and Japan, a greater percentage of Americans held negative attitudes toward Jews than toward German or Japanese Americans. Similarly, from 1938 until 1945, close to 45 percent of the population surveyed believed that Jews had "too much power" in finance, commerce, and business. In 1944, at a difficult point in the war for Americans, surveys in the United States revealed that 43 percent of Americans would "support a campaign against Jews." Only "Radicals" (as compared to foreigners, Negroes, or Catholics) garnered a greater percentage (46 percent), and radicals were usually interchangeable with Jews in many Americans' minds.[2]

This decade dashed the optimism that, even in the face of its virulent xenophobia, had pervaded American Jewish life in the 1920s. Now that the majority of American Jews were native-born rather than immigrants, two facts of life were unassailable: Jews were more uncertain about their place in the nation, and most of them were more comfortably members of it. Paradoxically, the years of crisis appeared to promote a truce of sorts, particularly between the prime participants in these battles in earlier decades, men and women who were either newly married or interested in marriage. Perhaps a growing solidarity of shared experience or the increasing economic pessimism that deflated hopes for the future stilled the anxious banter of those for whom only a decade before the middle class had seemed truly possible. Indeed, during the 1930s, the more Americanized Jewish family, even with its own internal conflicts, seemed to offer a shelter against an increasingly hostile world. At the same time, foreshadowing the stereotypes that would emerge in a new era of hope for American Jews in the 1950s, the outline took shape of new battlefields on which intimates could wage war.

Jewish Acculturation

As Beth Wenger found in her study of New York Jews during the Great Depression,[3] the majority of American Jews spent the years of the Great Depression and World War II among other urban Jews who also had increased access to American society. The family served as the most important set of relationships within which Jews, like many others, weathered their economic hardships.[4] Wenger also suggests that despite the economic devastation of those years, Jewish immigrants and their children, who had only recently found some measure of economic stability, continued to embrace middle-class values. Although it was difficult to manage, many Jews still idealized the middle-class family that kept women out of the workplace. And despite social workers' and other professionals' efforts to place young Jews in a variety of jobs, Jewish men and women persisted in their aspirations for middle-class work.[5]

Jews maintained dense ethnic neighborhoods and family ties, but neither these associations nor their growing anxiety for their own safety in America or for their families in Europe divorced them from their participation in an American culture. The majority spoke and read English, and consumed the burgeoning popular culture of film and radio that so successfully integrated a nation of ethnics and immigrants into one whose citizens began to share a cultural vocabulary.[6] The Jewish newspapers of Baltimore and St. Louis offered weekly listings of every movie playing in these cities. Radio, too, was extraordinarily popular during this period, and Jews were an avid audience. Success continued to be counted in American terms, even though during the 1930s a significant minority of Jews participated in leftist, highly secular movements that assailed those values.

"Cemented" as Jews were in the nation by America's popular culture, scholars of American Jewish life describe the 1930s as the period when Jews began to "vanish" as subjects from that American popular culture. Even films that began as novels or stories with Jewish characters usually ended up as feature presentations with Italian or ethnically bland characters.[7] Jews were in part so effective at combating the antisemitic portraits that dominated entertainment that they disappeared entirely from it.[8] Their banishment, ironically, coincided with Jews' presence at the production end of entertainment as well. For all of these reasons, the growing numbers of thoroughly acculturated children of immigrants and their children lived among Jews, but rarely encountered their cultural representations in the larger society, even as they were confronting antisemitism.[9] Their own venues for self-reflection were decreasing in number and changing in content.

Silences

If stereotypes of Jewish women as demanding and Jewish men as arrogant were circulated during the war years, there is very little evidence of them that remains. The *Day* was the last of the major Yiddish newspapers to carry English pages. By the early 1930s, whatever crossover appeal the Yiddish press may have had for the children of immigrants had been exhausted, and the Yiddish press itself had lost many of its readers. By 1927 its circulation had declined from its 1916 high of about 715,000 by 25 percent, to 535,000.[10] The *Jewish Daily News* had been absorbed by another Yiddish newspaper, the *Morning Journal*. The *Forward* and the *Day* continued to circulate among a smaller number of readers. The press no longer served as a prime mechanism of Americanization because Americanization had succeeded on so many other fronts.

Indeed, as the children of Jewish immigrants matured and came of age during the Depression and war years, their Jewishness found many other avenues for expression. For example, New York's 92d Street Young Men's and Women's Hebrew Association, a popular meeting place throughout the Great Depression for young and often unemployed Jews, featured a newsletter that detailed a lively organization. The newsletter made only passing reference to dating and love, commenting occasionally on the attractiveness of girls or their charms. Rather, it was concerned with employment and Jewish cultural events sponsored by the YMHA in particular, ranging from lectures on American literature to sports competitions.[11]

In the mid-1930s, a new journal, *News from the School of the Jewish Woman*, appeared.[12] The school, which began in 1933, was chartered in 1936 by the Regents of the State University of New York, and its journal allowed women to write about their experiences as students, as well as on matters of love, differences among women, and feelings about Judaism.[13] It offered courses in Hebrew, Yiddish, history, and synagogue skills. Its pages and curriculum were directed to daughters of immigrants and other acculturated Jewish women. It also featured an advice page with wisdom dispensed by a psychologist. Within a year, the journal became the *Jewish Spectator*, a magazine of Jewish opinion that remained under the control of its founder, Trude Weiss-Rosmarin until her death in 1989 and is still published.[14] The advice encouraged cooperation between young Jews rather than blaming either sex for their failures.

For example, in 1936, the advice section, "The Clinic of Personal Problems," addressed questions of compatibility between young men and women and the economic demands of marriage. A mother wrote to complain that her daughter loved a playwright and that they would have too little money to live on. She was advised by Dr. B. L. Wiseman, "It's hard to live on love, but be resigned to this."[15]

A young man of modest means wrote that he was afraid to ask his wealthy girlfriend to marry him because he could not provide her "hats for $15.00 and more, and dresses in the dozens." He received a lengthy reply about the children of successful Jewish immigrants. Dr. Wiseman explained that "wealthy men," only a short distance from "a cold flat on the east side and hard manual labor," have made "a grave mistake in the upbringing of their children by granting them every whim and wish." He advised the suitor to have a frank talk with his sweetheart to save her from the fate that awaited young women who had been given false expectations. He advised, "an expensive fur coat cannot drive away the chills of loneliness."[16]

Because of the hardships of the times, and likely because the magazine was directed to a rather serious audience of young women who were committed to night classes and Jewish study, the tenor of the advice differed starkly from that given in other columns. Rather than dramatic condemnations of young women, the reader found judicious suggestions about reasonable expectations and increased freedoms for young men and women. Even in the limited time that the magazine dispensed advice, problems of class differences and marriage were common subjects. Men and women were, however, less likely to portray themselves or to be portrayed as embattled with one another, and more likely to appear enmeshed in situations created by social class differences and parental expectations.

Images of American women as flighty, coy, or frivolous appeared beside contrasting images of serious women. Indeed, insofar as women's pages continued to appear in the Anglo-Jewish press, they reported on important positions held by women in Zionist and philanthropic organizations, and in national associations of synagogue sisterhoods. The St. Louis *Modern View,* the Philadelphia *Jewish Exponent,* and the New York *American Hebrew,* three newspapers that circulated over all four decades of the century (the latter two beginning around 1880), continued to report on ordinary life for Jewish families. They posted marriage announcements, and the *American Hebrew* featured fiction regularly and a yearly section on where to vacation.[17] However, these newspapers, which were both rich sources of commentary on women and families in the 1910s and 1920s, offered little on the subject during the 1930s and 1940s.[18]

Like virtually all Jewish newspapers of the decade, they charted the course of Hitler's rise to power, the relocation and decimation of Europe's Jewish populations, massive charitable efforts to help Jewish refugees there, efforts to create a national homeland in Palestine, and antisemitism in the United States. Once America entered the war, they also reported on the bravery and deaths of Jewish American soldiers. The press, reflecting the concerns of the war years, abandoned the images of intimacy to reflect on Jews' lives in America. Neither Jewish women nor youth symbolized American Jewish life for Jewish readers. Their lives became matters to report rather than emblems of cultural experience.

A New Generational Struggle

Prior to the war years there was, however, a detectable shift in discussions of Americanization and mobility, at least in the English pages of the Yiddish press. They revealed for the first time a certain discomfort with success and consumption that signaled not only a new level of economic comfort for Jews, but a new way of configuring American Jewish anxiety. With that hint of disenchantment came a new solidarity between young men and women against their parents. With the war not yet on the horizon, parents became the target for frustration about high expectations for success.

In 1927 the *Day*'s English section advertised a contest inviting its readers to submit letters on the topic, "Is the American Born Jew less fitted for success than his foreign born parents?" The paper offered small cash prizes for the best letters received. The winners' sentiments were to be echoed in the *Day* for the remainder of the decade and into the first years of the 1930s, when the paper's English pages disappeared. Emil L. Smith, author of the winning entry, wrote that there was more to life in America than economic success. Jewish parents' narrow view of life had led them to pressure their children to succeed.

> The living of an interesting life; the joy of doing what one desires most to do, (is true success). Then the American-born Jew has an immense advantage over his foreign parents. Many foreign-born Jews have become wealthy because they know no other way to satisfy the human craving for prestige and position. The American-born Jew realizes quite frequently that

enormous wealth is not the most satisfying possession spiritually.[19]

The next month the *Day* published Nathan Fibish's entry, in which he argued that the immigrant Jew's struggle to "amass a fortune to appease his inferiority complex did have a powerful driving force, and often he succeeded in gaining his goals—but how many never did?"[20] Fibish concluded that the American-born are "better off" even if they lack that drive for success.

Prior to, as well as following this contest, articles written by young men and women condemned parents, their own as well as immigrant parents in general, for insisting that their children pursue professions, and for misunderstanding the purpose of college as little more than technical training leading to a well-paying job. One anonymous writer contrasted himself to his brothers, who valued books only for their cost and fell asleep listening to the radio, unable to enjoy it as anything other than an "opiate." His choice of social work as a career, in contrast to his brothers' decision to become businessmen, allowed him much greater freedom, he claimed. He enjoyed his life, which he believed was all the better for lack of a car, excessive possessions, or an apartment on New York's prestigious Riverside Drive. Another condemned traditional "practical-minded" Jewish parents for ignoring the arts as worthy professions.[21]

In 1928 Erna Loeb accused Jewish parents of not "wanting their children's happiness." The author rejected Jewish parents' demands that children pursue "wealth and marriage and small careers for girls," and instead advocated their sons' right to study classics and writing. Loeb was particularly critical of parents who judged their children's suitors on the basis of how much money they had.

> They may have come to this land starved for comfort and education. They fought a fierce battle for their existence, and all around them they saw such openings into wealth and power, as had never been offered to them. And it is difficult for them to comprehend why their children who have been raised in comparative comfort, fail to appreciate these bounties. They cannot

conceive that education brings more than a craving for material success.[22]

In 1930, drawing on "personal experience and observations," a writer signing himself "B.L.T." pondered in the *Day*, "What's Wrong with These Parents?" He wrote that "hardly a mind goes untroubled by the thoughts of reconciling two forces," what a young man wants and "sparing of his elders." Speaking for both men and women of his generation he wrote,

> Our parents have made their sacrifices–true–but are not the returns expected somewhat disproportionate? For the boon of some truly excellent meals, are we to be robbed of sympathy when our desires take us in paths diverging from our parents (who) frown upon these pursuits as having no directly profitable values either in catching fortunes or a husband? Day by day we make concessions to another's beliefs, standards and laws.[23]

The American-born began to express some disillusionment, both with a life devoted to work and to the drive for upward mobility. B.L.T. asserted that parental love and protection, symbolized in the domestic and maternal terms of "some truly excellent meals," carried the excessive price tag of abandoning one's own dreams.

Tensions between immigrants and their children is a key theme in the literature and history of this period. These articles, letters, and stories, however, represent the struggle waged between the successfully acculturated immigrants and their native-born children. The American-born claimed their right to seek personal fulfillment. Many believed that their parents, because of the hardship of the immigrant experience, were concerned only with material success. Their common wish to pursue personal freedom created an alliance between young men and women that had not appeared previously in the songs, letters, and articles written by and for the children of immigrants. Parental expectations, their unfair demands for obedience, and narrowly imposed choices for acceptable marriage partners became a common set of experiences that they could reject in support of one another. Women argued that men should be able to study literature. Young men expressed outrage that their sisters' suitors were judged only on their wealth or earning potential.

The tone of these articles represented a shift in the battles engendered by love and marriage that had dominated the press during the century's first two decades. Young, unmarried American-born Jews began to express sentiments oddly reminiscent of some of the very immigrants who fled Europe in search of new opportunities and love. A reader of the *Day* wrote to the paper claiming that the reason there are "too many unmarried girls" is "the fault (of) their parents. Jewish girls' parents nowadays judge a man by his pocketbook."[24] In three short decades, from the columns of "the Observer" to the *Day*'s letter writers, the problem of bachelors and spinsters moved from a struggle between the sexes created by capitalism, consumerism, and membership in the working class to a generational struggle in which newly established immigrant parents forced their children into what they perceived as narrow, success-driven lives. Bachelor lawyers in 1899 were "forced" to marry for dowries. The *Day*'s letter writer claimed that they and their friends were "forced" to marry Gentiles, whose parents had lower expectations.

In 1932, in the midst of the Depression, Sol Davison wrote about changes in the meaning of marriage for his generation and their parents. He explained that most of the young men he knew were unemployed, and several wanted to pursue careers in the arts which would never provide them sufficient income to support a family. He called for "Fifty-Fifty Marriage" asserting that "the most frequent basis for this type of marriage is economic." As women once brought dowries to marriage, he asked why they could not now simply hold jobs. He concluded, "What is apparent is that few of us think of matrimony in the same terms as did our parents. The question has become one of economics."[25] By calling for equality in responsibility for the support of the family, Davison expressed little concern about his sweetheart feeling burdened. His anger was directed at the parents' expectations.

This flickering possibility of generational solidarity certainly suggested a new era in American Jewish culture in which alternative definitions of Americanization–rejecting professions and wealth–were offered and debated by young adults. The meaning of success, the purpose of education, and the ideal life in America all appeared to be contested, if only by a substantial minority.

The Homestand of American Jews

What critic Ted Solotaroff described as true of the "Jewish writer" is also apt for other media that featured Jewish self-representation. "What Walden Pond is to Thoreau or the West End of London to Henry James," he wrote," a family situation is to the Jewish writer; the homestand of his or her confrontation with life as well as the repository of distinctively Jewish and cultural norms."[26] Jewish acculturation reduced the number of settings in which Jews could express what made them "different." For the majority of American Jews, it meant that Jewish culture became the world of family and neighborhood. The period's pervasive secularization even made religion more of a family matter than of individual observance and study.[27]

In the mid-1930s, in the grip of the Depression and with the war imminent, second-generation Jews produced cultural works that focused on Jewish family life and were popular among both Americans and Jewish Americans. "The Rise of the Goldbergs," Gertrude Berg's popular radio saga of the Goldberg family that aired nightly throughout the 1930s and 1940s, and Clifford Odets's highly acclaimed 1935 play, *Awake and Sing*, both portrayed Jewish, New York, working-class families. But Berg's Goldberg family and Odets's Berger family shared few similarities beyond their Jewishness. Lighthearted, sentimental family situations on radio had little in common with the theater of a man known as both "the proletarian Jesus" and the "poet of the Jewish middle class."[28] Nevertheless, the mark of New York Jewish immigrant experience is evident in the work of both Berg and Odets, as their fictitious families come to grips with hopes for mobility, dreams for their children, and disappointments as well.

I am not suggesting that the Jewish family became a simple replacement for the complex intra-ethnic stereotypes of the early twentieth century. Rather, the Jewish family served as the context for the process of Americanization. In families Jews maintained ethnic solidarity and links to the past, and it became the most viable economic unit for them in the 1930s as well. It was a counterpoint to a homogenizing nation whose antagonism to Jews was very much on the rise. It was, then, an effective symbolic vehicle for exploring American life for Jews.

Gertrude Berg idealized the Jewish Mother through Molly Goldberg's good sense and care for others. Despite her character's apparent penchant to "meddle" or create problems, Berg spun Molly's nightly adventures around crises she created or inherited, and then resolved. In the 1930s Molly's humor was based on the heavily accented malapropisms that allowed her to misuse English words and syntax to make a sense all of her own. Although Gertrude Berg consistently contrasted herself with comics whom she believed degraded Jews by their use of accents that caricatured them, her maintenance of a Yiddish-inflected English was crucial to her character. Through the vehicle of language she portrayed the immigrant, but one who identified with American ideals and felt a sense of entitlement to them.[29]

Berg's ability to portray Jews as functioning, successful Americans, but ones who were still recognizably Jews, was critical to the appeal of her work. Donald Weber's analysis of the many letters she received from listeners suggests that those written by Jews most often expressed their approval and appreciation of her ability to describe Jews positively.[30] At a moment when there was a dearth of images of Jews in the public arena, the Goldberg family asserted that a successful American life was possible even with accented relatives, Jewish food, and a wise but meddlesome mother.

By contrast, Clifford Odets's Berger family hardly served to idealize the Jewish family.[31] To the contrary, through their collective life one saw the desperate toll poverty and the Depression took on each of its members. Writing about characters whose dashed dreams led them to inflict pain on their intimates, Odets staged Jewish life as unvarnished reality. It did what few plays about American Jewish life had done before. It turned the experience of immigrant American Jews and their children into a theater that was neither caricature, melodrama, or biblical epic. Odets peopled his stage with men who dreamed and men whose dreams failed entirely. Harsh and ineffectual, these men were held together within a single household by its pivotal character, Bessie Berger. Her husband worked at a dead-end, low paying job; her father was unable to change the world or support his family; her daughter was unmarried and pregnant; and her son yearned for love and to have something to show for his wages. Bessie supported, united, and often degraded them through sharp-tongued anger, tireless work, and manipulation of others. Neither her harsh strength nor powerless men, however, led American Jews to reject Odets.

Jews took him and his play up with pride. Interviewed by the Anglo-Jewish newspaper, the *Philadelphia Exponent,* for example, he was asked if his "characters were taken out of a real Bronx family and set on the stage." Odets denied it. The newspaper journalist, however, reported that Odets had "kept a notebook in which he jotted down the scraps of daily life which promised material for his work." *Awake and Sing* was drawn from these "stories and bits of conversation on the street."[32] Not unlike the fierce insistence that Molly Goldberg was real, the fact that Bronx street life found a place on the American stage demonstrated for many Jews that Odets wrote as one of them.

The Jews who listened and watched these sagas believed that their story was being told, and through these stories different groups of Jews found voices to express the dilemmas and hopes of their lives. One vivid example of that response is captured by Alfred Kazin, who recalled the impact of *Awake and Sing* on his life as a young, Jewish man hoping to become a writer. Kazin remembered the experience of finding Jews on center stage.

> For it seemed to me, sitting high up in the Belasco Theater,
> watching Odets' "Awake and Sing," that it would at last be possi-
> ble for me to write about the life I had always known. In Odets'

play there was a lyric uplifting of blunt Jewish speech, boiling over and explosive. . . . Everybody on stage was furious, kicking alive–the words, always real but never flat, brilliantly authentic like no other theater speech on Broadway. How interesting we all were, how vivid and strong on the beat of that style! Words could do it. Odets pulled us out of our self-pity. Everything so long choked up . . . was now out in the open, at last. And we laughed.

Sitting in the Belasco, watching my mother and father and aunts and uncles occupying the stage in "Awake and Sing" by as much right as if they were Hamlet and Lear, I understood at last. It was all one, as I had always known. Art and truth and hope could yet come together–if a real writer was their meeting place.[33]

What Jews–albeit rather different ones–found in both Odets and Berg was the writers' ability to capture how American Jews spoke and to portray the lives they lived, in the street, neighborhood, and at home. The critic Robert Warshow, writing in the 1940s, reflected on *Awake and Sing*'s poetic language:

It is a matter of language more directly than anything else. The events of the play are of little consequence; what matters is the words of the characters–the way they talk as much as the things they say. Odets employs consistently and with particular skill what amounts to a special type of dramatic poetry. . . . The speeches put in their mouths have the effect of poetry, suggesting much more than is said and depending for the enrichment of the suggestion upon the sensibility and experience of the hearer.[34]

Gertrude Berg did not match Odets's poetic use of language, but focused nevertheless on Molly's words as the most important sign of her Jewishness. Accented and fractured, she made a private language that was neither Yiddish nor English, but shaped a new form of communication with her audience. Similarly, Warshow argued that Odets's characters unknowingly "gave themselves away." A few words spoke volumes about the character's lives to the listener, who understood the shorthand. Alfred Kazin also alluded to this connection when he wrote, "Everything choked up for so long, and now out in the open . . ." And Kazin enumerated what that "everything" constituted through a long list of the indignities and particularities of immigrant poverty—graveled roofs and fire escapes of tenements that served as beds in the heat of summer, damp hallways, and the over-ripe smells of rotting food he associated with Coney Island—all of those experiences transformed into poetry.

Robert Warshow particularly commented on the poetics of Ralph Berger's line "It's crazy! All my life I want a pair of black and white shoes and I can't get them. It's crazy."[35] And Kazin responded to the humor he and other Jews of his generation heard in Ralph's line, "I never in my life even had a birthday party. Every time I went and cried in the toilet when my birthday came."[36]

These critics, themselves products of an immigrant Jewish American culture, underlined the power that came from the writer's capacity to communicate to his or her audience a great deal with a few words. In lines about shoes and toilets, both critics heard a new language on the American stage, a code for a culture that had been entirely overlooked: their own lives.

Odets's poetics and Berg's language play evoked a world of experience normally hidden from other Americans and absent from theater or mass culture—Jewishness itself. Replacing caricatures with families, a Jewishness that survived immigration and acculturation was what in different ways Molly Berg and Clifford Odets offered America, particularly American Jews.

Despite their cachet of "real" Jewish life, those families portrayed in the venues of radio and theater carried very little that was specifically or recognizably Jewish beyond a broadly conceived sense of language. They seemed to do little besides assert the persistence of Jewishness itself as a location of difference. Families maintained Yiddish, minimally enacted rituals, and cooked and ate special foods, a constant theme of "The Rise of the Goldbergs." Their "confrontation with America," as Solotaroff put it, lay in the fact that in large measure they worked to make sense of how to become Americans in their families.[37]

The Jewish family as the source of survival and conflict is illustrated in the one undefeated male dreamer of *Awake and Sing*. The Bergers' son Ralph, commenting on his father in the last lines of the play, declares, "Let me die like a dog if I can't get more from life." But when his sister Hennie, who is about to abandon the family and her own child asks, "Where?" Ralph replies, "Right here in the house." Conceding his mother's right to the money left to him by his grandfather Jake, a suicide a few days before, Ralph declares, "I'm twenty-two and kickin'! Did Jake die for us to fight about nickels? No! 'Awake and sing,' he said. Right here he stood and said it. The night he died. I saw it like a thunderbolt! I saw he was dead and I was born!"[38] Ralph remained at home by necessity, but with hope for his future against all odds. His sister's flight was precipitated by an unhappy marriage, not by the strife-filled, hard-pressed Berger family. In contrast with immigrant literature, in which separation and alienation proved the dominant theme, the Jewish and the American self were able to coexist in Jewish families, at least in the perceptions of critics from the period.[39]

With the temporary disappearance of gender-rooted stereotypes and venues to express them, so too did the idea of Jewish life as a battlefield between young men and women disappear. With antisemitism at an all-time high in the 1930s and 1940s, one might well assume that intra-ethnic stereotypes would also heat up to reflect that strife. I have found precisely the opposite. The anxious representations of embattled lovers flourished in Jewish life at times of greater hopefulness. The family, even in Odets's work, is as much anchor as battlefield. The massive anxiety of this period, along with increased Americanization, created representations of persistent Jewishness in a family beset by generational conflicts and tensions, which were anticipated in the press around issues of class mobility. A reflection of the importance of the family as an economic unit in this period, as much as a final holdout against cultural homogeneity, intergenerational Jewish intimates with all of their complexity became the grounding for American Jewish culture of the time.[40]

The Bridge

This focus on families in no sense suggests that issues of gender conflict disappeared for Jews. Beth Wenger's research about New York Jews and the Great Depression revealed that the economy took a terrible toll on Jewish marriage. The records of the Jewish Conciliation Court demonstrated abundant stresses and strains on Jewish families.[41] Nevertheless, this dramatic shift in Jews' popular cultural self-expression indicates that as powerful a medium of expressing anxiety as intergenerational relations proved to be for Jews, during the trauma of these decades something changed. The successful acculturation of American Jews, the difficulties of the Depression, and particularly the war against European Jews reshaped how that anxiety was expressed.

Gender relations were more often encoded cross-generationally. Mothers loomed large in these images and continued to do so for many decades. Unlike the mother from "home," the European mama, these Americanizing mothers bridged worlds. Sentimentalized and vilified, their full development as a symbol of American life found expression only after the end of World War II and in relationship to Jews' rising affluence. As economic and emotional manager of her family's world she maintained connections between particularity, intimacy, and American success. Just as the idealized Molly Goldberg could unfailingly succeed at the task, Bessie Berger and all of the other Jewish Mothers that would follow in the 1940s and 1950s would fail as the other side of the same anxiety.

The majority of American Jews were distinguished by the fact that they still tended to live in a relatively small number of urban centers. They continued to aspire to the middle class and chose male white-collar occupations as the most certain route to that end. Families often cooperated in making that goal possible for their sons. The patterns of Jewish life in the century's first two decades ended in the

1930s and 1940s, and new ones emerged firmly only in the 1950s, when Jews surged into the middle class definitively. These painful decades ultimately offered a bridge over which Jews moved from one era of optimism to another. However, these bridging decades did not shield them from the trauma of the Depression or the horror of a genocidal war that has marked American Jewish experience for the latter half of the century.

The structure of that bridge not only kept in place middle-class values, but it shaped a largely deracinated Jewish experience that relied on images of family to mark the power of Jewish experience as private yet persistent within the realm of American life. Jewish gender stereotypes shifted back and forth between intra- and intergenerational formulations throughout this period as acculturation took different forms. The love that formed new families and the complex ties and loyalties that transmitted Jewish life represented to Jews the process by which they defined their Jewishness within American life.

CHAPTER FIVE

Strangers in Paradise:
The Devouring Jewish Mother

The Jewishness that he wore so lightly as
one of the tall, blond athletic winners must
have spoken to us too–in idolizing the Swede
(Seymour's nickname) and his unconscious
oneness with America. I suppose there was a
tinge of shame and self-reflection. Conflict-
ing Jewish desires awakened in him by the
sight of him were simultaneously becalmed
by him; the contradiction in Jews who want
to fit in and stand out, who insist they are
different and insist they are no different. . . .
Where was the Jew in him? You couldn't find
it, and yet you knew it was there.

Philip Roth, *American Pastoral,* 1997

Judging from what many of our writers and
cultural observers have been telling us for
some decades now, being a Jewish Mother is
not only no honor, it is really a disease . . .
without a cure.

Samuel Irving Bellman,
Congress Bi-Weekly, 1965

The devastations of World War II left American Jews more certain
than ever of their place as loyal citizens of America and the possibilities of its promises. A once diverse ethnic community divided by
country of origin, political outlook, class, and religious and secular
expression of Judaism became, with astonishing rapidity, a middle-
class community committed to the New Deal consensus that supported the Democratic party's liberal wing. In unprecedented numbers Jews joined the synagogues of their new suburban locations and
pledged allegiance to an American religiosity that linked God, family, nation, and house of worship, although Jews continued to visit
theirs far less frequently than their neighbors.[1] Jews came ultimately

to join and even personify the middle class to which they so singularly aspired throughout the first half of the century.

At a period in American Jewish life that historians have called a "time for healing," "regrouping," and "conquest of suburbs,"[2] a familiar stereotype of American Jewish life took on a rather new shape–the Jewish Mother. She was not the Yiddishe Mama of the Old World, to whom immigrants longingly turned with sentimental songs and harsh comparisons to American sweethearts and wives. Rather, this representation of New World prosperity was an American-born Jewish Mother who pushed, wheedled, demanded, constrained, and was insatiable in her expectations and wants.[3] The guilt induced by the Old World was not her siren song; rather she demanded loyalty to herself and her impossible New World expectations.

The Jewish Mother often took the related form of a Jewish Wife to the husband who underwrote the suburban lifestyle of his family. As wife and mother came to dominate the Jewish popular culture as well as some of the fiction of the period, the husband faded away. The Jewish patriarch of some of the films and novels of the 1910s and 1920s did not even limp into suburban affluence; he vanished from popular culture.[4] No one laughed at Jewish father jokes in the 1950s and 1960s because there were none. When the father appeared, it was often as the passive foil to the monster wife. Mother/Wife dominated the scene. Her male counterpart spoke eloquently through his silence.

Neither would the unmarried Jewish woman appear again as a gender stereotype until the 1970s, when she would eventually eclipse the mother. Rather, the lineage of gender stereotypes among American Jews seemed to follow a developmental and historical path from the young, unmarried working-class immigrant Jewish woman, to the native-born working woman on the verge of marriage, to her postwar persona as suburban mother/wife. Each formulation articulated Jews' anxieties about their place in the nation through their relationships with one another, which were both inter- and cross-generational. The Mother/Wife became a vessel into which Jews initially poured their concerns about their arrival in the middle class in the context of postwar prosperity and the growing integration of Jews into suburbs.

In the decade following World War II, although antisemitism appeared to be waning, Jews' new affluence did not bring them the social and cultural acceptance that they anticipated from middle-class non-Jews. To the contrary, suburbs fostered the conviction that Jews were different, and Jewish women and their children became icons of excess and consumption. Rather than the immigrant Ghetto Girl who required control by the middle class, now suburban Jewish women and by extension in some instances their children were blamed by Jewish men and non-Jews for the parochialism and desires that barred Jews from their rightful place in America.

These new Jewish gender stereotypes appeared in different types of venues than had been available in the more limited worlds of interwar Jews. Jewish magazines were circulated to a national readership, and Anglo-Jewish newspapers continued to appear. Jews, however, increasing a trend begun in the 1930s, looked to reading material well beyond the borders of their own community and read *Life, Ladies Home Journal, Seventeen, Time, Newsweek,* and other magazines precisely because they shared the interests of the American middle class.

At the same time, many popular performers and writers commented on Jewish experiences for Americans both Jewish and non-Jewish. *Marjorie Morningstar,* Herman Wouk's 1957 novel, was the top grossing work of fiction of the year, selling over 191,000 copies, almost 40,000 more than its closest competitor *Auntie Mame.*[5] Its readers found in Wouk's story of a 1930s New York Jewish family a tale about their own lives—rapid economic success and loss, the death of a son in World War II, and a daughter's striking out and initially rejecting her parents' values and sexual mores.[6]

Films on Jewish topics in the 1950s were still a fraction of the number they had reached during the 1920s. Nevertheless, they were many more than had appeared in the 1930s and 1940s, when Jews virtually disappeared as characters in, let alone as the focus of, American films. Jewish Mothers, though a more prominent feature of 1960s American films, did appear in films like *Marjorie Morningstar* that were adapted from novels in which they were characters. Their fame preceded them.[7]

A great deal of American humor during this period was defined by Jewish comics, working as both writers and performers. Their material often focused on the Jewish family and provided for American experience an urban, ethnic frame that proved popular.[8] Jewish experience in general, and families and mothers in particular, had the potential to speak to a variety of Americans.

Jewish gender stereotypes, then, circulated not only within the Jewish community but in the many other parts of the society that were likely to read popular novels and see stand-up comics on television. At the same time the Jewish Mother/Wife was a stereotype that was widely articulated in Jewish life, and a source of speculation for Jewish social scientists and rabbis.[9] She crossed over from the specificity of American Jewish life to the non-Jewish consumers of diverse ethnic experiences. As a product of an increasingly mass media, her reality became even more convincing.

The Stereotype

The stereotype of the postwar Jewish Mother/Wife, drawn from Jewish comedy and popular Jewish magazines of the time, had three faces. First, her excesses knew no bounds. She thus suffocated her family, but especially her children, with food and nurturance that made giving and receiving a poisoned act. As an excessive giver, she never wanted or received anything directly, but she was highly manipulative. Her name was synonymous with guilt, her second attribute. Her demands were impossible to meet because she wanted what usually seemed impossible to give—total loyalty. Finally, she was often portrayed as naive, stupid, or hopelessly out of touch with the world of her children. These qualities, but particularly the first two, were the quintessential characteristics that marked her as a unique type of mother and woman.[10]

In the persona of the Wife, this Jewish gender representation was associated aggressively with wanting and demanding. Status, success, and suburbanization were some of the demands she placed upon her husband. The Jewish Mother was often less forthright than the imagined Jewish Wife in her demands, but each embodied a version of wanting.

It would be difficult to identify with equal precision a mother/wife stereotype of the dominant culture during this time. The postwar period is often associated with an anti-mother ethos of "momism" that I discuss later, but in general, its enshrinement of domesticity made a generic American mother less a source of humor and vitriol.

The Jewish Mother/Wife was a staple of the stand-up comedy that began in the Jewish summer resorts of New York's Catskill Mountains and took center stage in postwar America. Ed Sullivan's weekly variety show, *Toast of the Town*, long-playing albums, and nightclub floor shows were critical venues for these comedians. The prosperity of the decade made such entertainment accessible to a great many Americans, and Jewish comics played well nationally.[11]

Jack Carter was a young Jewish comic in the 1950s when he appeared on the Ed Sullivan show. He paid homage to older comics such as Myron Cohen and Alan King in his routine by complaining that as an unmarried man he couldn't joke about marriage as they did. But he explained his single status by "two words: my mother." Carter described his mother's attitude toward women who interested him. "She doesn't believe that the woman is born yet who is good enough for her golden boy. I found a girl, she can cook, sew, she can wash dishes. Mother says 'I'll use her on Tuesdays and Thursdays.'"

Jack Carter did not build his humor on the Yiddish accents of older comics, which had signaled that mother was foreign and an immigrant. He simply evoked the lineage of comics that would make his audience aware that the mother he described was a Jewish Mother, unwilling to let her "boy" go to another woman. If his sweetheart had wifely virtues, Carter joked, his mother was willing to hire her as a servant, not relinquish her son to her.

Carter's next mother joke was of course about food. "That's the trouble with America," he told his audience. "We all eat too much." Then he laid out the familiar images of the Jewish Mother forcing food on her children.

It all starts when we're little kids. The mothers start with the spoon barrage. They trap you in the crib or the high chair and they go, "a spoon for Daddy, a spoon for mommy [drum roll] one for Uncle Sam, one for President Eisenhower." No wonder everyone is blown up, we're eating for the whole country. [He lunges aggressively].

Have you ever seen kids in the morning eating cereal? Meanwhile the mother is filling up a bag with sandwiches, and pears and apples, and pies and cheese. She puts it under your arm and when you get to the bus she yells, "Don't forget to come home for lunch." Isn't it true whenever you go to your mother's she has food ready? It's murder. You can never catch her short. She has 80 courses already. And she's always running and up on her feet, and then they stand behind you like an umpire. "How's the chicken liver?" "Fine." "It needs salt, pepper; you don't like it?"

"No I like it; I like it."

"Don't eat too much; there's soup coming."

My mother has what I call warning food. Everything is "watch out."

She puts down the soup, "Watch out; it's hot."

"Put it down Ma, I'm 37, I'm not an idiot. I'll know if it's hot."

"Watch out for the fish; there may be bones."

"I know there's bones. As soon as you hear [he makes sounds] you'll know I'm choking to death. I cross the street by myself Ma, wave bye bye; leave me alone."

"You're hollering. All I am is a servant to you and your father."

And is he going to get it after I leave. Look how she dragged this poor soul in. This man hasn't said a word in 40 years.[12]

In fewer than ten minutes, Carter mapped the 1950s comic terrain of Jewish Motherhood. She offered excesses of food and criticism as part of an arsenal of weapons to infantalize her son. His father was worthy of passing mention for his silence and weakness.

The powerless, put-upon husband and father was not a developed comic type in the same way as the Mother/Wife was, but his presence loomed large, particularly in the sociology of the period that I discuss later. Harry Golden, a popular humorist of the time, not unlike Jack Carter, sympathized with Papa. In his comic sketch, "It Was Better When Papa Was the Boss," Golden wrote nostalgically,

> If only the American world . . . also adopted the patriarchalism of the Jews of two generations ago. We'd probably all live to one hundred and twenty, like Moses. It was much better when papa was the boss and ruled the family.
>
> We have most of the automobiles, telephones, washing machines, and beauty parlors in the world, but it is all a mad dash from sun-up to sundown, and a growing alienation from life.
>
> Many wives of course, tell the truth when they say that they do not apply any extra pressure on their husbands, but this does not diminish his own needs, what he thinks his obligations to her to continue to stew in this economic pressure-cooker that is the America of 1958.
>
> And then she says, "No, I do not want a new coat this year– we cannot afford it"–it is the unkindest cut of all. She is sincere, of course, but "the times are out of joint." She has merely added another ton of pressure to his shoulders and he is more determined than ever to become Top-Man-in-Sales for the ensuing month.[13]

Passive and dominated by the Wife and what she must have, the Jewish father represented nothing so much as a silent reminder of the failure of patriarchy.

In not such gentle terms an army of Jewish comics–Myron Cohen, Milton Berle, Shecky Green, Henny Youngman, and Alan King–joked about their wives' demands for the houses, appliances, trips, and clothes that were impoverishing their husbands. "My wife has a black belt in credit cards." "Marriage is a great institution. Ask any man who has been put in one." "Take my wife, please."

In fact, the fault line that fractured the nearly seamless stereotype of the Jewish Wife/Mother in the postwar period was constituted around desire. While Wives were represented with bottomless wants, Jewish Mothers appeared to want nothing. Comedian Jack Carter joked, "And you can never give them gifts. They always resist it. Eventually they take it, but they fight you. I wanted to give her a fur coat. 'Don't spend the money. You'll throw it out. I'll never wear it; I don't need a fur coat. Maybe a mink would be nice, a small one.'" Carter's humor relied on the same indirection as Harry Golden's. Women of course wanted things. Their denial required their husbands and sons to learn to divine their true desires because they could not acknowledge what they wanted.

What mended the fracture of want between these women's images was their equally insatiable demands for love and obedience. Another humorist, Dan Greenburg, focused on the demands of the Jewish Mother. His 1965 novelty book, *How to Be a Jewish Mother*, was a remarkable success, the top grossing nonfiction work for the year. It sold 270,000 copies and provided a model for a variety of humor books for decades.[14] *The David Susskind Show*, a popular talk show that brought together groups of politicians, writers, or experts to address a contemporary issue, devoted a program to Jewish Mothers.[15] The idea was obviously derived from the book, and Greenburg was one of its guests. He defined the Jewish Mother for Susskind as "an expert in instilling guilt and manipulating." The humor of his "how to" book was derived from breaking down Jewish Mother behaviors into teachable units: "The Basic Techniques of Jewish Motherhood," "The Jewish Mother's Guide to Food Distribution." Greenburg created a Jewish Mother vocabulary built upon words and syntax that evoked a Yiddish-inflected English. In a section called "Practice Drill," Greenburg wrote, "(1) Give your son Marvin two sport shirts as a present. The first time he wears one of them, look at him sadly and say in your basic tone of Voice: 'The other one you didn't like?'"[16] The Jewish Mother demanded conformity from her son, could not tolerate separation and fed and overfed others constantly. She was, however, miserable. Greenburg offered a section on "the technique of basic suffering," to distill her fundamental outlook.[17]

Finally, the Jewish Mother's simplicity rendered her foolish. Dan Greenburg, for example, provided his readers with Jewish Mother's opinions on a variety of subjects from Fidel Castro ("A man that cannot take the trouble to shave, comb his hair and put on a suit and clean shirt would not get my vote, I can tell you that much"), to Nasser, and the moon landing that revealed her complete lack of knowledge about world events.[18]

The comic Myron Cohen told the audience of the Ed Sullivan show a story in this genre. He explained that his mother received champagne and caviar from a friend of his and when he asked how she liked them, she said "The ginger ale was good, but the herring was too salty."[19] Myron Cohen's Jewish Mother was not entirely part of the New World, even in the 1950s and 1960s.

Sociologist Gladys Rothbell noted in her analysis of American joke books that the Jewish Mother emerged as a subject of humor only in Jewish and not in non-Jewish collections of jokes. These Jewish Mother jokes appeared for the first time in books printed after World War II; they formed a substantial percentage of the jokes about women. The themes Rothbell found in this humor included overprotection, boasting about children, ethnocentrism, and incompetence about most things, the same themes that pervade the humor of Greenburg and the stand-up comics.[20]

The Jewish Mother stereotype, then, not only appeared in the media just after World War II, but also in relatively new venues. On television, in print, in widely circulated long-playing albums, and in novelty books, she personified, often through her son's vision of her, an American Jewish culture in transition. She was funny because she was out of place. Her excessive and dangerous nurturance held back her sons–the producers of this humor–from moving forward into adulthood.

Like all other stereotypes, the postwar Jewish Mother appeared to be thoroughly real, and she served as fodder for Jewish comics because she appealed to a broad audience of Americans who, in laughing at her demands and her excesses, laughed at something familiar in their own lives.[21] She became popular not only with humorists, but also with a cast of experts in an era much taken with expertise. Deconstructing her power and significance reveals the anxieties of postwar life that were brought on by a fundamental transformation in American Jewish experience.

What Is Wrong with This Family?

These comic images of nurturance gone awry appeared in tandem with an anxiety that beset suburban Jews. Amid their prosperity and growing confidence, their leaders sounded the alarm over the Jewish family and the future of the Jewish community. With great regularity, and with some of the same excesses of the stand-up comic, these experts blamed the Jewish Mother in her suburban world for the many crises American Jews faced.

The sober sociology of suburban Jewish life, as well as the commentators in popular Jewish magazines, described the troubled moral order of the Jewish family of this era. That Jewish women had too much "power" was commonly used as an explanation for the persistence of problems in the Jewish community and family. These problems included preoccupation with status, sons' alienation from their fathers and domination by their mothers, and Jews' diminished religious practices. For example, Leon Feldman argued that the "predominant parental influence of the mother," was reflected in the Jewish college student having "more ignorance than knowledge of Jewish life."[22] Sociologist and rabbi Albert Gordon passed on the observation by "some" that in "class conscious families," Jewish Mothers set "false standards for their daughters." He quoted a respondent who decried the purchase of expensive clothes for daughters because it created a competitive atmosphere.[23] The Jewish family had lost its traditional patriarchal focus, confusing its children, argued others. And, perhaps most ingenious, the writer David Boroff asserted in 1960 that Jewish women had ruined Jews' reading habits.

Blaming the "curious transposition of roles in contemporary life," he argued, that women now induced their husbands to read books rather than books serving as the "sancta" of Jewish male existence. Lacking "his passion," Jewish women created "the Jewish best-seller." Because Jewish women were the book buyers, they foisted these inferior works onto a best-seller list, which in turn increased their popularity. As a result, "lightweight" books were popular because "lightweight" readers (Jewish women) usurped Jewish literary culture.[24]

Jewish women ascended to power, in the minds of so many of these writers, through a cruel trick of acculturation. Writing in 1966, Earl Grollman declared that "the former jurisdiction of the patriarchy is handed by default to the wife." He did not imagine that women relished this role because they had "too many duties and burdens without this authority," but he noted, using a common term of the period, "the vacuum is there."[25] Albert Gordon declared that suburban Jewish women formed a matriarchy that unseated the normal Jewish patriarchy. He wrote, "The Jewish woman has acquired her position of executive leadership by default."[26] Gordon quoted a teenage boy saying, "Mother makes all the family decisions in our home,"[27] simply to illustrate what seemed to be an agreed-upon crisis.

The dominant and dominating mother even found her way into an early 1960s religious school curriculum. *Modern Jewish Problems*, a book directed to teens, presented students with the problem, "Should we intermarry?" It was a common topic for the religious school curriculum at a time of new anxiety about intermarriage because of the greater opportunities created by suburban life for young Jewish men and women to meet non-Jews. The case study of Sidney and Louise concerned two college-aged students who decided to marry after dating for a few years. Sidney's parents, like Louise's, did not greet the news happily. Louise's Christian parents together expressed their concern. But Sidney's parents responded as "His Mother." She burst into tears and sobbed, telling him, "All my life I've dreamed of the day when you would marry a fine Jewish girl." She added, "That's not what father and I have sacrificed so much for in all the years since you were born."

Here in a capsule is a Jewish representation of Jewish life. Christians speak together; Jews speak through mothers. Jews and Christians hold the same opinions about intermarriage, but Jewish Mothers delivered their concerns with threats, emotions, and recriminations. Jewish Mothers, in short, dominate and render Jewish men silent.[28]

Jewish women's "unnatural power" was widely believed to further corrupt a family form altered by immigration. Samuel Irving Bellman, whose "Jewish Mother Syndrome" appeared in *Congress Bi-Weekly*, psychologized the matter as a "confusion of sexual roles." He pontificated that the Jewish family structure was "essentially patriarchal," and had not responded well to the "administrative tampering on the part of the wife and mother." She filled the "power vacuum" left by a father concerned with work. He concluded that her children created negative stereotypes of the Jewish Mother because of that "administrative tampering," and the push for "upward mobility."[29]

A variety of Jewish commentators noted that the Jewish woman's increasing importance in the synagogue was parallel to, and as problematic as, her power in the family. She lacked sufficient religious education to serve as a lay leader, according to Albert Gordon, who found her dominant role "not a healthy condition for the synagogue."[30] Marshall Sklare, in his suburban study, described women's increased participation in synagogue life as "a symbol of newly won status" reflecting their class mobility and acculturation, but he attended very little to understanding their other motivations for their religious lives.[31] Sklare certainly acknowledged women's important role in synagogue and community life, and Albert Gordon concluded, much to the contrary of the rest of his book, that suburban Jewish family life was both intimate and important. However, they could not seem to help themselves from blaming women, or at least noting their centrality to the problems that beset postwar Jews. Commentators most often presented their dominant role in suburban Jewish life, in fact, as an accident that women took advantage of, rather than one motivated by articulate values and ideas of their own. At their most neutral, Jewish sociologists of suburbia noted that women's commitment to Jewish communal life represented a fundamental transformation in Jewish values. With men abandoning their traditional roles and women taking them over, most commentators foresaw disaster for the Jewish community.[32]

Herbert Gans's study of Park Forest, Illinois, and its Jewish community provided a variation on this theme. In 1949, about one hundred Jewish families formed the core of the Jewish community of the new "planned garden city." Gans documented the families' debates over what institutions to create first–a synagogue or a Sunday school. The debate divided along gender lines. Men favored the congregation, and women the Sunday school.

The women's triumph, according to Gans, led to a "child-oriented community." That approach, he argued, guarantees "the existence of the ethnic group for another generation, despite the ambivalence or rejection of the culture by the adult carrier." Gans suggests that the women were the architects of this approach to Judaism because of their dominance in suburban life. Men, according to Gans, were no longer "traditional" fathers who were "adult-oriented," and had lost their position as religious leaders of the family.

While Gans never makes an overt value judgment, the implications are clear. Women created a Judaism that failed to sustain adults. Although Gans wrote about the lack of religious involvement or education of the vast majority of these one hundred families, the fact that women supported religious education, and men lobbied for a synagogue became the basis for his assumption that the changing sexual division of labor made the Sunday school the mechanism that excluded adult Jewish practice from the community.[33]

The views of the Jewish Mother/Wife as the source of the failure of Jewish values and Jewish religious and intellectual life were

A fathers and children's breakfast held at Rodeph Shalom, a Conservative congregation in Los Angeles, around 1953. Events such as these were clearly designed to involve fathers with their children and with the synagogue as well. They were in part motivated by the pervasive anxiety of the period about mothers' dominance.
(Courtesy of Riv-Ellen Prell.)

starkly polemical. Commentators, whether sociologists or Jewish communal leaders and journalists, expressed nostalgia for the learned, patriarch-dominated Jewish family that simply was not the norm of American immigrant families or their children.[34] Leon Feldman claimed, speaking of the parents of Jews who were college students in the mid 1950s, "The[ir] Jewish educational background . . . is meager; less than four years and less than five hours a week. His [the student's] father had more Jewish education, but less secular education than his mother."[35]

These minimally educated, secularized Jewish men hardly seemed likely to provide the highly learned lay leadership that rabbis longed for. Women were accused of either sentimentalizing or reducing Judaism to "ceremonial" practice. It is hard to imagine what Judaism these men would have offered as an alternative. Rabbi Stuart Rosenberg, for example, was horrified to discover in 1943 at his first New Jersey suburban pulpit–a newly organized synagogue–the young, Jewish male leaders knew no Hebrew and had not attended a Sabbath service in decades! He described them as typical of American Jews of their ages.[36]

Like the other stereotypes encountered, the Jewish Mother/Wife has far more to teach us about Jewish acculturation beyond the Jewish world than about "administrative change" in the family. The connection is all the more powerful because this Jewish stereotype had a powerful analog in America generally known as "momism." In 1942, and then in twenty-seven subsequent printings through 1960, Philip Wylie's book *Generation of Vipers* gained extraordinary attention by arguing that American mothers had destroyed the morale of the nation by their treatment of their sons.[37] Wylie reflected on the significance of his book in his twentieth edition, in which he informed his reader that his discussion of motherhood is "one of the most renowned passages in modern English Letters."[38] He argued that deprived of their "social usefulness," and with control over their husbands' money, they amassed excessive power in their families, in politics, and in the church, while doing nothing productive in return. Wylie claimed that men's only hope was to "make the conquest of momism, which grew up from male default," to take away their money and disavow Mom's "perfidious materialism," and resume a life of dreams and conquest.

Wylie was recognized as extreme even while his work was popular. Nevertheless, the uncanny similarity between his prose and that of sociologists and Jewish commentators suggests the extent to which the Jewish Mother/Wife was the product of American culture.[39] Like other Jewish gender stereotypes, nevertheless, the Jewish Mother/Wife was more powerfully marked as "Jewish" than as "mom" by those who circulated her image. The Jewish Mother was an icon of difference from, not similarity to, the broader American culture. She appeared to be the opposite of Wylie's alcoholic narcissist; after all, she nurtured and disavowed her desires. Nevertheless, in the poisoned atmosphere of "momism," Jews not only reflected dominant cultural images, but in rendering them Jewish looked to that source of difference to discover how they undermined their ability to be either "really" Jewish or American.

Suburbanization

Postwar Jewish life was defined by suburbanization, particularly for its young middle-class families. Between 1950 and 1960 the Jewish population in the suburbs more than doubled, in contrast with the total suburban population, which increased only 29 percent.[40] Although they began to leave the cities, Jews continued to live near one another. By 1960, 75 percent of American Jews lived in only five states.[41] Gerhard Lenski's study of Detroit and its suburbs found that Jews were the most geographically concentrated of all other religious groups, a particularly striking fact because they exceeded "Negro Protestants," whose housing choices were the most restricted.[42] Jews retained their prewar residential patterns of living in close proximity to one another, but they did so by abandoning urban life en masse.

One of the dramatic changes for Jews created by suburban life was that it introduced them to a more diverse set of neighbors. Rather than living among immigrants and their children, most often Catholic, Jews now shared their neighborhoods with Protestants whose parents and grandparents had been born in the United States.[43] Following a great surge of antisemitism in the 1940s, suburban life appeared to be far more tolerant.[44]

Opinion polls conducted in the 1950s revealed an increasing openness to Jewish participation in American life. The Gallup organization, for example, found that in 1959 white Christians overwhelmingly supported a Jewish family moving next door. At the same time an Anti-Defamation League's poll that asked if Jews' moving into a nice neighborhood would "spoil it for other people" revealed that more than two-thirds disagreed. Similarly, two-thirds agreed that "I would like to have Jews in my neighborhood."[45] These attitudes, in their own time, were perceived as a dramatic transformation in American non-Jewish attitudes toward Jews.[46] Nevertheless, white

American prejudices persisted. This group did not support discrimination against Jews; they simply held antisemitic beliefs. On the other hand, the same group strongly supported discrimination against African Americans, but disapproved of racist stereotypes. In particular, respondents to the survey were more willing to have Jews as neighbors than African Americans.[47] Jews rested firmly within the color line of their suburban neighbors.

The promise of these newly tolerant attitudes, however, was not born out in other studies of suburban life in the 1950s and early 1960s. While Jews represented the Jewish Mother as an oppressive, intrusive, and powerful woman, they were experiencing an unyielding prejudice in suburbs. Not only did a third of those surveyed by Gallup and others express their reservations about whether Jews were undesirable and would "spoil it for others," but sociological studies learned that non-Jews left the suburbs when Jews moved in because they thought that Jews and their children were undesirable.[48] The Jewish Mother/Wife came to embody both the demands of mobility and the parochialism that kept Jews out of the world they sought.

Strangers in Paradise

Social scientists (primarily Jewish) were particularly interested in the experience of Jews within the newly developed suburban neighborhoods that grew up after World War II. Despite a wide range of topics, from synagogue membership to occupations, in the end what interested social scientists of Jewish experience most consistently about suburban life was how successfully Jews were able to integrate with their non-Jewish neighbors. The mass immigration of Jews was long over. Nevertheless, with suburbanization, America's "Jewish problem" reemerged.

On the basis of a variety of community studies published in the early 1960s, it appeared that Jews were not finding interaction with their new neighbors at all easy. Studies of Jews and non-Jews in the suburbs of Chicago, Boston, New York, the pseudonymous North City, and Canada's Crestwood Heights pointed to a phenomenon that respondents termed "the 5:00 shadow," "the invisible gate," or "the drawing of silken curtains."[49] Socializing and intimate friendships were slow to transcend religious boundaries. Young Jewish families asserted that they felt unwelcome in non-Jews' homes. As one Jewish suburbanite told a sociologist,

> Our husbands do business with them. We see them in the town's shopping area. It's always a very pleasant "Hello, how are you?" kind of superficial conversation. We may even meet at a meeting some afternoon or even perhaps at the PTA affair at school, but it's seldom more than that. It's a kind of "9 to 5" arrangement. The ghetto gates, real or imagined, close at 5:00 PM. "Five o'clock shadow" sets in at sundown. Jews and Christians do not meet socially even in suburbia. If we do, you bet that it is to help promote some cause or organization where they think we Jews might be helpful. But after five o'clock there is no social contact, no parties, no home visits, no golf clubs– no nothing.[50]

The social class mobility and government funded opportunities from the G.I. Bill that allowed Jews access to new housing brought with it continuing uncertainty, and even anxiety, about whether they belonged in their new homes, or if they belonged in the same way that others did. Unquestionably, these opportunities positioned Jews to obtain the advantages of middle-class life in an unprecedented way, leading to far greater opportunities and success.[51] Nevertheless, seizing these opportunities did not end their journey to become middle-class Americans who would be indistinguishable from other white, middle-class Americans.[52]

A variety of surveys during this period revealed that Jews, young and middle-aged, most fervently believed that "Jews are like everyone else." In their 1959 study of North City, sociologists Kramer and Leventman found that 62 percent of the third-generation men and women in their sample (those most likely to live in suburbs) claimed "there are no differences, except in religious affiliation," between Jews and Gentiles.[53] Marshall Sklare's suburban Chicago study found that "to gain respect of Christian neighbors" ranked fourth of twenty-two statements respondents believed to be essential to being a "Good Jew" in 1957. Ranking above it was "to promote civic betterment and improvement in the community." The second highest ranked essential component of being a good Jew for respondents at 85 percent, was "to accept his being a Jew and not try to hide it." The highest, at 93 percent, was "to lead an ethical and moral life." These four ranked far above belonging to a synagogue, attending religious services, knowing the fundamentals of Judaism, and marrying another Jew.[54] In suburbia, then, Jews wanted very much both to be accepted and not to hide their Jewishness, although hardly to live it with much specificity. Nevertheless, they continued to be barred from the personal lives of their non-Jewish neighbors.

Those barriers were usually barbed. Not only were Jews to some degree still unwelcome, but their neighbors provided rationales for why social interactions were not possible. A variety of questions posed by researchers led Gentiles to explain precisely why Jews were "different." Non-Jews at P.T.A. meetings, in interviews with sociologists, and in neighborhood organizations, often said that their Jewish neighbors represented values that they found alien. In Newton, Massachusetts, for example, a special committee of the Parent Teacher Association investigated charges that Jewish parents (coded as newcomers) "give children huge sums of money for which they do not have to account," and that children were left unsupervised while their parents went off on winter vacations. Gordon wrote that the committee found no proof of either accusation, but another group concluded in 1955 that there were considerable tensions between "old and new residents." The new residents were overwhelmingly Jewish.[55]

In a Chicago suburb, more than one-third of Gentile residents stated that the newer Jewish residents lacked "refinement."[56] The older residents of the community, like those in Newton, were distressed by Jewish children and families. Sixty-five percent of the respondents believed that the problem created by Jewish residents whose children were "spoiled and unruly" affected their own children. The sociologists who spent five years in the suburban Crestwood Heights quoted a "woman informant" who explained that the presence of Jewish children forced Christian parents to enroll their children in private schools if the parents could afford it. "Children learn materialistic values in the schools, mainly because of the insecurity of the Jews," she explained, "which has driven them to make a materialistic display of their position and wealth."[57] During a period of time when teenagers in America purchased ten billion dollars' worth of goods in a single year, consumption patterns of Jewish teenagers were hardly the cause of adolescent "materialism." Rather, Americans projected onto Jews their concern about their own children becoming "the lords and ladies of discretionary spending."[58]

Benjamin Ringer's additional study of the pseudonymous Lakeville suburb concluded that the Jewish child, "aggressive, unrefined, hedonistic, and materialistic–is a mirror image of the adult Jewish newcomer" in the eyes of their Gentile neighbors. He reported that Gentiles felt that their "traditional values" were under attack, and that consumer-oriented Jewish newcomers had corrupted their world.[59]

The Iconic Jew

Suburban life promised to be a coming-out party announcing Jews' arrival in the middle class. Jews had, through the 1940s, created a parallel system of prestige and sociability in the United States. Through a vast structure of organizations–fraternal and philanthropic–they had created a dense network of virtually all-Jewish relationships, aided by their location in a relatively small number of urban centers. The move to the suburbs widened definitions of status and valued interaction, access, and contact within a single prestige system defined by the American middle class. Expanded social and economic opportunities increased those desires and made barred access more disappointing. Jews found few Gentiles interested in participating in their "coming out," or celebrating their arrival.

As Kramer and Leventman argued in their 1961 study of Jews in a midwest suburb, the third generation inherited a "mixed blessing" from their successful fathers. They absorbed "the tensions of a new status" that came with their parents' increasing economic security. That new status, according to the sociologists, pressed suburban children into increasing contact with the non-Jewish world.[60] These sociologists concluded that the children of the "gilded ghetto" had broadened "their status audience" and now set about to acquire the refinements that invited its applause. In short, sociologists of the period understood Jews' success to create anxiety both for themselves and for the Gentiles into whose midst they moved.

As strangers in the postwar suburban paradise Jews found themselves serving as icons for many of the criticisms of American life—permissiveness, indulgence, and a focus on consumption. Jews who participated avidly in conspicuous consumption, as well as those who decried it, were perceived as the same by their detractors. Packard's discovery that corporate America found Jews too aggressive parallels the findings of sociologists Ringer, Sklare, and Gordon that suburbanites believed that Jews corrupted traditional American values. They expressed a sense of Jews as different, outside the norm, and unable to appreciate American traditions, the very charges made against new immigrants from Europe thirty years previously.

Jews understood that what made them "different" was their Jewishness. In fact their behaviors—consumption, child orientation, and increasing freedom for adolescents—were typical of suburban life, not the exception. Gerhard Lenski's study of the "world views" of various religious groups in Detroit and its suburbs of the 1950s demonstrated that along many measures Jews resembled no group as much as wealthy Protestants.[61] But studies of Jewish-Christian interaction revealed that suburbanites believed their problems were caused by an influx in the number of Jews, and their children's corruption by the attitudes and values of the newcomers.[62]

It was precisely during this period and under these very pressures that the Jewish Mother/Wife stereotype made her debut. For Jews, she lurked on their side of the silk curtain–their image of unspoken and unspeakable division between Jew and Gentile. As the suburban Jewish experience of increased access to a larger world proved bruising, Jews were able to read Jewish experts or tune in on Sunday nights to hear successful Jewish comics decry their Jewish wives and mothers. Their excesses were as corrupting as their neighbors feared. If they were wives they spent too much money. They were insatiably demanding as mothers, wanting more success and attention. They would not let their children, principally their sons, go into the world as "normal."

Above all, the Jewish Mother/Wife marked difference. She was parochial. As Ringer noted, the complaints against Jewish children mirrored classic antisemitic stereotypes. The complaints against Jewish Mother/Wives mirrored ongoing intra-ethnic stereotypes. They were synonymous with excess. They wanted too much–whether it was love, loyalty, or mink–precisely as antisemitic attitudes suggested that Jews did. The food which Jewish Mothers forced on their family members, like the children Jack Carter imagined restrained in their high chairs, reflected the excesses of difference. The foods such as chopped liver, soups, and matzo balls that were among the few remaining acceptable marks of difference for many American ethnics were the weapons of the Jewish Mother. She forced Jews to eat, to internalize their differences. The innumerable jokes about that excess might well be read as associating difference with the dangers of infantilization and being made "other." How might Jews find common cause with their reluctant neighbors if a Jewish Mother was waiting to entrap them? If what made Jews dangerous was their polluting children, then families were the source of suspicion, and Jews saw in the personification of that family–the Wife and Mother–a parochialism and excess that they called on to explain their troubles. For both sociologists and comics Jewish patriarchy had fallen on hard times, producing a family out of kilter. For reluctant Americans who were finding it more difficult to exclude Jews than they had previously, the

Jewish family remained an unattractive feature of their new neighbors. Gentiles blamed Jewish children, and by extension, their families. Jews blamed Jewish women.

Writer Vivian Gornick reflected on her experience of life in her postwar Bronx neighborhood. She noted a change in the air. "It was awful; it was wonderful. It was frightening; it was delicious." Signs of this change included kids going to college as a matter of course. A girl in her building had a nose job. A male friend got a job in the city by changing his name from Braunowitz to Brown. The sea change, however, put men on the front lines of access to the larger world in a way that women were not.[63]

She associated this difference in experience for men and women with the humor of Jewish male comics stretching from Milton Berle's generation to Woody Allen, who was exactly her age. Though her mother disliked Milton Berle for his "Jewish self-hatred," Gornick recognized a humor applied to the "grosser materials of my own environment." Watching a Woody Allen film in the '70s, she recalled feeling, "This is dis-gust-ing, and as I said it I knew I'd been feeling this way all my life; from Milton Berle to Saul Bellow to Woody Allen. Every last one of them was trashing women. Using women to savage the withholding world. Using us. Their mothers, their sisters, their wives. To them, we weren't friends or comrades. We weren't even Jews or gentiles. We were just girls."[64]

"Where Was the Jew?"

A growing number of memoirs provide evidence of how middle-aged Americans reflect back on their own coming of age in that era. They provide an additional perspective on how Jews experienced the postwar period. Some of their writings focus on a "double consciousness" that is the patrimony of groups who serve as representations of others' frustrations and disappointments.[65] These autobiographical writings indicate a keen consciousness of being Americans entirely, and yet not quite full participants in American life. For example, Calvin Trillin's exploration of the 1991 suicide of a college friend, Denny

Hansen, led to his reconsidering his years at Yale College in the 1950s. In *Remembering Denny* he described a time of Jews' both unprecedented access to elite institutions and their constant consciousness of their differences from other students at Yale. Even within that non-elite group there were invidious distinctions. For example, Denny was chosen to be the subject of a *Life* magazine photographic essay on graduation weekend not only because he was not a Jew, but because his last name was less "Jewish sounding" than the other non-Jewish Rhodes Scholar who was the alternative choice.[66]

Writing about the same decade from the point of view of an adolescent girl, Nancy K. Miller, a distinguished feminist literary scholar, recalled: "The power of these conventions in the 1950s [looking like idealized Christian women], especially in families where American identity was newly acquired, is not to be underestimated. In the 1950s girls like me obsessed about our appearance with a single-mindedness that closed out the larger world of history, politics, and paradoxically Jews. Our corner of the diaspora [a word I didn't know then] was a lonely place."[67] On the one hand, Miller commented on her sense of similarity to those around her. Her only active experience of difference came with weekly trips to a Sunday School, where she was to learn what it meant to be a Jew. On the other hand, she was constantly conscious of physical features that made her feel different from other Americans.

This double consciousness that Trillin and Miller both tried to grasp in their memoirs is wonderfully illustrated by Lois Greene's adolescent diary, which was written in 1946.[68] The diary is distinguished by nothing so much as its ordinariness, reflecting the life of a teenage girl, born in 1932, who lived in suburban Flushing, New York.

Lois's father Leo, a button manufacturer, on becoming head of the synagogue's Education Committee, urged congregants in 1951 to "overcome" their fear and shame of being Jews.[69] He asked them, "What more glorious feeling [is there] than to say 'I have helped cement Judaism in the world, I have helped keep its mighty heart pul-

Lois Greene in her Flushing, New York home in 1948, cutting a cake to celebrate
her graduation from junior high school. She labeled the photograph with the fact
that she is wearing a dress that she made herself.
(From the Lois Greene papers, P-587. Courtesy of the American Jewish Historical
Society, Waltham, Massachusetts, and New York, New York)

sating so that Jews everywhere may spread their wisdom and love of
Judaism so it many continue to live and flourish forever?'"[70]

Yet for all of the family's pride in both their synagogue and their
commitment to Judaism, what Lois's diary described was a girl who
was virtually indistinguishable in her behavior from any other Amer-

ican girl.[71] Her diary describes boyfriends, Friday night parties, Saturday outings, including one she described as "a day I never want to forget as long as I live" when she and a friend had "two frozen malteds and two hot dogs" while roller skating at the World's Fair.[72] She listed the films that she saw and the songs that she listened to on the Hit Parade, and wrote a great deal about the parties she attended, the boys that she liked and those who liked her. She pledged herself to take the cooking and hostess badges in Girl Scouts.[73] She mentioned piano lessons and a recital. She recorded the fact that "mother gave me a brazzire [*sic*] . . . and with a few pins it fit. Of course I don't really need it,"[74] as well as "Today I am a woman. I have just begun to menstruate."[75] On July 7, 1946 she wrote to her diary on an airplane, "Yes I said AIRPLANE," from Washington D.C. to New York.

The diary records very little of a Jewish life. Lois mentions Sunday school once. On a Saturday she writes, "I didn't do anything today. I didn't even get blessed," but it is hard to tell if that is connected to a home or synagogue ritual, and why this occurred on Saturday, rather than the accustomed time on Friday night.[76] She attended a class for confirmation at the Flushing Jewish Center, and her father delivered the speech to the young women at their confirmation ceremony.[77] She also noted, "Tonight is the first candle of Chanaha (or some correct spelling.) I lit it and said the prayer."[78] But on December 24 she wrote, "This evening is Christmas Eve. This is what I got. . . ." She then listed seventeen gifts and concluded, "Ain't life wonderful?" The next day she wrote, "Santa left me this morning . . ." and listed five more gifts.

The Greene family appeared to experience no disjunction between their active participation in synagogue and celebrating Christmas at home. Lois was an American Jew. She reflected the lives of most Jews in disregarding the Sabbath and violating dietary laws. She did "pledge" a Jewish girls' club, "Bnai B'rith girls," but only described that she had to give up lipstick for three weeks as part of her hazing. One of her few comments on a Jewish observance was recorded on April 16, 1946, and concerned "Passover," which she put in quotes, and having "matzo meal pancakes for breakfast," and dinner at her aunt Rose's.[79] She reported that on April 17 she went to the movies to see "The Three Strangers and Tarzan and the Leopard Woman inasmuch as it is Passover."[80] Lois missed school to observe the holiday, but her observance included going to a movie theater in Long Island, a very American adaptation to the festival.

In short, the Greene family was very much like other suburban American Jewish families who retained an ethnic uniqueness through an engagement with Jewish life that did very little to differentiate them from other Americans. Nevertheless, eventually Lois did comment on the ways that she had felt different from those around her.

When she gave her diary to the American Jewish Historical Society in 1988 Lois Greene left a letter for those who might try to understand this adolescent journal. "While Public School 32 was a difficult place for a Jew, like then and like now, I look for and at the meaningful, happy, and positive aspects of my life. Even in this private dialogue with my leather bound book, I saw and recorded what was my day or growing-up-boys feelings and not the hurts and hates from some classmates because of my faith. My parents gave me space to develop and encouraged my talents and abilities."[81]

Miller, Trillin, and Lois Greene framed their late 1940s and early 1950s memories in a late twentieth-century perspective. In so doing they underlined the condition of immediate postwar Jewish life. Jews were like other people, but they were also conscious of their differences, and yet they barely found articulate form in their day-to-day lives. Whether it was the mass media or the unkind comments of school chums, their acculturation and access to mainstream life was always tinted by their experience of difference. At best being different created a sense of uncertainty and discomfort. If for Jews being Jewish and being middle-class were hard to extricate from one another, it was their Jewishness that was the vulnerable side of the equation.

This decade, so rife with status conflict, ongoing discrimination in housing, and continued exclusions in other social relations is generally regarded by social scientists and Jewish leaders as the period when antisemitism was in substantial decline. In keeping with Jews' increased access to middle-class American life, what most concerned Jewish defense organizations of the 1950s was "social discrimination."[82] The "pocket of middle class antisemitism" engulfed suburbanites. Their similarity to their neighbors only intensified their own discomfort as stubbornly different while being oddly the same.

Gender Coding Jewish Experience

The suburban Jewish family encoded many of the contradictory experiences of suburbia for Jews. Their growing economic success led to access to middle-class American life. At the same time they continued to feel closed out of a variety of opportunities available to others in their class. But Jewish women and men experienced this duality differently.

Jewish men's opportunities were expanding, and both occupations and work places, their defining arena, were broadening men's expectations for success and social life. Women, by contrast, embodied the triptych of Jewish suburban life—family, consumption, and synagogue. The structural separation between men and women linked their genders to their different experience of Jewishness, the middle class, and the economy. As managers of the private sphere, Jewish women, even while they were activists in their communities, synagogues, and often politics, represented family and Judaism. Jewish men continued to personify the successful provider.[83] On behalf of their families Jewish women "wanted," while they maintained the family's collective Jewishness, and Jewish men were cast as marginal to virtually anything beyond "providing." Not all Jewish men succeeded economically, but in their successes or failures, their productive role, reflecting the values of the period, was the sign of their Americanization.

The changing construction of the Jewish father is evident in the transformation of the era's most famous media Jewish father, Jake Goldberg, of the popular radio and television program, *The Gold-*

bergs.[84] In 1931, two years after the radio program first aired, when it ranked second only to *Amos 'n' Andy* in popularity, Jake was a formidable presence, although dependent on Molly's wisdom and warmth. In the episode called "Molly Saves the Day," Jake was introduced in the following way, "Steps tramped through the flat. The Father of the family had arrived." His presence was a constant concern to his wife and children. For example, Molly often kept the bad news of their son's report card or failures to attend Hebrew school from him.[85]

In "Molly Saves the Day," Jake was frustrated by his inability, because of lack of money, to fulfill his dream of starting his own business. He told Molly, "I can see you're only a voman [sic]. You don't understand life." However, when she produced the money he needed, saved for five years from pennies, Jake was overcome and confessed that dream to her. When he listened to the sewing machines in the factories where he worked he heard their song, "Jacob Goldberg, Jacob Goldberg, go, do, be–become somebody!"[86] Molly recognized the importance of his dream, just as it must have resonated with hundreds of thousands of working-class listeners.

Jake's life was nevertheless anchored in the family, and his dream of success ultimately was facilitated by his wife. He was vulnerable, powerful, and hard-working, and Jake and his family needed one another.

By the early 1950s, the television program went under two names: *Molly* and *The Goldbergs*. "Rosie's Nose" was a 1955 episode devoted to the family's discovery that their youngest child, seventeen-year-old Rosie Goldberg, was suffering from "an inferiority complex," and she wanted "a plastic job" on her nose. Jake huffed and puffed his disapproval and ineffectually threatened to "put down my foot" to forbid the surgery. But Molly and her now entirely cooperative college-student son Sammy together took a "psychological" approach to this "trauma," and handled the problem themselves through a ruse that convinced Rosie she did not have to alter her nose.

Jake continued to work hard as a successful manufacturer, but his presence was marginal, and without symbolic or literal footsteps in their house.[87] No one ever followed his advice, and he increasingly appeared as a blustering foil to Molly's abundant good sense. His simultaneous marginalization at home and success at work suggested an uprooted masculinity contained within his business. Jake was reduced to being ineffectual in a family in which he had once been more fully integrated. By contrast with its radio counterpart, the television program "de-ethnicized" the Goldbergs. Their accents disappeared and their Jewish specificity was unstated. Only an aroma of difference remained, to be read into the episodes by knowing viewers. Along with Jake's marginalization, the medium itself erased the vitality of ethnic specificity, presenting a family in which the mother assimilated by understanding the psychology of the family and the father assimilated through a singular focus on work.

Molly Goldberg's presence on television from 1949 to 1955 certainly provided an alternative view of the Jewish Mother and Wife. Her positive image in that medium, however, obliterated her Jewish uniqueness. The comics who were her contemporaries, and whose humor relied on the Jewishness of the women in their jokes, followed a different course. Their focus on the Jewishness of the Mother emphasized ethnic differences rather than universal features of motherhood.

The postwar era presented dramatically different opportunities for Jewish men than the interwar years had offered. During the war years and thereafter, education increasingly served men as an important foundation for success and occupational mobility. Economist Barry Chiswick's analysis of Jewish participants in the General Social Survey (GSS) underlined just how striking was the generational transformation of occupations for Jewish men of this period.[88] The study demonstrated that the 14 percent of Jewish men in the sample who were sixteen years old during the immediate postwar period had fathers who were professionals. Forty-three percent of the respondents who were adults in 1980, hence young children in the 1950s, were professionals. Similarly about half of the fathers were self-employed, while one-third of the sons were self-employed from the 1950s to 1970s.[89] Jews of both generations shared the desire for sons to achieve mobility and to enjoy higher status jobs. The series of choices that led Jewish male workers from factories to the trades and offices, to management and professionalization, suggested a high consensus about the status and meaning of work.[90] Suburban Jewish fathers and their sons, then, anticipated that work and success would be their primary focus.

The Jewishness represented by the Jewish Mother/Wife offered a parochial, suffocating identity of excess. Indeed, Jewish women experienced a dramatically different fate than their husbands, encoding every feature of family, religious, and private life. They stayed in the suburbs. Sociologists, along with other experts, underlined the important role of the Jewish Mother and Wife as the emblem of private, hence Jewish, life in setting material and status expectations. Kramer and Leventman, for example, argued that the third-generation Jews' problems were created by "status tensions," and hence the domain of wives who were inevitably arbiters of taste as "the principal bearers of status in middle class American life." She guarded the "family's social position."[91] Jewish sociologists explained that women's desires for attractive furniture, appliances, and other niceties, as well as "good" neighborhoods, kept their husbands hard at work providing for the family. The television Molly Goldberg, while an immigrant, was both suburban and acculturated when she dictated in "Rosie's Nose" that the family's gifts to Rosalie for her birthday should include a cashmere sweater and a third watch. Her knowledge of what a young woman should own demonstrated how much more successfully she had Americanized than Jake. She understood both psychology and consumption.[92]

Vance Packard learned that Jewish women were one of the primary reasons Jewish men were not invited to hold social club memberships. Corporate men claimed that their wives disliked Jewish women for their style and demeanor. Wives, he explained, were more concerned about social status because women were more isolated. His Gentile informant commented that "their" wives might be jealous of Jewish women's furs, for example. Packard concluded that more self-segregation occurred "at the wife level than at the husband level."[93]

The status that obsessed the sociologists of the time was also closely linked to the Jewish family as a consumer unit. Herbert Gans described suburban Jews as typical of American "middle class consumer society."[94] But their Americanness seemed constantly to be subsumed by the Jewishness of their consumption, as the Jewish Mother/Wife was criticized for her purchases, indulgence, and expectations of her children. Women were entirely associated with the materialism of suburban life.[95] Men were made invisible as consumers.

Anxiety about the inequality between men and women seemed to grip social scientists and rabbis. Ironically, Jewish men were a problem of home and synagogue life because they were not present. But Jewish women were dangerous because they were. Active and committed to the life of their children and community, they were continually represented as the problem in the Jewish family and in the synagogue. Jewish women were coded as usurpers of power and excessive consumers in their suburban life.[96]

The Jewish family reflected the fact that Jewish social class aspirations did not differ for men and women. Jewish women, for example, had slightly fewer years of education than men of their own ages but considerably more than non-Jewish women.[97] Rather, the strongest difference between Jewish men and women was in work force participation. During the late 1950s, nearly 60 percent of Jewish women aged 18 to 24 participated in the work force, but only slightly over 20 percent of Jewish women aged 25 to 34 worked outside the home. The overwhelming majority of Jewish women had the support of a husband during their twenties and thirties. About 30 percent of women aged 35 to 44 moved into the labor force during that time, and nearly 40 percent of Jewish women participated in paid labor between the ages of 45 and 64. This was a period in the United States when women were working in greater numbers. In 1950, 29 percent of the labor force was women; 31 percent of all women worked, and 52 percent of female workers were married, the largest number of paid working women in the nation's history.[98] Jewish women reflected this change, but appeared to work to a lesser extent during their childbearing years, most likely reflecting their solidly middle-class status. They lived the lives of the idealized American middle class and bore the burden of its definition as a unit of consumption and socialization.

An Anxious Nation

The postwar period established Jews' presence in the middle class and allowed them to epitomize two of its most important features of that time. American Jews lived in suburbs and American Jewish women stayed at home during their childbearing and childrearing years. In sharing these patterns with the dominant culture, Jews of course also fell prey to its anxieties. The ideology of the breadwinning father and consuming/childrearing mother confined and constrained middle-class women to the domestic world.[99] It also associated women, and the "unemployed stay-at-home-mother" in particular, with consumption. Because women did not earn the money, by "default" they had the time to spend it. Advertisers directed their products to women and hence, as Barbara Ehrenreich argued, "in the temple of consumption which was the suburban home, women were priestesses and men were altar boys."[100]

Americans who wished to follow an alternative path were made to feel like unnatural and disloyal citizens. Marriage, childbearing, and consumption were all declared good for the nation. Yet, the pervasive "momism" of the era only underlined the discomfort with women who were at once idealized as mothers and yet often portrayed as preying on husbands. The problem family beset by juvenile delinquency and materialist children also reflected Jewish Americans' and middle-class Americans' growing concerns about their un-containable offspring.

Although Jews shared the anxieties of the American middle class, their concerns were by no means identical with the larger culture's.[101] As Americans were fully experiencing their age of anxiety, Jews were recovering from theirs. Jews shared with other Americans a powerful sense of purpose and solidarity during the 1930s that placed them in the New Deal coalition, on the front lines of labor alliances, and within many cultural and political movements. Through these various important coalitions they felt a new level of acceptance within a newly envisioned, pluralist United States.[102]

Nevertheless, the 1930s were a devastating time for American Jews. Antisemitism was at an all time high, and occupational and residential discrimination was widespread. Jews lived with the growing realization of the genocide that engulfed a world in Europe to which they felt deeply tied by kinship, religion, and shared destiny. Whatever anxiety they felt in the nuclear age, it probably could not compare to what the Depression and the Holocaust wrought. They were deeply indebted, quite simply, to the nation that fought the Nazis. They entered the postwar era with great anxiety and loyalty, with hope and fears, and with the trauma of watching their own pasts destroyed.

At the same time the era's optimism remained partial for more than two decades. While a variety of Jewish intellectuals—writers, historians, and critics—may have articulated a critical vision of the United States and rejected its consumerism and Cold Warrior stance, the majority of Jews remained concerned about their ability to be accepted within the middle class. Antisemitism persisted, even if diminished. The stuff of their nightmares—the Holocaust and antisemitism—as well as their appreciation of greater integration into the nation created an alternative experience of postwar life, even as they appeared to epitomize it.

The accusations against Jewish families and women about their "values," their spending habits, and their indulgence of their children were all too reminiscent of other times when Americans projected their anxiety about a changing nation onto Jews who reshaped those slurs into representations of one another. In everyday life, then, Jewish women were not only aware of their comic portrait, but of how limited the cordial relations with non-Jewish neighbors might be. As Mothers/Wives they carried the double burden of representing Jews to their neighbors and of demanding women to Jews.

Jews' gender stereotypes before World War II focused on Jews' anxieties as they looked toward life in the middle class. The Jewish Mother/Wife signaled a different anxiety. Arrival in the middle class appeared not to have solved the problem of whether Jews would feel fully integrated as Americans. Disenchantment with the middle class came to be expressed in conflicts between intimates. Gender stereotypes that portrayed mothers in conflict with their sons (and by silent extension daughters), and wives and husbands with one another only reemphasized the fact that Jews continued to be one another's mirrors for the pain of their difference from the nation.

CHAPTER SIX

The Jewish American Princess:

Detachable Ethnicity, Gender Ambiguity, and Middle-Class Anxiety

> As Prince Charles was born to be king, as Robert
> Kennedy, Jr. was born to serve, the authentic
> Jewish American princess was born to shop.
> Perhaps needless to say, the desire for a bargain
> runs as deep within the JAP consciousness as
> Zionism or love of one's Daddy.
>
> *The Official JAP Handbook*, 1982

In 1985 a popular American Jewish magazine interviewed a contemporary Jewish matchmaker from Boston. Linda Novak could not have been farther from the nightmarish *shadhan* (matchmaker) of the 1910s and 1920s. Trained as a social worker, she was a sensitive listener to the needs of her clients. She found them to be vulnerable adults who were in search of Jewish partners, often because relationships with non-Jews had not worked out. She explained that her clients repeatedly expressed certain concerns. She told the magazine, "I don't want someone who is 'too Jewish,' is a common phrase. The men are afraid that the women are going to be 'JAPs' and the women are afraid that the men are going to be 'princes.' I don't think, incidentally, that this is a particularly Jewish problem; rather, it's an 80s phenomenon. But the fears and the worries get focused on these Jewish stereotypes."[1]

In 1988, the (American-born) Israeli journalist Ze'ev Chafets wrote about his journey through the United States to learn about American Jewish life. He came to the same conclusions as the Boston matchmaker. At a singles weekend at a large hotel in New York's Catskill Mountains, he found that "Jewish men and women seemed both attracted to and angry with one another." Jewish men told him about their search for "down-to-earth" women, while Jewish women complained that Jewish men were "spoiled." Evidence of this concern appeared in the bold print of the *Digest,* where participants placed their notices advertising the ideal qualities they sought in a companion. They frequently stated, "JAPs need not apply." What struck Chafets in his travels was how few young Jews he met who resembled the caricatures that they feared.[2]

Through the shorthand of these slurs, these men and women expressed their anxieties over such matters as materialism, self-absorption, competence in the physical world, and their desire to share a life with a partner committed to equality. Novak and Chafets both noted that Jews in the 1980s saw what were fairly common anxieties among unmarried men and women about compatibility and love through a different lens. On the one hand, they sought out a Jewish match in the hope of finding a compatible person to love; on the other hand, they dreaded what they took to be Jewish behavior on the part of the opposite sex.

These young Jews came of age in the 1960s and 1970s, when the Jewish American Princess made her debut as an ubiquitous stereotype of Jewish life. One writer described how familiar her students at Colgate University in 1987 were with the image. "I had been raised on Moron jokes," she wrote. "They had been raised on JAP jokes."[3] The JAP had become the predominant Jewish gender stereotype of the period. For much of the 1970s and 1980s, American Jews found this representation of their recent affluence available in multiple forms—including jokes, joke books, greeting cards, T-shirts, jewelry, novelty dolls, handbooks, magazine articles, comedy routines, and novels.

Until the late 1980s no one could quite agree on how to regard the stereotype. Some women boldly claimed the identity as proof of their power and entitlement.[4] Others thought it was all in good humor. In 1983 *Moment* magazine received a letter that asserted that "JAP" was not a derogatory term, because it has been "at least in part co-opted [by Jewish women themselves]." The author claimed that "Jewesses in their 20s to their 50s almost regard the term as endearing." By way of illustration he offered the "cutesy toddler t-shirts emblazoned with JAP, and princess necklaces that dotted the letter i with a Star of David" worn and purchased by Jewish women.[5] Many of course thought the stereotype was simply true, an accurate description of the women around them.

A vocal group of Jewish feminists—men and women—condemned the JAP stereotype as antisemitic and sexist. They suggested that the Jewish community tolerated the stereotype because it was about women, and a comparable stereotype of men would have been swiftly attacked.[6] Within the Jewish community a consensus that publicly condemned the image was finally reached following the publication of a 1988 issue of the Jewish feminist magazine *Lilith*, which devoted a section to the discussion of the stereotype and how it was used on college campuses.[7] *Lilith* reported on the work of a Syracuse University sociologist, Gary Spencer, who documented the extent of graffiti and personal attacks focused on JAPs. In addition, he found, as have others on campuses with large Jewish populations, that the slurs were used by non-Jews in overtly antisemitic ways. JAP graffiti praised Hitler, made sexual references to Jewish women, and focused on their wealth. At Syracuse University athletic events, women who dressed a certain way were "JAPped." If they walked in front of the fans, the marching band played a tune as sometimes four thousand students screamed, "JAP," and pointed at them.[8]

The organized Jewish community then made systematic efforts to condemn the image. In calling on Jews to abandon the stereotype and stop purchasing the novelty items, organizations explained that the humor encouraged antisemitism, possibly abetted intermarriage, and harmed women.[9] Commercial venues for JAP commodities dramatically diminished when Jewish women's organizations refused to advertise or carry items with JAP on them.

In addition, several adult and teenage women's magazines carried articles about the stereotype.[10] In contrast to the 1970s, when *Cos-*

mopolitan and *New York* magazines reported on the JAP with the zeal of investigative journalism, these 1980s articles, often written by young Jewish women, were not only critical, but talked about the pain caused by the stereotype. The work of *Lilith* was successful not only in drawing attention to the stereotype, but in cutting off its commercial markets. In the 1990s, JAP merchandise has largely disappeared.[11]

However, the stereotype remains not only alive and well, but it has essentially eclipsed the image of the Jewish Mother as the dominant American Jewish stereotype.[12] It remains a touchstone of American Jewish experience, and its advocates are convinced that they are describing Jews, not caricatures. The JAP is most widely known by the jokes that have developed around her, starting in the 1970s. The early 1970s humor does not refer to her by the acronym JAP; at this point she was just the Jewish Princess. By the end of the 1970s, however, both acronym and humor were firmly established in popular culture.[13]

The JAP Stereotype

The Jewish American Princess is withholding and passive, and at the same time she displays an aura of entitlement. She is a mirror image of the Jewish Mother who exaggerates all forms of maternal nurturing, only to invert them by her demand to be compensated through the burdensome demands she will never directly make. By contrast, Jewish American Princesses require everything and give nothing. If housekeeping, cooking, and overstuffing her children were the Jewish Mother's métier, then the JAP's withholding qualities are best characterized by the simple joke, "What is a JAP pornography film? Debbie Does Dishes," a send up of *Debbie Does Dallas*.[14] A pornographic film about a Jewish woman, the joke suggests, is not about her sexual insatiability, but about the mere suggestion of her performing housework. A JAP joke classic, "What does a Jewish American Princess make for dinner? Reservations" underscores the point. The JAP will not labor or nurture.

The JAP fails to care for the needs of others because she asserts the right to be cared for, particularly by men. Her father sometimes, her husband at other times, and often both serve her wants and desires. What the JAP wants amounts to the fantasy life of the American consumer. She wants everything that calls out luxury. Gilda Radner's 1978 *Saturday Night Live* "commercial," at the height of the designer jeans fad, for "Jewess Jeans" offered a visual and verbal tour de force of the stereotype. Radner, in her JAP persona as Rhonda Weiss, wore tight jeans embroidered with the Star of David on her hip pocket. She adorned herself in gold chains, a gold Star of David, and dark glasses. Backed up by a multiracial chorus of women wearing identical tight jeans they sang:

> *Jewess Jeans.*
> *They're skintight, they're out of sight.*
> *Jewess Jeans.*
> *She's got a lifestyle uniquely hers,*
> *Europe, Nassau, wholesale furs.*
> *She shops the sales for designer clothes,*
> *She's got designer nails and a designer nose.*
> *She's an American princess and a disco queen.*
> *She's the Jewess in Jewess Jeans.*

If the viewer had any doubts about the meaning of the commercial, the narrator proclaimed, "You don't have to be Jewish to wear Jewess Jeans," and Gilda responded, "but it doesn't hurt."[15] This late 1970s comic piece responded to the popular commercial assertion that "You don't have to be Jewish to enjoy Levy's rye bread," by suggesting that the Jewishness of the jeans wearer was very much to the point. It is only the Jewish American Princess who travels, who uses plastic surgery, who likes both sales and expensive clothes, and truly fits the Jewishly adorned tight jeans. If a minstrel-like "Jew face" existed in the world of entertainment, Gilda Radner's routine perfected it.

Radner's focus on consumption is part of, to continue the metaphor, "Jewing Up." The Jewish Princess has a single obsession:

to own things. Her pursuit of the "right" furniture, linens, clothing, shoes, accessories, carpets, china, and hundreds of other objects, not to mention neighborhoods, cars, and vacation spots, defines her. American playwright Wendy Wasserstein evoked the entire cultural milieu of the JAP in her play *The Sisters Rosenzweig*. The only sister who is a practicing Jew lives in a Boston suburb and speaks an arcane language of designer shoes and clothing. She and the synagogue sisterhood women she escorts on a tour of London were defined by nothing so much as their owning or yearning for such items.[16]

The JAP is knowable by what she buys, owns, and wears–the Jewess in the Jewess jeans. She does not, however, finance this consumption. Unlike the hardworking Jewish Mother, she consumes without producing, and she takes without giving. "Daddy" is often the source of her consumption. In Anna Sequoia's *JAP Handbook* he is one of the two essential ingredients in the life of the JAP. "Without Daddy [whether Daddy the doctor, or Daddy the lawyer, or Daddy the businessman], there could never have evolved the new American aristocracy of achievement, taste, intelligence, and conspicuous consumption: the JAP."[17] The father pays off the charge cards and creates the JAP's expectations for entitlement and indulgence. Her lineage appears to be from father to daughter with little mention of mother. The economic relationship is central. Father underwrites all of the relationships and it is economic dependence that is at the root of the JAP caricature.

The JAP is also portrayed as wife, in which case her husband, in addition to her father, finances her desires. By contrast with the father, however, the husband of the JAP experiences another form of his wife's lack of productivity. Not only does she fail to earn any money, but neither does she give sexually in her marriage. The JAP, in part a product of the more sexually open and permissive decades since the 1960s, denies her partner sexual pleasure, and appears to be indifferent to it.[18] Her sexual pleasure is a means to an end. After she marries and secures her source of support, she withdraws sex. One JAP joke asks, "How is a Jewish man like a ceramic tile? You lay

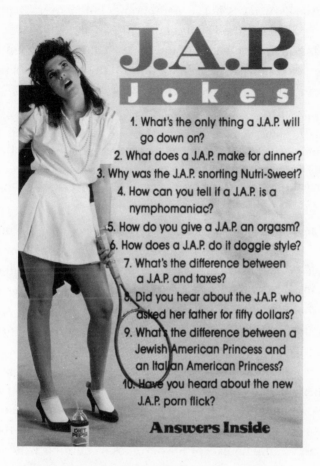

A greeting card produced in the 1980s that features the JAP and jokes associated with the stereotype.
(Courtesy of Noble Works Cards, Hoboken, New Jersey)

it well the first time and then you walk all over it." Another more explicit joke poses the question, "Why does a Jewish woman smile walking down the aisle at her wedding?" "No more blow jobs," is the punch line.[19] This genre of joke offers innumerable examples in which the male partner is deprived of any pleasure. However, the humor never casts him as a cuckold. His wife is as passionless in the jokes as he is. "Mildred and I had doggy sex last night. I sat up and begged and she rolled over and played dead."[20] Various versions of a joke that asks what is a JAP nymphomaniac answer, "Sex once a month," or sex after the JAP has her hair coifed.

The JAP is more often than not portrayed as dead when she has sex. One of the more elaborate versions of this joke makes the point without any of its characters being Jewish.

> A prince enters a castle, and finds a beautiful woman lying on a bed. He tiptoes into her room and ravishes her. As he leaves, he is approached by the lord of the castle. Lord of the Castle: "Have you seen my poor daughter? She's been in a coma since her horse threw her last week." Prince: "In a coma! I thought she was Jewish."[21]

The Jewish woman is sexually passive; she does not move, respond, or express pleasure in her sexual relationships. Her passion and even her orgasms are related only to her consumption. She reaches orgasm by holding a credit card or facing in the direction of a large New York department store. The only thing she will "go down on" is a store's elevator. She and her partner neither give or receive any pleasure.[22]

The JAP is personified by a passive body. She exerts energy to adorn herself, but otherwise she moves neither to labor nor for pleasure. In the slurs unleashed by the social worker at the session described in the Introduction, Jewish men described women as "never being athletic except for aerobics." The men who held this view suggested that a Jewish woman will not exert herself, even while exercising. Because the JAP is a consumer she lives without exertion.

The widely circulated humor about the JAP is increasingly codified in Jewish joke books and reaches beyond them into print, television, and film venues as well. Following on the successful *How to Be a Jewish Mother* and the *Official Preppy Handbook*, the JAP found her way into paper doll and game books, greeting cards, jewelry, and clothing, as well as her own handbooks and humor books. They rehearsed and elaborated the jokes and provided visual images for the princess, and subsequently a prince. Because they were "humorous," they were framed as unobjectionable in their evocation of indulged daughters who loved credit cards, diamonds, sought marriage to a wealthy Jewish man, and attended synagogue in order to parade a wardrobe. Mass-marketed items other than greeting cards rarely dealt with sexual themes. Instead, they emphasized the JAP's passion for designer items purchased on sale or at below retail prices, and her timidity about the physical world, worrying over a broken fingernail, needing to rest, and above all indulging herself because "you deserve it."[23]

In Pursuit of Truth

The films, jokes, and novelty books are all framed as humorous entertainment. The JAP stereotype, however, has never been reduced to the world of "let's pretend." Throughout the 1970s and 1980s journalists and nonfiction writers steadily explored the JAP not as stereotype, but as a unique phenomenon.

In 1971 Julie Baumgold wrote for *New York* magazine about Jewish American Princesses, who she referred to as JPs. Her essay drew on her own experience and that of a group of writers interviewed by David Susskind, whose 1970 show "How to Be a Jewish Son" involved a conversation among Jewish men that quickly turned to the existence of the Jewish Princess. Comedian Mel Brooks, among others, focused on her sense of entitlement and her parents' slavish commitment to all of her needs, which made her overly dependent on an ever-disappointing husband.[24]

Baumgold observed that princesses had "toned down from the throbbing sixties." She too emphasized the key feature of the Princess as an attitude of utter confidence and entitlement. The "JP" she said, can "feel the pea under 74 mattresses," and assured her readers that one had to be neither rich nor Jewish to be a Jewish Princess, just confidently sure of her own specialness. Her specimens were "two girls bent over with laughter" who are exiting a play that has left other patrons in tears. Her Jewish Princesses are "above it all," "thin," and "fur clad," and they "nestle all over the city."[25] Baumgold's only point appeared to be that JPs are "inevitable," appearing in literature from centuries ago to the present, and that such women will and do exist.

In a 1975 book called *Nothing but the Best: The Luck of the Jewish Princess*, Leslie Tonner undertook a more detailed analysis of the Jewish Princess. Her book was excerpted the next year in a *Cosmopolitan* series on "princesses." The magazine told its readers, "We brought you the Southern Belle, the WASP Princess, and now with a mite of trepidation we give you the most exotic of all the birds–the JP. Some say she doesn't exist. Well, if you happen to be a JP, you'll surely recognize her, if you're not you may wish you were one."[26] In an article advertised as "the truth," Tonner assured her readers that Jewish Princesses, like the author herself, are "well equipped to stand up for myself, to work hard and to believe in my abilities." However, she also told her reader that she had pursued the "funny side" of being raised female and Jewish, and that "every one and everything mentioned in this book is real."[27] Ms. Tonner delivered on her promise. She found Long Island middle-class mothers who treated their daughters' bedrooms like holy shrines to clothing and bedding. She found newly married women who devoted years to decorating and redecorating, and who shopped and lunched out five days a week. She found Jewish men exasperated with the sexual timidity of Jewish women who, said one man, required being "raped, because she can't just want to go to bed," and a sexually adventurous Jewish woman who after a night on a waterbed with two men called her parents at 2:00 A.M. to say she was staying late at a party. She described grotesque Jewish wedding celebrations in Chicago as well. However, she also described art collectors, feminist writers, and doctors who were princesses by dint of their ambition and drive to underscore her point that the Jewish Princess should in no way be taken to be a criticism of Jewish women.[28]

And most provocatively, Leslie Tonner actually sought out "Jewish explanations" for some of these attributes, which was remarkable because none of her interviewees behaved in ways that might be labeled classically Jewish. Nevertheless, in Tonner's view "ancient" rituals of women's immersion at menstruation, for example, explained sexual reluctance on the part of some women. Tonner cited lines from the Book of Psalms to remind readers that Jewish women's self-adornment was a long-standing issue. And the good fortune of life in America turned European ideas about the lack of value of Jewish girls on their head and produced highly valued daughters who were showered with love and attention. Similarly, Anna Sequoia suggested that poverty and pogroms in Europe were erased from memory by owning beautiful things.[29] Their contortions to render a stereotype "true" and humorous took on heightened proportions by their search for explanations in Jewish history and customs.

Humor and media were successful enough in formulating the JAP stereotype to introduce it in American courtrooms. A California judge in 1987 was disqualified from handling a case concerning the timing of visitation of a child because he called the mother a Jewish American Princess. The Court of Appeal decided that the judge had lost his "impartiality" when he chose to use the epithet. The judge and his supporters disagreed, arguing that the judge's language was merely a neutral designation of "a spoiled brat-type female who always gets her way." The judge noted that it was a term he used to his own wife and daughters when they were being equally unreasonable as a woman trying to renegotiate her children's custody schedule with her ex-husband.[30]

However, the courtroom also served as the setting that reified the JAP. Steven Steinberg murdered his wife Elena in 1981 by stabbing her twenty-six times with a kitchen knife in earshot of their children, one of whom called the police. He was found innocent because his lawyer successfully demonstrated that his wife was a JAP who had driven him temporarily insane by her insatiable demands, her constant shopping, and whininess.[31] His severe problem as a compulsive gambler was blamed on her materialist desires. Finally, and most improbably, a team of psychiatrists persuaded the jury that Steinberg's vicious act of homicide was performed while he was completely asleep and unconscious.

The JAP representation of Jewish women took on the appearance of reality because "she" appeared in print and because legions of experts suggested that "she" was real. Leslie Tonner reinvented the concept by associating it with professional women at the same time she was searching out outrageous examples of consumption. On the whole, in comic or journalistic form, like other images of Jewish life, the Jewish American Princess carried the cachet of "reality" by the late 1970s.

The Sisterhood of Jewish Stereotypes

Undoubtedly, the Jewish American Princess that women and men both feared is the sister of the Ghetto Girl, the Jewish Woman in Search of Marriage, the Jewish Wife, and an inversion of the Jewish Mother. The telltale marks are there. She wants. Her consumption is excessive. She threatens the men who should or will support her abundant needs. Her desire is ambiguously cast as both and alternately sexual and consumerist, neither simply material or sexual. Her qualities share common elements with other affluent American women, but her Jewishness also stigmatizes her as different. Her pursuit of consumption follows a different path than that of the normal elite, because her luxuries are obtained by shopping and buying on sale or through wholesale. She is powerful and dependent, active and passive, unproductive, yet all consuming.

Jewish gender stereotypes of the twentieth century, like a pack of cards that offer a finite number of combinations, appear repeatedly to remind us that the limited differences between cards have very real consequences. What determines the significance of the hand is the game. The reshuffling of the gender stereotypes' attributes reveals the construction of an American Jewish identity in a nation that has defined the pack.

The Jewish American Princess creates quite a different hand from the Ghetto Girl or the Mother. She is the product of a moment in which Jews had far wider access to American society than previously. She coincided, for example, with the first significant rise in

Jewish–non-Jewish intermarriage rates. She developed in response to the experience of Jews' fully entrenched suburbanization, in the context of significantly decreasing antisemitism and of a post-Holocaust era during which there was little said, portrayed, or displayed about the genocidal campaign against European Jews. Perhaps most significantly, the JAP stereotype arose in a period not only of unprecedented American Jewish affluence, but one that anticipated the continued success of the stereotypes' purveyors through advanced education and professionalization.

The JAP therefore feminized the experience of being a middle-class Jew. No longer excluded and blamed for American Protestants' failings, as was the feminized suburban Jew initially, the JAP represented ill-gotten affluence purchased through the subjugation of the labors of others. Her tie to "Daddy" underlines the fact that the relationship is economic and not simply indulgent. He is the source of the support.

Over the course of the life of the generation which embellished the stereotype, America experienced a breakdown of its "cultural consensus," and sexual and gender expectations were radically challenged. The movements of the 1960s and 1970s challenged, among other things, the natural order of the family and gender roles, as well as the nation's right to conscript its youth to fight wars that its citizens did not support. During the same few decades, American identity was acknowledged as far more plural and was the source of regular contestation in the United States. The place of gender, race, sexuality, and class became a matter of concern on the nightly news and in situation comedies as much as among scholars. The JAP, then, was surrounded by a high-stakes card game in which the meaning of being a Jewish man or woman, a participant in a Jewish marriage, and holding on to a unique identity were dramatically redefined.

These transformations, not unlike immigration, acculturation, and mobility, were signaled in new variations on Jewish gender stereotypes. Humor, media, journalism, sermons, and other venues of Jewish life reflected those changes. What has persisted is that those shifts continue to be expressed through ties of intimacy between Jews within economic realities and relationships. Connections in private life–among spouses, family members, lovers–reflect the tensions implied in changing definitions of being an American Jew. The anxieties that created the need to carefully police boundaries between acceptable and unacceptable behavior on the body of the Jewish woman of the early twentieth century continued to frame, at the end of the century, the dangers of a Jewish woman who had distorted the rewards of mobility by her excess and dependence.

Detachable Identities

The peculiarities of the era and the medium of the JAP stereotype created one important contrast with the pre–World War II stereotypes. With few exceptions, the books and jokes about the JAP suggest that one does not have to be Jewish to be a JAP. Julie Baumgold described Bette Davis, Yoko Ono, and Diana Vreeland as JAPs.[32] The humorist Anna Sequoia included in her list Princess Di, Zelda Fitzgerald, Nancy Reagan, Jackie Onassis, and Cher. "Because we live in a democracy," she asserted, "one absolutely does not have to be Jewish to achieve even an advanced state of JAPitude."[33] Just as humorist Dan Greenburg declared in 1964 that one had to be neither Jewish nor a mother to be a Jewish Mother, the 1960s ushered in an era in which identity was reputed to be detachable from culture, race, ethnicity, and gender.[34] Gilda Radner joked, "It doesn't hurt," in response to such denials, but the language of consumption and ethnicity dominated the era. In the consumer culture that grew ever more powerful from the 1960s on, one could be anything in America by eating it, wearing it, or appropriating its qualities.

For example, Anna Sequoia suggested that there is a virtual rainbow of JAPs. She included the "Male Gay JAP [who is] utterly dedicated to the pursuit of the Good Life" and the Black JAP whose "nose job [has] stunning results. Her passion for status and style is rarely equaled in contemporary society."[35] However, her multicultural embrace broke down around Lebanese and Greek JAPs, whose taste in clothing and jewelry, she explained, would never equal other JAPs. Sequoia "joked" that some ethnics are incapable of good taste.

In chapter 1 I discussed the turn of the century *Harper's Bazaar* that featured a story in which a plagiarized schoolgirl essay insisted that the "woman Jews" who perpetually sought bargains were not necessarily "the pretty, black-eyed daughters of Israel, conspicuous chiefly for their inordinate fondness for cheap jewelry and proportionate distaste for swine's flesh." Any woman, according to this essay, with the inclination to seek a bargain was a "woman Jew."[36] However, the sentiments that were more typical of that period documented "types" who possessed racial and hence biological characteristics. In the case of Jews, irrefutable proof of mental inferiority and tendencies toward dishonesty were constantly advertised as unique to their type. Similarly for African Americans, Asian Americans, those of Nordic stock, and any other group who could be similarly designated, an essential racial identity linked behaviors to groups. Virtually every social issue of that era, including birth control and immigration, as well as every form of entertainment, like film and drama, largely offered a discourse of racial types that carefully positioned America's diverse population around a genetically determined hierarchy. Race was the primary social category, usually encompassing religion and what would subsequently be called ethnicity.

After World War II, the rejection of Nazi racialism led Americans to be cautious about their assertions of racial types. Nevertheless, the constant trope of the period beginning in the 1960s, "You don't have to be a (racial/ethnic type) in order to want, buy or appear to act in a certain way," revealed a continuing effort to link differences in racial or ethnic identities to specific behaviors, even while asserting the arbitrariness of the connection. This cultural move that denied and reasserted racial difference appeared in a moment when social movements attempted to protest race discrimination and many Americans continued to assert and theorize a liberal tolerance that denied the existence of differences.[37] For one school of sociologists the proof of America's tolerance of difference was founded in Euro-

pean immigrants' upward mobility. As ethnics joined the marketplace, differences between them seemed to have disappeared. Where
racial difference persisted it was easily explained by the failure of
minorities to succeed. Their success would otherwise have integrated them.[38]

Therefore, the JAP is, in this conception, a detachable Jewish mask
over a more essentially confident consumerist/American middle-
class core. Everyone can be a JAP who enters the middle class. If
Blacks can be JAPs but Greeks cannot in Sequoia's typology, what further proof is needed that what "melts" Americans is a matter of class
and taste embodied in consumption? No form of identity is critical,
just certain "qualities" that appear to be entirely "neutral": "self confidence," "a little sac of specialness,"[39] "a JAP aesthetic–I am terrific;
Daddy will pay,"[40] perfect taste, and obsessive consumption.

Writing for a popular Jewish magazine in 1983, Jeffrey Mallow explained that science fiction had also discovered the JAP. *The Magazine of Fantasy and Science Fiction* reviewed a television show noting
that "Princess Ariel, [a character], is a thoroughly unpleasant bitch, a
Jewish American Princess who doesn't happen to be Jewish or American." The outer reaches of space offered up a character with all the
unsavory characteristics of the American elite, and the character was
labeled Jewish.[41] But Jewishness didn't count because anyone could
have these qualities. Jews were not different because they could be
repulsive, yet the repulsiveness of their character revealed them to be
Jewish and female.

However, the JAP signifies not only a collection of traits, but ethnic and gender "types." The difference signified by the signs "Jewish"
and "female" are not erased, but only reinscribed. They reinforce difference. Only the Jewish authors and tellers of these jokes insist anyone can be a JAP. None of the favored Gentile icons of models and
great beauties used the term for self-reference. Indeed, the detachable identity of the JAP is the outsider's fantasy that "we" are all the
same.

The JAP's qualities are evocative of earlier intra-ethnic and racist stereotypes. The JAP's body, for example, calls to mind the Jewish woman's large Oriental body, about which Jewish journalists wrote in the 1920s. The constant references to the JAP's need to exercise and diet evokes the fear of a body of too large proportions. Other humor relies on the JAP's "passive body" to explain her unwillingness to labor and her demands for adornment.[42] These accusations reiterate not only classic antisemitic slurs about Jewish males described in chapters 1 and 3, but focus on the link between a nonproductive woman and her use of male wealth. The loser in JAP humor, the father/husband, simply highlights the woman's lack of productivity and her symbiotic nature. Images such as these were as current in the nineteenth and early twentieth centuries as they are in the 1980s and 1990s.

The circulation of this humor into mainstream film, fiction, and television underscored the fact that for Americans, Jews personify affluence. The association of wealth, passivity, and the Jewish woman then reinscribed simultaneously the Jew as different and the Jewish woman as even more dissimilar. The strategy of denying an essential or typical Jewishness to these stereotypes demonstrated the fact that differences, along some measures, were not assimilable to American life, and became increasingly aggressive and ugly in slurs, graffiti, and humor. The liberal consensus of equality in America was accessible to Jews but also illusory.

Ethnicity, then, was a detachable identity from a Jewish core only because that core had a clear set of traits and tendencies that were easily identifiable. As Jewish men and women stereotyped Jewish excess and parochialism in the person of a woman from whom they separated themselves, they continued to assert the Jew in the woman and the woman in the Jew as pariah. The evocation of "type" inevitably reinforced a repugnant difference that Jews, even in the last decades of the century, associated with being Jewish. What gender reiterates in the Jewish stereotype is that Jews may differentiate themselves from one another through identification against a woman or man. I may be a Jew, the image tells us, but not a JAP.

Merging Gender Differences

The JAP is usually a woman, but the humor encompasses men as well in two ways. The JAP victimizes her husband, who suffers her domination and demands. He cannot participate in the patriarchy that should allow him control over his wealth or "his" women. He is expected to give without receiving sexual compensation or obedience in return. There is no JAP without a Jewish male partner.

The Jewish man is woven into the stereotype in a second sense, because JAP is a gender ambiguous term which implies a prince or a princess. Jewish men and women use the acronym, often interchangeably. Nora Ephron's novel, *Heartburn,* provided the most famous sustained humor about men.

> You know what a Jewish Prince is, don't you? If you don't there's an easy way to recognize one. A simple sentence. "Where's the butter?" Okay. We all know where the butter is, don't we. The butter is in the refrigerator. . . . But the Jewish prince doesn't mean "where's the butter?" He means "Get me the butter." He's too clever to say "get me" so he says "Where's." And if you say to him (shouting) "in the refrigerator," and he goes to look an interesting thing happens, a medical phenomenon that has not been sufficiently remarked upon. The effect of the refrigerator light on the male cornea. Blindness. "I don't see it anywhere. . . ." I've always believed that the concept of the Jewish princess was invented by a Jewish prince who couldn't get his wife to fetch him the butter.[43]

Ephron's protagonist caught the stereotypes of arrogance and entitlement that are often associated with the young Jewish man. Though few popularly circulated jokes concern the Prince, Linda Novak, the matchmaker, and participants at seminars on Jewish men and women all used the term commonly and consistently. He was alternately cast as demanding, easily threatened, weak, and financially successful. And in the disturbing accounting of Syracuse University undergraduates shrieking "JAP" at women who walk across a gym, there are also examples of the same being done to the Jewish male students.[44]

The consumption and desires that equate all groups in an American middle-class utopia are reflected to some extent in the gender ambiguity of the JAP. The ambiguities of the acronym suggest certain indistinguishable features between Jewish men and women: they are both royalty and victims. Given the long history of Jewish men's feminization at the center of antisemitism, the gender ambiguity of the JAP is especially powerful.[45] This image of consumption gone mad embraces both male and female, and victim and victimizer. Ambiguous categories such as these almost always signify considerable cultural anxiety over an indeterminate social reality.

The JAP stereotype articulates the anxiety over cultural and ethnic difference as well as who is the perpetrator and victim of the consumer economy.[46] With the rise of second-wave feminism during this period a major reevaluation of who was breadwinner was very much at the center of American life as well.[47] Not unlike the cultural upheavals of the 1920s, the questioning of fundamental categories of American cultural life, particularly relations between men and women, dominated the period of the wide circulation of the JAP image. Sex, work, adornment, leisure, and consumption were related to American Jews in the image of the JAP.

Suburban Life Transformed

The JAP storm gathered its fullest force as Jews entered the middle and upper reaches of the American middle class during the late 1960s and progressively thereafter when Jews became almost indistinguishable from middle-class white Americans. By the end of the 1970s most university and college quotas on Jews finally did cease. Housing, country clubs, and other "pockets of middle-class anti-Semitism" were sewn up.

Jews were acculturating so successfully that intermarriage and Jewish assimilation began increasingly to preoccupy Jewish leaders.

The 1990 National Jewish Population study reported an unprecedented degree of intermarriage in the preceding decade that confirmed what many rabbis and lay leaders had been predicting.[48]

In this same period a Jewish feminism flourished, nurtured by the second wave of secular feminism in the United States.[49] Reform Jews were the first to ordain women, and during these years the number of women rabbis increased. Conservative Judaism responded as well; its Seminary faculty voted to allow the ordination of Jewish women in 1983 as rabbis, following a 1973 vote by the Committee on Law and Standards of the organization of Conservative rabbis to allow individual congregations to count women as full adults in many Jewish rituals from which they had been previously barred.[50] Because Conservative Jews still work within a framework of Jewish law, deviation from that law and further separation from Orthodox Judaism was a weighty matter. Only judgments rendered by the organization's law committee can be binding, and the decision to ordain women was taken within a framework of Jewish law.

Jewish feminism created visible groups and publications that criticized the role of Jewish women as second-class in the family, the religious sphere, and in communal organizations. Virtually every work on American Jewish women of this period discussed the Jewish American Princess and Jewish Mother in order to explain her ubiquitous presence in Jewish life and its difficulties for Jewish women.[51]

These powerful signs of Jewish acculturation also coincided with another change in Jews' occupational structure. Jewish men moved even more rapidly into white-collar professions. The independent Jewish entrepreneur gave way to the Jewish professional, who was less likely to be self-employed. And Jewish women—the quintessential dependent consumer—began to work in unprecedented numbers and began to close the gap between educational and occupational differences from Jewish men.

In the 1950s and early 1960s, as detailed in chapter 5, Jewish males entered a set of occupations different from those they had held only twenty years before. By the 1940s, few Jewish men worked in craft or blue-collar labor. By the mid-1960s, in Boston for example, most were in business, and about one-fifth in professions. Based on the census and a 1963 study, demographers hypothesized that for the first time in the United States more Jewish men would work in corporations than in family establishments.[52] In addition, the sons of those proprietors would increasingly opt for professional occupations that required longer educations, and that put off earning a salary until well into their late twenties and early thirties.[53] Sociologist Marshall Sklare anticipated this trend in his 1957 study of Jews in a Chicago suburb. He learned that 61 percent of the male earners in his sample were self-employed or owned a business. At the same time he characterized these men as "the last of their breed," arguing that it was unlikely that their children would be able or would want to maintain this same level of self-employment in the American economy.[54]

The very young Jewish men whose success was much anticipated often complained about their father's obsessions with making money. The third-generation respondents to a sociological study of Jewish suburban life during the 1950s indicated that their "most vivid memory of their fathers" was of men so busy earning money that they didn't have time for their children. Sons not only condemned their fathers for being unavailable to them but for failing to devote time "to the finer things in life."[55] Younger Jewish men questioned their fathers' ideas about life. Their access to education and their entry into a different set of occupations created a new relationship to the United States.

These educated young professionals were also born to middle-class Jewish families during a time when the economy was booming and consumer items were widely available. As members of the middle class, their ability to maintain their affluence and success depended on their ability to "defer gratification," precisely as their parents were learning how to gratify themselves through household consumption and as teenagers were receiving their own funds.[56] Lacking the patrimony of the property and wealth of the upper class, it fell to the middle class to ensure its children's success through academic achievement.[57] The tensions around consuming and its demands, and the costs of desire and its requirements, were squarely before the eyes of the Baby Boom generation.

By the time this high-achieving generation joined the middle class they encountered a far less booming economy than their parents had known, and vastly expanded opportunities for consumption. Unlike their fathers, they may have learned to enjoy life's finer things, but those things were still only available through their own hard work. What repeatedly and insatiably demanded more and more from young Jewish professional men was the middle class they had joined. It required far greater resources than their parents could have imagined in the 1950s. Neither economic nor personal horizons were any longer imagined as unlimited.

The JAP stereotype emerged from the clash between the high expectations of professionalized middle-class Jews and the 1970s and 1980s economy of, which could not always meet those expectations. The innumerable cultural protests that questioned gender roles and the need for men to support women also operated to challenge some of the cherished assumptions of the middle class. Jews belonged at the center of American middle-class life because they could consume, according to the reigning wisdom of liberal tolerance. Jewish men's ability to consume depended on successful professionalization. The demands of the middle-class male role were embodied by the JAP who always wanted more and had little to give. She represented the dangers of Jewish difference (the Jew in the Princess) and desire (the Princess in the Jew) that were both excessive.

A small but significant number of American films about Jews during this period challenged the promises of middle-class affluence for men and women. *Private Benjamin* introduced one of the screen's classic JAPs, Judy Benjamin. Widowed on her wedding night, in despair she enlisted in the military because of her naive belief in a military recruiter's promises of pleasure and luxury. She stayed in the military and distinguished herself to challenge her father's assertions of her stupidity and his need to rescue her. She was even able, by the end of the film, to dump an unfaithful Jewish doctor at the wedding canopy. She emerged autonomous and independent because she broke with the expectations for women of her class.[58]

Isabelle of *Crossing Delancey* abandoned her hopes for an affair with a European poet when she realized that her greatest attraction for him was her secretarial ability. She turned instead to a Lower East Side (albeit college educated, of course) pickle man who had pursued her throughout the film, and whose intelligence, kindness, and comfort with himself allowed him to remain on the Lower East Side rather than abandon it.[59] The film, less focused on matters of social class, asserted the value of personal integrity and identity over the appeal of elite culture.

The 1987 film *Dirty Dancing* featured the romance between Baby Houseman, the daughter of a Jewish middle-class doctor and Johnny, a working-class dance instructor at a Catskills resort where they occupied different sides of the class divide between worker and guest. The film was set in the early 1960s, and Baby's idealism not only allowed her to find the genuine goodness and integrity in Johnny and the rest of the largely nonwhite staff, but with them to discover her own sexuality and passion. In the process she rejected the Jewish resort owner's grandson for his pretentious and self-important qualities.[60] Similarly, an earlier film, *Baby It's You* linked another young Jewish woman—Jill Rosen—to her white, Catholic, Italian high school boyfriend, Spano, as they found a shared passion that transcended class.[61]

The 1990 *White Palace* was the most explicit in its portrayal of class relations. In this film, what began as a momentary fling between a working-class waitress and a recently widowed young Jewish man grew into a true love that allowed him to reject his close circle of Jewish friends, his career, and his luxury apartment to follow his lover to New York, where he planned to become a teacher. He found himself by abandoning the Jewish middle class that had grounded his life.

The protagonist of each of these films dissolved the equation between Jewishness and affluence in order to establish an authentic and meaningful identity.

None of these films demonized Jewish women per se, as did the popular films about Jews of the 1970s–*Portnoy's Complaint, Heartbreak Kid*, and *Goodbye Columbus*. To the contrary. *Private Benjamin* and to some extent *Dirty Dancing* offered the development of a young Jewish woman into an autonomous adult actor. Even *The White Palace* rejects a middle-class Jewish life without depicting Jews in general or Jewish women in particular as undesirable. What is familiar, however, is that each of these characters, with the exception of those in *Crossing Delancey*, find themselves by rejecting a cultural double in the person of a Jewish man or woman. What is undesirable about the Jewish life that is left behind–its bodily inhibitions, cultural pretensions, or lack of passion–is its tie to the middle class.

It is certainly worth noting, if only for its irony, that in 1927 when Al Jolson initiated the sound age with *The Jazz Singer*, Jake was a sensual figure. His music, the movement of his hips, and even "the tear in his voice" that was linked to the history of the oppression of the Jewish "race" were all exceptionally appealing to the successful (non-Jewish) actress whom he loved. What changed over these sixty years is that all the future Jakes ended up in the middle class, alienated from their sensual beginnings as America's outsiders.

The powerful association of class and Jewishness in the 1980s, however, worked in tandem with the JAP stereotype and the affluence that defined her. Both represented disenchantment with the demands of the middle class, and in the case of *The White Palace*, rejected the Jewishness that was subsumed by it. In the 1980s the love of opposites was grounded in Jews throwing off middle-class demands. As Jews entered that class and became indistinguishable from it, Hollywood idealized an authentic self that rejected class and cultural differences.

These desirable film heroes and heroines circulated in the same cultural spaces as the JAP, the stereotype of the avaricious Jew whose wants and demands were bottomless. Like the films that protested the inauthenticity of the middle class, the JAP warned Jews that life in the middle class was one of unrelenting demands by a woman who could never be satisfied or provide any satisfaction. Jews actively pursued the economic success of the middle class, but as they–particularly Jewish men–used education and professionalization to advance themselves they remained vigilant against the JAP who shackled them to debt, demands, and cultural difference. The women who joked about JAPs, who ambivalently wrote the humor books that praised and attacked them, who boasted of their entitlements to affluence be-cause of their own successes and wore "JAP" and "Born-to-Shop" T-shirts simply reinscribed their lives with the conviction that anyone could be a JAP, but only Jews ever were.

Princess as Earner?

Paradoxically, the JAP's threat of entrapment developed not at the height of Jewish women's dependence, but during their growing eco-nomic independence. Like the "feminist backlash" that began in the same decade that the JAP stereotype flourished, women's small eco-nomic gains became associated with a cultural rage at them. Women created fear and anxiety as a result of their autonomy, not their de-pendence.[62]

Since World War II, but particularly since the 1970s, Jewish women and men have begun to resemble one another in education and employment as they never had previously, according to the re-search of Israeli sociologists Harriet and Moshe Hartman. For exam-ple, in 1990 Jewish women born between 1954 and 1965 were slightly more likely to have received Bachelor of Arts degrees as their high-est degree than Jewish men (46.2 percent to 43.1 percent). By con-trast, Jewish women born between 1946 and 1955 were slightly less likely to receive terminal Bachelor of Arts degrees than men (32 per-cent to 35 percent). The education gap between Jewish women and men is closing. At the same time, Jewish women born between 1946 and 1965 had on average about sixteen years of education. U.S. white males and females of those ages each had on average about thirteen years of education. Only Jewish males had more than Jewish women did, slightly more than sixteen years on average.[63]

Jewish women did not pursue their education simply as an end in itself; it served as the basis of the women's occupations. What determined whether or not women worked was neither her husband's education nor his income, often key determinants of women's labor force participation. Rather, what was decisive for a Jewish woman's participation in paid labor was her own education and the number of children she had. In 1990 nearly 57 percent of Jewish women eighteen and older were in the paid labor force; 71.5 percent of Jewish men were gainfully employed. Only when Jewish women reached their mid-thirties did a workforce gender gap appear between Jewish women and men. For example, Jewish women with graduate degrees were less likely to be fully employed than comparably educated Jewish men during their main childrearing years from 35 to 44. Although Jewish women stayed out of the labor force because of children longer than other white women, they were more likely to stay in the workforce for longer than all white women. Jewish women aged 25 to 34 with no children participated in the paid labor force at nearly the same rate as men of these ages.[64]

These statistics demonstrate that as humor about Jewish women's dependence on men increased and became more virulent, the percentage of Jewish women in the workforce dramatically increased.

As shown in Table 6.1, the proportion of Jewish women in the workforce rose dramatically over the three decades ending in 1990.[65] Although women's participation remained below men's levels of participation in the labor force in 1990, the increase in women's employment was evident in every age group.

The information on Jewish labor force participation reveals that Jewish women and men experience marriage and children differently, and their effect on Jews' occupations and labor force participation differs as well. Jewish men are far more likely to be highly paid

TABLE 6.1

Percent of American Jewish Women's Participation in the Workforce
by Age Groups, 1957 and 1990

Age Group	1957	1990
18 to 24	57%	43%
25 to 34	26%	76%
35 to 44	34%	75%
45 to 64	38%	66%
65 and older	9%	10%

professionals than women. Marriage serves their work life effectively.[66]

Jewish women, despite the fact that younger women are moving
into more professional work, are in occupations more like the over-
all white population than like Jewish men. Nearly 40 percent of Jewish males have professional occupations, while somewhat less than
30 percent of Jewish women do. Professional occupations for Jewish
women are still a relatively recent phenomenon, by contrast with
Jewish men.[67] Women's economic power grew just as JAP jokes became more popular and more aggressive. In the 1980s, when Jewish
women were the most professionalized, the humor built on symbiotic JAPs peaked.

The picture of Jewish women's life derived from these data certainly suggests that contrary to the cherished beliefs of so many Jews
and Jewish commentators, Jewish women are not primarily characterized by excessive wants subsidized by the resources of husbands
and fathers. If a twenty-five-year-old unmarried Jewish woman vis-
ited matchmaker Linda Novak in 1985, she was almost certain to be
a college educated, full-time worker earning at least a middle-class
salary, and more likely to end up marrying a person of lower occupational status than was a Jewish male or other whites.[68] Were she to
marry in 1986, she would have been likely to continue to work until
she had at least two children, and she would probably return to the
workforce as her children reached school age. She would likely stay
in the workforce past the ages of most white workers.

The JAP stereotype, like the others that have represented American Jewish experience to Jews, is not a mirror image of American Jewish life, unless it is the carnivalesque imagemaker of fun houses. No wonder journalists and matchmakers puzzle over unmarried Jews' anxieties about the demanding, whining Jewish women whose expectations are for luxury and support. Those who seek out "real" Jewish American Princesses must look long and hard to find them. The wounding images of affluence, success, excess, and greed attached to Jewish women portray nothing so successfully as anxiety about the demands of the American middle class.

Gender Tension

JAP jokes and humor appear clearly to coincide with changing patterns of Jewish men's and women's education and occupations . The Jewish family was becoming a dual career unit directly in response to the rise of second-wave feminism and women's interests in work. As middle-class white Americans, Jewish women were uniquely placed to take great advantage of the increasing opportunities for women in graduate and professional schools and employment. They worked, and in so doing the nature of Jewish family life began to change. As in all other dual career families, children needed care, and working women became less likely to define themselves primarily through family and voluntarism. Middle-class families remained intensely child-centered, but not with mothers always at home. The result was that Jewish women could no longer be defined by the needs they served or their primary focus on family.[69]

The stereotype that skewers both men and women as mutually inflicting pain suggests a fairly profound anxiety about the family. The JAP humor of the late 1970s and 1980s shares two characteristics. First, its participants are always childless. Wife and husband are not only passionless and defined by consumption, they do not reproduce themselves. Here are Jewish families that do not play their central function of recreating the Jewish people. Their passionlessness implies a particular sterility. The passivity of the JAP's body exchanges adornment for productivity.

The other feature of the JAP stereotype is that it adds "American" to its acronym. The JAP is the first and only of a great panoply of figures in Jewish humor to be designated as an American. Neither the Jewish Mother, nor the rabbi, nor the older schlemiel were ever described as American. European Jewish humor certainly designated certain characters by their geographic location, whether it was the fools of Helm or the hard-edged Litvaks. As JAP humor evolved into the male–female dyad, it underlined the Americanness of the figure. She was indistinguishable from her American, middle-class setting. In fact, she epitomized it–demanding and withholding. Not only was she consumer to her male counterpart's producer; she consumed his energies and rendered him a servant. The increasingly aggressive and angry humor that compared JAPs to vultures and placed their husbands beneath their heels heated up in relationship to the growing demands of the middle class, and the transformation of the Jewish middle-class family into a dual-career unit with professional Jewish women competing for professional jobs with men, and with Jewish men in particular.

As the United States was increasingly driven by a consumer economy and the Yuppies made their debut as a new class of Americans, the JAP became the image of the American middle class itself, cast as an unproductive Jewish woman consumer demanding the sweat of her husband's brow.[70] Unlike the parochialism of the Jewish Mother who made her children different, the JAP makes her husband/father just like everyone else. To be rid of her is to be free of the discipline of work. The demands of the middle class were, as they have been for the duration of the century, laid at the feet of women. Jews' active participation in both the consumer culture and its professional/ managerial class is reflected in the representation of the woman's body that does not sweat and personifies the middle class. Freed from labor, but requiring others to work, she reveals the anxiety that is the patrimony of the middle class. The passive body, and the bitterness that creates its representation, incorporates this anxiety.

Philip Wylie, whose work was best known for his attack on "momism," advanced an American princess as the source of the problem in the 1940s. According to Wylie, Mom is the product of a perversely American version of the Cinderella tale. He explains, "She is conditioned to get the hell out of those chores. There is, the American legend tells her, a good-looking man with dough, who will put an end to the onerous tedium of making a living."[71] Women, therefore, in the United States have become for the first time in human history "an idle class, a spending class, a candy-craving class."[72] Wylie concluded that women were doomed to be disappointed when they realize they never really would be the Princess that the Cinderella story promised. Their only revenge then, was to institute "mom worship," which made it possible for women to be idolized, to control 80 percent of the nation's wealth (!) and to enslave males.

Decades before *Cosmopolitan* thought to reveal the life of the Jewish Princess to its readers, Philip Wylie had invented her. He just didn't know she was Jewish. She was the demanding consumer who refused to work, and controlled men as husbands and children. The JAP is the creation of the consumer culture that finds a group—gender, racial, or ethnic—to blame for the excesses shared by all its citizens. Specific members of the family who constitute the consumption unit are often particularly blameworthy. Children or wives generically, African American males, Asian American women, or Jewish women specifically, bear the sin of consumption to explain why everyone works so hard and must keep spending.

Jewish Life as Middle-Class

The classic stereotype of the excessive and demanding Jewish woman could only become a Jewish American Princess with postwar affluence. However, other markers of American life were equally important to her image. The insistence that there was nothing particularly Jewish or female about the JAP was a critical feature of the

American insistence that all Americans could join the middle class and that the nation was capable of incorporating all differences. The liberal pluralism modeled on the American marketplace created the JAP as surely as Jews' membership in the middle class.

The JAP stereotype emerged as Jews really did appear to be like others. Jewish men and women and middle-class Jews and non-Jews became harder to differentiate in terms of where they lived, where they were educated, and what their occupations were. The specter of assimilation was not only frightening for Jews who wanted their community to maintain its uniqueness, it was also illusory.

The embourgeoisment of American Jews once again raised boundaries that required new forms of policing. The JAP embodied a largely undesirable middle class that, whatever its pleasures, simultaneously embraced its punishments. The JAP reminded Jews as well as non-Jews of the dangers of a middle-class life that was excessively consumerist, overly dependent on designer labels, and that embodied the JAP credo, "More Is More." JAPs spoke a "secret language" that was the tongue of consumption. The stores, restaurants, resorts, shoes, belts, purses, clothing, and furniture that were acceptable to the JAP were poisonous to the enslaved husband whose work purchased it. He was reduced to the butt of jokes about sexual depravation, the sucker who got nothing for what he gave. She was so empty that her desire to "get a deal" was equivalent to nationalist yearnings for Zion.[73]

The JAP, because there was seemingly ample evidence that she was real and not even Jewish, proved that what was most undesirable about life in the middle class could be thought of as Jewish, and under most circumstances female. To excise those features of middle-class life made consumption safer for everyone. Every classical antisemitic stereotype—the body, passivity, the tone of voice, the failure to work or do physical labor—was embodied by the Jewish American Princess.

When Jewish men and women told matchmakers and journalists, not to mention one another, that they were in search of a Jewish partner who wasn't a JAP, they gave eloquent testimony to their anxiety about being Jewish in America. Linda Novak was genuinely puzzled about why her Jewish clients in the 1980s were convinced that they understood an American problem to be a Jewish one.

Men and women who wanted to retain their Jewishness in a culture committed to homogenization were acutely anxious about the dangers of being Jews. They no longer feared antisemitism. They were not turned away from jobs, housing, education, or even a private club if they had wanted to join it. They were afraid, it seemed, of the demands of the middle class, of expectations for wealth and display. And they were also afraid of being seen as weak, undesirable, unsuccessful, or unattractive–in short, "too" Jewish. Jewish difference was a nightmare to those imagining a future and a family.

Just as ragpickers and secretaries were frightened that they would not be found desirable to other Jews who wanted to marry and make a life in America in the 1910s and 1920s, so unmarried Jewish men and women in their twenties and thirties in the 1970s, 1980s, and 1990s saw in the image of the JAP their hopes for a future wrenched from them. To love and marry a Jew became the equivalent of being a slave of middle-class life.

CHAPTER SEVEN

Talking Back through Counter-Representations:

The 1970s to the 1990s

> In a world saturated, perhaps even dominated, by
> the image it is close to impossible to understand
> any given interaction without reference to the
> multitude of mass produced images that often
> seem like only so much background noise to the
> real business of social forces.
>
> Suzanna Walters, *Lives Together*
> *Worlds Apart: Mothers and Daughters*
> *in Popular Culture*, 1992

A merican Jewish women have, throughout the twentieth century, served the nation and other Jews as a medium for representing difference, excess, and desire. The burden of being an empty canvas on which others inscribe their anxieties and fears has not, however, erased Jewish women's ability to find ways to represent themselves. They have always talked back, so loudly in fact that their voices, often described as a threat to Jews' acculturation, have also served as a complex source of their own empowerment.

The lively newspaper debates of the century's first decades revealed the gender dynamics that created the stereotypes that Jews held about one another. The vast majority of columnists in the Jewish press were men, and the readers who responded, at least through letters to the English pages, were overwhelmingly working-class women. For the most part these young Jewish women's letters both rejected how they were portrayed, and offered alternative versions of their lives, which sometimes included condemnation of Jewish men's values and attitudes as the source of those portraits.

Jewish women's rejection of these widely accepted stereotypes was not confined either to the Jewish press or to the early years of mass immigration. Throughout the twentieth century, Jewish women defied stereotypes of themselves as domestic and dependent, becoming bawdy entertainers and influential figures in politics and other public roles.[1] It was not, however, until the 1970s, when American Jewish women's marriages, family lives, and work patterns changed so substantially that they began to reject the stereotype publicly, even as they gained in popularity.

Jewish women began to talk back loudly and persistently to their stereotypes by challenging, reformulating, and referring to them in their writing, art, and comedy. They created literary characters who responded to the JAP, television sketches that mimicked her, and art that drew on and flaunted her qualities. This interest by Jewish women in engaging their own stereotypes marked a shift both in women's entry into the workplace and in their contesting of key definitions of what it meant to be a Jewish man and a Jewish woman. Autonomy, independence, family, class, and culture were all questioned in Jewish women's talk-back strategies.

Some of these works shone a spotlight on the Jewish men whom they saw as the perpetrators of the stereotypes; no one was in that limelight more consistently than the American Jewish writer Philip Roth. Just a few years following the appearance in 1969 of his highly successful novel, *Portnoy's Complaint,* several of the novels in a genre of popular fiction that was dominated by Jewish women writers evoked and attacked Roth and his portrayal of Jewish women in general, and Jewish mothers in particular.[2] But Roth was most likely simply a lightning rod for women's frustrations with their representation by comics, writers, and other commentators on American Jewish life. What was particularly significant about the images created by these Jewish women was that they responded to being stereotyped at so many levels—to what was said about them, to who was saying it, and to the forms in which it was being said.

Yet these women's works were neither didactic nor narrowly political. In contrast to the writing of the nascent Jewish feminism of the period, they did not provide outright condemnations of the stereotype.[5] Instead, while reformulating some of the JAP's supposed qualities in literary characters and art, they parodied the American world that created her, and in so doing, began finally to drive a wedge between what was Jewish and what was middle-class in Jewish self-representation. They drew on popular cultural images associated with Jewish women–middle-class consumption, designer label clothing and accessories, and styles of speech–to, in one form or another, comment upon Jewishness in the United States and the place of women in it. In short, as soup cans were to Andy Warhol–icons of mass culture reconfigured as an aesthetic reflection upon America–so JAPs were to a variety of Jewish writers, comedians, and artists. They were popular images of Jewish women that served to assert Jewishness in a challenge to a monocultural America.

These artists' focus on Jewish women complicated their attack on that monoculture. With their circulation of gender stereotypes, even in the service of asserting Jewishness and the power of women, their critique is blunted in a way that more overtly feminist statements are not. The stereotypes consistently draw on complex images of both self-hate and liberation. Their ambiguity, whether in novels or art, asserts an ongoing ambivalence about the ways in which women are associated with middle-class consumerism as a central feature of American Jewishness. The talk-back art often reproduces the stereotypes even while using them to criticize what they represent.[4]

As Jewish women engaged these stereotypes as artists, they nevertheless began to add a new layer to what Sander Gilman identified as "the outsiders' acceptance of the mirage of themselves generated by their reference."[5] They did not embrace the "mirage" so much as dissect it and parody it. In the act of recreating the representation–of marriage-driven, consuming women–they flaunted their lives as Jewish women. Stereotyped images of body parts that have been associated with Jewish women in particular throughout the century–noses, large breasts, and the curves of the "Oriental body"–were positioned as central to fiction, art, and humor. These artists mocked and parodied middle-class consumerism, its objects and obsessions, by labeling it as Jewish and underlining and exaggerating the stereotyped links between women, consumption, and Jews. They also revealed marriage and family as problematic conditions. Unable to count on either, Jewish women in these works are unmoored from the promise or support of a husband, and hence are radically redefined as both Jews and women.

In this way, women authors and artists asserted the centrality of Jewishness to their identities that, though secular, provided a striking contrast to a homogenized American identity. By relying on humor and parody, Jewish women talked back to their stereotypes during the eras in which feminism, sexual freedom, and multiculturalism created new possibilities for fashioning selves in America. These writers, artists, and performers reconfigured their Jewishness through their representation of their experience as women, particularly in regard to sexual relations and the middle-class economy. In the process they redefined and reinvented an American Jewish womanhood that refused to be confined to the family.

1970s Popular Literature

One of the venues for this process of reconfiguring Jewish womanhood is a group of eight popular feminist novels about unmarried Jewish women in search of love written by Jewish women between 1973 and 1976.[6] Certainly no such clustering of novels about Jewish women written by Jewish women existed previously.[7] All eight novels are comic and draw on certain of the feminist conventions of the time. They are coming-of-age stories about women in search of love and independence, and they center on the protagonists' anxieties and brief triumphs.[8] Most of the protagonists are sexually active and very interested in relationships with men, and their boldness signifies an era of unprecedented sexual freedom and women's assertiveness.[9]

The fact that almost all of the characters in these novels are Jewish, however, alters the shape of the genre substantially. Although none of them engages in activities that might be thought of as normatively Jewish—attending a synagogue, uttering a prayer, studying a text, or participating in a ritual–they are continually represented by a Jewishness that is inseparable from the suburban Jewish family and its conflicts and values. These stories transformed the feminist coming-of-age novel from a "universal" experience of young womanhood to one inflected with the specificity of middle-class Jewish experience.

What marked these novels as particularly Jewish, in addition to the world of middle-class consumption, was the protagonists' struggle to launch themselves into adulthood through marriage to a Jewish man. All of the promises of Jewish success–home, comfort, and suburban life–crashed on the shoals of the simple inability of these young Jewish women to find husbands. The novels pose that failure as attributable to a variety of problems. Each protagonist finds her hair, weight, nose, or lack of beauty has created a crisis, intensified by the possibility that Jewish men are especially reluctant to make commitments to Jewish women.

These mishaps and struggles provide the narrative thread for each novel. Paradoxically, these narratives of failure reveal precisely how engaging, funny, and sympathetic each young Jewish heroine is. They are powerful characters who confront and manage crises, and who likely did so with the empathy and affection of the reader. If their bodies are wrong, their noses and hair vexing, if their parents are exasperating, and their love interests unworthy, their capacity to endure and to comment upon these problems provided them with voices whose ultimate power lay in the narration of their lives within this Jewish world, with its challenges and possibilities. The novels announced a transformation in Jewish women as symbols of American Jewish culture, just as in a more general feminist vein they proclaimed the ability of young American women to be sexually liberated and assertive.

The JAP Inverted

These eight novels narrate the lives of seven young women and one man who "becomes" a woman. The youngest are college-aged; the oldest are in their late twenties. The source of the novels' comedy is simultaneously the source of their pathos. In contrast to the JAP, the characters are not imperial and self-confident, and they do not feel entitled to have every whim satisfied. They are instead the JAP's nightmare: they can control neither their appearances nor their loves. Their Jewishness, unlike the JAP's, is not detachable. They are uncontained rather than contained, unable to command rather than commanding. As failed JAPs, they dismember the JAP, drawing the reader's attention to how, in contrast to their own bodies, the JAP's body is constructed, how her beauty and her ability to command attention are created. These women all comment upon the JAP in their coming-of-age stories as the unachievable ideal against which they measure themselves with envy and anger. But in their failure to achieve her status, they triumph over her and the world that has created her. Because they are not JAPs, they cannot be a source of scorn or attack in the same way that she is.

Each Jewish woman must, in the course of her story, undergo major transformations in order to achieve her goal of marriage. In the novels that portray women setting out for college–Susan Lukas's *Fat Emily*[10] and Louise Rose Blecher's *The Launching of Barbara Fabrikant*[11]–the scenarios seem straightforward. The protagonists are beginning to separate from their families, to explore their sexual freedom and desires, and to create independent identities. However, even the novels about women approaching their thirtieth year require their heroines to undergo dramatic changes. Uniting all of these women is their heroic quest to establish an adult identity through love and marriage.

For each young woman the act of transformation is more than a matter of course. The challenge results from the burden laid upon her by one or another of her body's fatal flaws. She must either become smaller or keep herself from growing too large. The protagonists battle not only fat, but noses which must be reshaped to make them beautiful, and hair that, like their bodies, needs constant management. Their incessant focus on their physical imperfections is comic: a parody of the obsessions of American culture and American women, but seen through the lens of Jewish experience. Their fatness and their frizziness, their large, bumpy, or otherwise undesirable noses all code their struggles as Jews to be found beautiful, particularly by Jewish men.

In these novels, as in subsequent works by Jewish women artists, issues of physical imperfection serve as a trope of difference: icons of Jewishness in a non-Jewish, American world. The physical differences become inseparable from the protagonists' struggles to find love. Most of these women travel a course between the despised and envied perfection of the JAP and the American-defined unattractiveness of the Jewish woman to claim their bodies as a territory for struggle and self-assertion.

In *The Launching of Barbara Fabrikant,* Barbara describes her eighteen-year-old body in this way: "At this moment I'm wearing a bra that cuts deep into the skin underneath my breasts whenever I sit down and a 'long line' girdle that pushes the flab up; it feels as though there is a war going on between my bra and my girdle. When you lose in one place you gain in another, and all the bra salesladies and mothers in the world cannot prove differently."[12] This body cannot be masked or liberated. Its grotesque and slapstick dimensions are such that flesh can be redistributed at will. Barbara's twenty-five pounds of excess weight define her life.

Barbara Fabrikant's "launching" into womanhood is a tale of weight lost and gained, because her body expresses her Jewishness, her capacity to attract husbands, and her relationship to her family. She and her mother fight about her need to lose weight if she wants to marry a proper Jewish husband. Her temporarily successful dieting during her freshman year yields her the love and attention of Jewish men who had previously ignored her. Throughout these adventures, and in reflecting on her life as the daughter of a rabbi, Barbara Fabrikant, a smart Jewish woman, feels the weight of her parents' desires and her own wish to complete her life through marriage to a Jewish man who will care for and support her well.

The women of these novels–Gail Parent's protagonist, Sheila Levine,[13] Emily Howard's Emily of *Fat Emily,* Barbara Fabrikant, and others–are stigmatized by imperfect bodies that block their access to love and marriage. But even in the case of a "relatively" normal Jewish woman, there is no freedom from a pathological physical self. Florida Burns, the protagonist of Marie Brenner's *Tell Me Everything,*[14] works hard to keep her body trim, but she is burdened by what she describes as grotesque breasts: "Breasts. I have a few words to say about big ones. You think you've got problems, well . . . try adding an 'ample bosom' to your list. I'm not just concerned with Edith Lance's custom-made 'flattener' fittings, or a monthly swell to honeydew melon size. I'm talking about something much, much more. Nobody looked sillier than a girl with big tits."[15] A successful gossip columnist in her late twenties, Florida developed her proclivity for humor as a Texas high school student who needed to overcome the burden of her breasts. She feared then, as she does in contemporary New York, that only boys from the working class found large-breasted women attractive; the success-bound men appeared to prefer the flat chests of thin women.

Like the rest of their bodies, women's noses demand alteration. They too must be transformed to create attractive and desirable women. Sheila Levine's novelistic suicide note describes 100,000 women, all of whom need their noses and hair straightened, looking for husbands in New York. Barbara Fabrikant is the daughter of a rabbi who beams at her face transformed by plastic surgery and proudly declares "she looks like a shikse." Musing on her father's contradictory pleasures, Barbara says, "They want us to sound like the British Royal family and still be proud that we're Jewish, a Jewish heart and a Queen Elizabeth exterior."[16] Barbara's parents urge her to become a "finished" person, to be transformed by changing her body.

Perhaps the most striking nose transformation belongs to Suzanne of Myrna Blythe's novel *Cousin Suzanne.*[17] Suzanne Goldfarb is the wealthy and extraordinarily beautiful cousin of Aileen Walker, the novel's narrator. Suzanne's parents indulge her every desire, and see no need for her to change. But Suzanne demands the transformation of a nose she comes to understand as grotesque and that shatters her high school tranquillity. She confronts her cousin who is brought to comfort her.

> "Why didn't you tell me I was grotesque?"
> "Well–because you're not."
> "I AM SO!" She began to cry, great breaking sobs. The night before, when she should have been studying her vocabulary lists, she thought it would be more fun to observe her oval face from a new and different angle. She was quite content with what she saw as usual until she caught an unexpected glimpse of her profile. When with mounting horror she noticed for the first time ever, the sixteenth of an inch mound of flesh that separated the pert nostrils of her nose. A dip, I think it's called, a slight excess of flesh, barely noticeable. In Suzanne's case it was a family characteristic. "It's just grown there" she insisted, beginning to sob again. . . .
> "It's the nose God gave you," said Aunt Bea.
> "The hell with that," said Suzanne.
> "So you'll have it fixed." Aunt Bea said after a moment.[18]

Both body and noses must be transformed from their God-given state to an altered one. The fat daughters of this fiction, for example, have fat mothers. Aileen explains that Suzanne's "dip" is a "family characteristic." But transformations from what "God gave you" are required, nonetheless, to make possible necessities of life–the love which secures suburban households and comfort, children, and a purpose.

These Jewish women's' novels depend on a *perceived* grotesqueness, whether it involves one-sixteenth of an inch of flesh or excess pounds of weight. The protagonists' bodies need to be changed and contained to be made lovable. Consistent with the twentieth-century stereotypes of Jews, these women's "excesses" render them unacceptable and undesirable. The Russian literary critic Mikhal Bakhtin, however, noted that the "grotesque" body has power in its unacceptability. Large bodies and over-sized orifices—in this case noses—transgress tidy social norms and violate order. Like tricksters and demons they reveal how the world is put together by unraveling it.[19]

These novels' authors wielded these stereotypes in their own writing to reveal that the world that rendered them unlovable and unattractive ultimately gave them some power and autonomy. Although "difference," signified by the narrators' bodies, was a source of despair and their deepest desires for love might have been frustrated, from that loss they gained their independence and power.

For instance, Emily Howard, despite her weight, eventually finds a lover. But ultimately she ends the relationship because it does not satisfy her. Rather than returning to her dominating family, she moves out to a place of her own where she has to please no one other than herself. Barbara Fabrikant rejects the Jewish college professor she had ardently pursued when, in the midst of lovemaking, he asks her to put on a cross so he can become sexually aroused. His request makes her realize both that love is not worth abandoning oneself, and that he is not worthy of that self.

In these novels there are no happy endings according to the conventions of the middle-class fairy tale that put women at home, supported by their husbands. Florida Burns is one of the characters who gets her man, but only after he loses his business, goes bankrupt, disappoints his father, and is unable to support her financially. These novels tell complicated stories of loss and victory, and what these heroines achieve is the ability to tell a story of partial triumph.

The Gaze

The grotesque bodies of these novels are created by the gaze of those who judged these women and found them wanting. Mothers, friends, and potential boyfriends all have the power to determine the right proportion of these women's bodies.[20] The narrators most often tell their stories from the outside looking in. For example, Sheila Levine, in *Sheila Levine Is Dead and Living in New York*, repeatedly uses the metaphor of the camera. Describing herself from the perspective of an audience viewing a film, she evaluates herself brutally. In the following vignette Sheila begins her adult life looking for work in New York:

> We open on the exterior of 1650 Broadway, a dirty old building. Pan down to Sheila Levine. She is in a size fourteen black sheath, which is a little too tight so that if one looks closely with the inquiring eye of the camera, one can see exactly where her panty girdle ends. The shot should not be too tight because Miss Levine neglected to shave under her arms this morning. Well movie lovers, there it is, the Sheila Levine Story. The critics loved it. Sheila Levine was played by Ernest Borgnine.[21]

Similarly, the title of *Fat Emily* is derived from a dream Emily Howard regularly has in which others view her humiliation. In the dream she spins plates dressed as an obese clown for the amusement of children. A ringmaster announces, "And Now, Ladies and Gentlemen, in the center ring, performing her hilarious acts of physical dexterity, the world's greatest plate spinner, FAT EMILY."[22] The dream becomes agonizingly detailed: she moves clumsily, cannot keep all of her plates spinning, and is pulled off-stage by a giant hook as hundreds of people, young and old, look on.

The self-conscious externalized gaze also appears in two novels which differ from the others, but in ways which only reinforce the basic messages of how Jews' bodies are linked to the need for transformation. The first, Gail Parent's *David Meyer Is a Mother,*[23] is the only novel of this group written about a man, but one who by the book's final pages is transformed into a "woman." David muses on his transformation from a confident 1950s seducer to a 1970s male entirely confused and "mixed up" about the sexes. As a result of cystitis, a medical condition, he bleeds regularly–"menstrual period style"– keeping him from sex. When his own credit card is rejected, he is forced to use his girlfriend's MasterCard at a restaurant. He finds himself upset if he misses his hair appointment, wants commitment and security from a lover who wants freedom and independence, and finally yearns for a child. David's symbolic transformation to a feminized body reveals a profound change. He constantly views himself through the eyes of others, underlining his uncertainty about who he is. David narrates himself not through the camera, but through his fantasy of being put on trial by a feminist tribunal presided over by Gloria Steinem, one of the founders of second-wave feminism. In each of his fantasy trials David is called upon to justify behavior that was once acceptable–seducing women, for example–and has now, in another era, become "criminal." He has lost his ability to defend and hence define himself.

The gaze is not only externally imposed by critics, but by the culture itself. These novels powerfully express the centrality of the consumer culture to their characters' lives. Many of them find in that culture a world of images created by what they own, buy, and wear–in short, how they appear to others. Who one is–his success or her desirability–is reflected in the garments and things displayed by these protagonists. Like the clothing that could confer Americanization on immigrants, the desirable objects of the consumer society, obscure as they might be to outsiders, carry the weight of belonging and status to those who embrace them.

Consumption is critical to Rhoda Lerman's *The Girl That He Marries*. Like David Meyer, the novel's main character is not a Jewish woman but nevertheless provides a powerful representation of Jewish womanhood. Stephanie, the story's protagonist, is a Christian art historian who is intrigued by and then wants to marry a Jewish lawyer, Richard. She is failing at this goal and turns to a Jewish woman friend for advice. Miriam teaches her how to win a Jewish man by imitating a Jewish Princess. Consumer items are critical in this quest.

> Then she burst from the closet. "Here! Are they gorgeous?" Triumphantly, she tossed me an old white T-shirt and a grimy shoulder bag. "See this ratty thing . . . plastic piece of junk. That's my Louis Vuitton bag. The shoulder strap is leather. In the sixties, this bag then cost one hundred and eighty five bucks and the older it is, the longer it looks like you've been rich."
>
> "I don't really like status symbols, Miriam, It's really outside of my . . . uh experience."

"Oh sure. That's because you are a status symbol yourself.
Listen, now you have your princess uniform. The secret motto
of the legion is: attack. But subtly. See? Do their possessions, not
them.
Mothers attack them. Princesses have a more delicate touch.
If he brings you rye bread with seeds, sigh and say you have
been lusting for rye bread without seeds, and if he brings you
without seeds sigh and say, et cetera. Always an A minus. If you
want to marry him, you have to keep him in line."[24]

As David Meyer did not have to be a female to become a Jewish
mother, so Stephanie does not have to be Jewish to become a Jewish
Princess. What makes their world unstable is precisely its link to the
middle-class preoccupation with images, objects, and illusion. What
continues to promise what they want, a good hair style or the love of
a man, fails to produce it. The more they try to acquire that illusion,
the more frustrated they become.

The world of the JAP, because it is a middle-class consumption-
driven world, lacks solidity. For the novels' protagonists to become
more JAP-like and to attract men they are required to constantly alter an imperfect "Jewish" reality to achieve the ideal middle-class
aesthetic; they must transform what is given. As Suzanne Goldfarb
remarks to her mother's weak insistence that her nose was God-
given: "The hell with that." Neckties can be changed, weight can be
lost, and Vuitton bags can be purchased or shared.

The protagonists' inability to achieve transformation, whether
they gain back lost weight or find that the man who they imagined to
be Prince Charming does not alter their worlds, points up the empti-
ness in those expectations of middle-class life. Realizing this, in each
novel the narrator takes back her voice from the control of others. By
rejecting families, lovers, or growing weary of pursuing men or perfect bodies, these women reject the world that finds them wanting.

Jewish gender stereotypes have an important role to play for these
protagonists in their narratives of sexual warfare in postwar life. They
position themselves in relationship to them. For example, Florida

Burns defines herself as like or not like self- consciously Jewish char-
acters from novels by writers Nora Ephron and Gail Parent. Several
writers refer to Philip Roth and his literary Jewish mother, Sophie
Portnoy, often positioning themselves in contrast to "her" and him.
Sheila Levine attributes Jewish men hating Jewish women to what
Roth called "Portnoy's Complaint." Stephanie, in *The Girl That He
Marries*, imagines a tribunal in which Richard will be tried for his attachment to another woman. She puts the great twentieth-century
Jewish philosopher Martin Buber on her side, and leaves Philip Roth
for Richard. Barbara Fabrikant even describes her father's hair as salt
and pepper "like Philip Roth's."

These novels are peopled with characters who talk back to literary representations. Their "inter-textuality" reveals that these Jewish
women protagonists are part of American Jewish life, but they are not
subsumed by it. They narrate a world of Jewish women who can tell
stories, shape lives, and determine a future that would have been
unimaginable to the male Jewish writers who dominated what came
to be thought of as postwar American Jewish novels–Saul Bellow,
Philip Roth, and others.

Both literary and popular writers about Jewish life dissected and
critiqued the world of the American Jewish middle class, but what
sets apart these comic novels from the 1970s is that Jewish women
wrote them not only to question the synthesis between what was Jewish and middle-class, but to undermine the view of themselves as the
nexus point connecting them. The novels' constant comments on
other Jewish novels, their writers and characters, underline this parodying protest of Jewish women's place as symbol of that synthesis.
The women refuse the role by refusing to be the poisoned prize of
American Jewish life, a role given them no place so powerfully as in
the 1950s fiction by American Jewish male writers.

The Poisoned Postwar Prize

The American postwar period dawned with several works devoted to
Jews; among the most controversial were two that featured young

Jewish women–Herman Wouk's popular 1955 novel *Marjorie Morningstar*, and Philip Roth's critically acclaimed 1957 novella *Goodbye, Columbus*.[25] Their beautiful, confident, and even imperial young women protagonists became for their writers, but especially for their readers, the embodiment of American Jewish life in postwar New York and the suburbs of the Northeast. These women personified the success and excess of that world, which the writers linked to Jews' upward mobility and their changing relationship to work and pleasure in suburban families. Marjorie and Brenda, the novels' protagonists, provide the context for the "talk back" literature created by young Jewish women in the 1970s.

Although *Marjorie Morningstar* and *Goodbye, Columbus* focused on young Jewish women, these novels are more profoundly about relations between Jewish men of different generations. The women– daughters of fathers and wives-to-be–are conduits through which the males transact their cross-generational relationship. They are portrayed as prizes that the senior generation plans to bestow on the junior one, the batons one generation of men will smoothly pass to the next as they continue to build a successful American Jewish life. Neither novel focuses on the gory details of father and son entanglements, but instead uses tales of heterosexual love to show that the race is unraveling and the prize is unclaimed.

In both novels younger Jewish men show no interest in carrying on the torch of either hard work or economic success. They portray unmarried, young Jewish men refusing both the partner and the dance of American middle-class life. Therefore, each man inevitably rejects the women whom the novels represent as embodying the reward of suburban success–the family's ability to consume the objects of middle-class affluence and to raise beautiful daughters.

These early Jewish princesses, Wouk's Marjorie Morningstar and Roth's Brenda Patimkin, provided their readers with an intimidating specter of beauty and affluence. At the same time, they were cast as entrapping, insufficient, and doomed to failed love. At a point when few films were made about Jews, and even fewer about Jewish women, each was adapted for the screen starring beautiful and appealing young women.[26] Both the novels and the films created an image of the Jewish woman as a poisoned prize, which became central to her reformulation in novelistic representations of the 1970s.

Herman Wouk's character Noel Airman, an attractive but troubled man of thirty, never succeeds despite his youthful promise. His decision to fail at law school distinguishes his dreams from those of his father, a New York judge. He reigns instead as a successful writer and musician at the adult summer camp where he works, and is adored and pursued by virtually everyone as he creates show after show for devoted followers. At this camp he encounters Marjorie Morgenstern, ten years his junior, who sneaks in and falls under his spell. After years of pursuit, attraction, and breakups they become lovers. During all of this time Marjorie believes in Noel's talents and constantly encourages him to write the great musical he longs to create, giving his career more importance than her own ambition to become an actress. He finally has a musical produced on Broadway only to have it fail, and in his letter to her ending their long affair, he attributes the flop not only to his lack of talent, but to Marjorie's constant confidence:

> I'm responsible . . . for the fact that Princess Jones was an old-fashioned piece of tripe that closed in five days. You're responsible, however, for my exposing myself and my limitations in such a wretched and crucifying way.
>
> I'm tired of playing the horse to your rider, and I'm throwing you. People who didn't know the situation as well as I do would be appalled at this statement of it. You're the innocent victim, of course, and I'm the bored old seducer casting you aside. But the fact is, you seduced me as much as I seduced you. If I seduced you to go to bed with me you seduced me to go to work for you. You have ridden me mercilessly. Your left spur has been the American idea of success, and your right spur the Jewish idea of respectability. I have disbelieved in both ideas with all my heart since I was seventeen. But you have used the miserable fascination you had over me to make me conform to those

ideas, or to break my heart trying. Princess Jones was at bottom
your big bid for a house in New Rochelle, and for that reason
I'm glad it flopped.[27]

One of the ten best-selling novels of the year, this postwar work
placed at its core a doomed love affair.[28] Airman refuses to enter the
respectability of Jewish life with its taint of suburbs, empty synagogue
piety, and marriage.[29] His anger at his father both fuels and pales in
comparison to his deeper rage at Marjorie's wish to create a family
and move to the suburbs with him. Finally, he flees New York for
Paris, leaving behind a love that he claims drove him toward work
and success, and by the novel's end is in a sexually ambiguous marriage with a "mannish" German woman.

This same anxiety and disenchantment is depicted in *Goodbye,
Columbus*. Neil Klugman, the novella's protagonist, works at a New
Jersey public library, has no plans for his future, and feels only contempt for his colleagues who devote their lives to ascending their tiny
ladders of success there. Instead, he dreams of Tahitian islands and
a sensuality that is just out of his grasp. In the library he attempts to
protect the dreams of an African American child who seeks refuge in
the library's art section and admires beautiful color plates of Gaugin's
paintings.[30]

Amidst those dreams Neil falls in love with Brenda Patimkin,
whom he meets at his wealthy cousin's country club, to which he is
invited once a year. Their easy sensuality is played out in the suburban New Jersey home where the Patimkins live, and Brenda's eager
eroticism coexists with the conventional and tense life of her wealthy,
hard-working father and shrill, nouveau riche mother. Neil, like Noel,
resists these aspirations in his own life, but his passionate affair with
Brenda Patimkin brings him to the very precipice of the world he has
rejected.

Like Airman, one of Neil Klugman's most pressing concerns is
whether the object of his love is just another Jewish woman bound
for suburbia. Both Noel and Neil initially believe that a sexual rela-

tionship is proof that their loves are not really simply Jewish "girls" in search of marriage and respectability. Noel's description of the "Shirley" parallels Neil's musings about the women he knew in high school–the "immortals" and "goddesses"–who devoted their lives to homes, hair styles, and clothing that all resembled one another and were always dictated by the style of the moment. "Shirleys" and "goddesses" may be desirable, but they are a prize that always contains a hidden punishment. No matter how they initially appear–adventuresome, free spirited and sexually available–ultimately they demand that men work and give up their dreams, so that they can settle into the comforts of affluence.[31] They are entrappers who, like mythological goddesses, set their snare with beauty and guile.

When Noel first explains "the Shirley" to Marjorie, what she finds most cutting is the equivalence he draws between a young woman and her mother. Noel explains that he encounters Shirleys in the person of one or another young woman awaiting his arrival at her Upper West Side apartment door:

> The respectable girl, the mother of the next generation, all
> tricked out to appear gay and girlish and carefree, but with a
> terrible threatening solid dullness jutting through, like the gray
> rocks under the spring grass in Central Park. Behind her, half
> the time, would loom her mother, the frightful giveaway, with
> the same face as Helen's or Susan's, only coarsened, wrinkled,
> fattened, with the deceiving bloom of girlhood all stripped
> away, showing naked the grim, horrid, respectable determined
> dullness, oh God . . . the smug, self-righteousness mixed with
> climbing eagerness.[32]

Neil, like Noel, fears the illusion of attractive Jewish women, and learns that Brenda is after all simply one more "immortal," dooming their passionate affair to failure. Roth cast Brenda as the embodiment of her parents' values, and thus she abandons Neil when forced to make a choice between the pleasures of their forbidden sexuality and her parents' approval. But Neil leaves relieved and liberated, and Roth makes Brenda just unattractive enough to convince the reader that he is better off with his freedom.

Both Neil and Noel calculate love in terms of a consistent set of dimensions—loss/win, victory/defeat, resist/seduce—because their passions are inseparable from their fates. Which American dream will they pursue—to supersede their fathers' economic success, or to remain free to pursue adventure and art? The men in the senior generation of both novels are manufacturers. Their occupations are portrayed as involving unrelenting work with no apparent intrinsic value beyond the affluence it brings these families. As these younger men taste the sweet fruit of desire and sexuality, they begin to lose their autonomy and independence to the taskmaster of hard work. As they lose these women, they win their freedom from fathers and productivity. Whatever their ultimate fate, each refuses the middle class by refusing its daughter. They flee hard work and the creation of a family, personified by the father-producer and embodied by the beautiful, sexual daughter and her less attractive mother.[33] The novels' male characters provide the reader with images of a Jewish postwar masculinity that rejects middle-class success.

Entangled Stories

Most of the eight novels of the 1970s about the lives of Jewish women feature protagonists who simply said "No thanks" to the role of poisoned prize created by male Jewish writers. Each of these women, during a complex and even distorted coming of age, announces that she is not Sophie Portnoy, she is not Marjorie Morningstar or Brenda Patimkin, and she is not confined to the life of the Jewish daughter or wife. These works present women as sexually active with multiple partners. Sometimes their sexuality is motivated by capturing a man, but more often women engage in the chase and indulge their desires. "Grotesque bodies" keep women from love but also reveal their independence, autonomy, and the possibility of pleasure. As classic "losers" these women are funny; their voices control the novels, providing commentaries on contemporary Jewish life, the family, and the impossible dilemmas that beset women. Drawing on familiar styles of Jewish performance–the self-effacing, the comic, the hyperbolic, and the iconoclastic–they transform the language of hopelessness into one of power. These writers not only "talk back" to Philip Roth and others, they tell the jokes, violate decorum, and push the limits. In their fiction they find the voices to narrate American Jewish experience as women.

In the 1970s, as master narratives of gender, assimilation, and the family fell apart, these women writers reformulated the loser/outsider as a woman bursting out of cultural restraints. Jewish women writers declared themselves capable of narrating lives at the same time that their narratives asserted that the future would not be as they imagined it as children but, rather, a reality full of terror and possibility. Love, solidity, social class, and Jewishness were all in question, their shape uncertain, and their relationship to one another fractured and cracked open.

What the novels achieve is neither a triumphant assertion of a Jewish women's art, nor an uncompromising rejection of the pleasures of middle-class life. Instead, they reject the role of poisoned prize to declare that coming of age as a Jewish woman is a new tale to tell.

The 1970s was also the period when the comic Jewish American Princess made her television debut. Neither as complicated nor as painful as these novels, television became the medium for a more affectionate critique of the middle class represented as a young Jewish woman.

The Comic JAP: Gilda Radner and Saturday Night Live

Saturday Night Live debuted in 1975, bringing a new form of humor to weekly television. Lorne Michaels, a Canadian Jew, assembled an extraordinary group of writers and actors to create an ensemble that produced intelligent, contemporary, and very original comedy. The program's young comedians and culturally relevant and often outrageous humor became an immediate critical success, and ultimately a popular one as well. Gilda Radner was one of the many Jewish members of this group, and in 1978, in the show's third season, as she moved into greater prominence, she introduced to television its most outrageous Jewish American Princess, Rhonda Weiss.[34]

Rhonda was an unmistakable JAP parody. Her nasal, New York-accented speech was devoted to commenting on what she bought to wear and to display, and the bargains she was able to find. She was by turns sweet, demanding, banal, and obsessed with her weight and appearance. Her viewers encountered her at her surprise wedding shower, and stoned on marijuana in her living room with one of her best friends. She sang the praises of a sugar substitute just as she exclaimed over her favorite possessions.

Rhonda Weiss was a popular *Saturday Night Live* character, and Gilda Radner, with her remarkable gift for comedy, portrayed her so effectively and affectionately that few people seemed to take offense. A Jewish woman played a Jewish woman stereotype without making her audience hate either of them. Rhonda Weiss had an appealing vulnerability about her that marked Gilda Radner's performances and humor.

Radner's JAP was young, eventually newly married, and most significantly, a consumer. What she consumed was so trivial that she lampooned the world of consumerism more than the consumers. At her "kitchen shower" Rhonda Weiss received a "melon baller," an "egg tweezer," and an apron emblazoned with "For this I went to college?" She wept with gratitude over the gifts she had first noticed in the Bloomingdale's sale catalog, and thanked her friends for the event she described as "the major niceness of my life."[35]

Rhonda Weiss's consumerism, however, also made her aggressive. When her MasterCard was suspended because of excessive spending, she was forced to meet with a counselor about her debt. Rhonda, who chewed gum constantly and wore her trademark oversized glasses, sat down for her ordeal armed with receipts of purchases. She patiently explained that each was necessary. When she pointed out that the "silk blouse I'm wearing cost only $65.39 on sale," the counselor, played by Laraine Newman, retorted "You call that a sale?" The two women became fiercely competitive about who had found the best deal on silk blouses and emerged as good friends from the fray.

The most innovative comedy sketch about Rhonda's life as a consumer portrayed her high on marijuana and having a frightening experience. She and her best friend Barbara, also played by Laraine Newman, sit in Rhonda's suburban living room sharing a marijuana cigarette. Rhonda complains that "I'm completely wacked [stoned] and I get paranoid." As they drink diet sodas and eat popcorn, Rhonda explains what she does to calm down to deal with her paranoia: "I imagine the ideal wallet, key case, and cigarette holder set." But her technique fails her. She says bitterly, "It keeps coming out in vinyl."[36] Rhonda's comfort in things is defeated by the cheap imitations she imagines during a "bad trip." Vinyl expresses her paranoid fear of a dangerous world.

Through Rhonda Weiss, Radner and her writers inverted the classic women's comedy that looked at the foibles of everyday domesticity. It was not exasperating husbands, children, and laundry that were the source of this humor, nor did Rhonda rise above the domestic. She recreated it as a site of consumption, and a young married life that included wedding showers, Hanukkah parties, telephone conversations with Mother, and getting stoned. In juxtaposing drugs and suburban women's anxieties about what they own and eat, Radner simply renders funny and absurd what is stereotypically represented as a Jewish woman's life.

Rhonda Weiss is certainly portrayed as one-dimensional, but she is funny because Gilda Radner, a Jewish woman, made her funny. Her audience laughed at the absurdity of suburban life, at her exaggerated style, and at her passion for a bargain. But there is no pretension that this comedy was about "real" life. Rhonda was recognizable because she was a suburban everyman/woman. The audience understood that they lived in a world that offered "egg tweezers" and other absurd items for purchase, as well as the promise of bargains as they spent money they did not have. The slapstick, physical humor of *Saturday Night Live* only underlined the fact that Rhonda Weiss was no more real than other sketch characters such as the Cone Heads or Radner's Roseanne Roseannadanna.[37] Vulnerable, exaggerated, and recognizable, Gilda Radner created a JAP that no one hated. At the same time, Rhonda's trials and tribulations, like those of the women protagonists of the popular novels, were funny because their struggles were recognizable.

Indeed, Rhonda Weiss exposed American middle-class women's profound anxiety about weight as the lead singer in one of *Saturday Night Live*'s most famous sketches. Writer Marilyn Miller immediately wrote a song for the character when she learned that the sugar substitute saccharine caused cancer in laboratory mice.[38] Backed by the Rondettes, Rhonda Weiss sang about her body and her love for what she could no longer have. It is to saccharine that she attributed her "first chance to wear my clothes without imprinting in my skin the elastic from my underpants" and her ability to "zip my jeans without lying down." Radner captured American women's anxiety about weight when the chorus asks, "What did you weigh in college?" She answers, "I went up and down between 115 and 125." When they persist in asking "closer to 115 or 125," she shouts out "Bitch!"

Gilda Radner's tremendous success on *Saturday Night Live* was a breakthrough for women comics of this period. Her capacity to be funny as a Jewish American Princess was neither a feminist critique of representations of Jewish women nor a pioneering effort to create a self-conscious Jewish women's humor. But Gilda Radner did not create a Jewish American Princess through the eyes of men, or blame her for the troubles that beset them. Rhonda Weiss was a cleverly drawn caricature of suburban, Northeastern, Jewish middle-class life. She was seen by a little more than 25 percent of late Saturday night television viewers as one in a panoply of sketches by a talented group of young comedians. It was her ordinariness, her place in the pantheon of the ensemble's characters, and the vulnerability and attractiveness that Gilda Radner brought to this role that made her a very different send-up of American Jewish life. Radner reformulated the JAP to make her more funny than pathetic or dangerous.

Like the popular novels' literary JAPs, Rhonda Weiss made transparent the absurdity of the links between Jewishness and suburbanization, and women and consumption. Humorous send-ups by talented Jewish women underlined the simple fact that women were not only sources of representations but also their creators. Like the novelists, Radner continued to circulate the image of the JAP, leaving it a popular stereotype within the mass media. However, her humor sufficiently refashioned the JAP to at least remove a substantial part of its sting.

"Acts of Provocation": 1990s Art and Representation

Jewish Princess jokes, greeting cards, and novelty items flourished throughout the 1980s and, as noted in chapter 6, during this same time Jewish feminists began a direct assault on the humor. In the 1990s, however, a whole new genre of "talk back" art appeared that drew on the symbols and images that had been linked with Jewish women in the consumer culture.[39] Clothing and accessories that were clearly associated with renowned designer labels were incorporated into art. These icons of beauty and affluence were juxtaposed with overt signs of Jewishness, Yiddish words, the festival of Hanukkah, and Jewish food, making explicit the artists' self-consciousness about their difference as Jews from the larger society. That art should take up and trade in images circulating in the mass culture was a phenomenon well established by pop art in the 1960s. That these vernacular images should create an art explicitly linked to issues of identity in general, and Jewish identity in particular, was a far more recent phenomenon. For Jews to "talk back" through art was as much a challenge to American Jews as to the art world.

These artists, born after 1960, entered a multicultural dialogue about art and identity with their work. Several of them had produced art that expressed other identities as gays and women. Their "Jewish" art integrated gender, sexuality, and Jewishness to explore the experience of being an American Jew. As I have argued, Jewishness largely disappeared from popular culture during the period of the 1930s to the 1960s. It re-emerged with the resurgence of white ethnicity in the late 1960s and throughout the 1970s. Those images, however, were frequently posed as masks to be taken on and off at will and interchanged in a pluralist America.

The Jewishness with which these artists contend is of a different order. Inspired far more by assertions of racial difference and sexuality, they are concerned with the problem of an identity that is marginalized by the dominant culture, and often simultaneously contested by the person who explores and claims it. The very act of contesting, nevertheless, is a way to continue to assert opposition to the larger culture. These Jews challenge how they are represented by drawing on the topics of those representations—for instance, excessiveness, consumption, and icons of Jewish celebrity like Barbra Streisand—to reconfigure them. Rather than creating a Jewish art per se, they literally trade in images in order to reimagine being an American Jew. The brashness and provocations of their art are the product of exploring Jewishness at that meeting ground of difference and otherness.

These artists, like other Jews taken up with the multicultural issues of the last two decades, experience a special challenge.[40] Unquestionably, these decades have been characterized by Jews' greatest access to American society because in this period, as a group, they became solidly middle- to upper middle-class. As beneficiaries of civil rights legislation they have also experienced the removal of barriers to institutions, neighborhoods, and clubs once denied to them.

However, in a period during which wider access to America was possible, the assertion of cultural uniqueness and difference became increasingly a project of those Jews who wanted to resist the domination of the larger society. Similarly, this period was one in which the Holocaust emerged as a matter of public concern through the work of scholars, artists, performers, and religious leaders and thinkers, and it became an important element in many artists' exploration of their Jewish identities. Both inside and outside of the dominant culture, Jewish artists explored the meaning of a Jewish identity in their art.

A multicultural Jewish art faces two tasks. It positions Jews within the critique of a society as hostile to cultural diversity, and hence opposes a modern art that rejects particularism and identity. At the same time, it broadly defines a Jewishness that is non-normative and which explores sexuality, secularity, and feminism, all of which challenge traditional Judaism.

The Jewish identity/multicultural art that emerged in the 1990s in large part drew on American Jewish comic traditions that transgressed boundaries of decorum and propriety. Like other multicultural art, it addressed issues of gender and sexuality and was often rooted in the body–particularly for Jewish artists, the parts of the body that were so often objects of antisemitic slurs. It portrayed the experience of difference and marginality of American Jews through vernacular images that were ambiguously grounded in the middle class. The images of shopping and buying that constitute activities of middle-class Jewish life served both as a critique of the culture that collapsed Jewishness and the middle class, and an often witty recognition of some Jews' participation in that world. That ambiguity ties this art to the popular feminist novels of the 1970s. However, the art of the century's last decade has a broader and more encompassing cultural critique at its core.

In addition, these artists avoid didactic renderings of "identity." In contrast to classic 1950s definitions of identity as a coherent, singular set of meanings that might be seen at work in voting behavior or choices of employment, in the hands of these artists it is quite a different matter. It is neither coherent nor straightforward. For them, Jewishness, for example, is fluid and not particularly stable. Their artwork challenges a polarizing "pro" or "con" approach. It draws on clichés, experiences, and contradictions that are worked out within the life of the individual, rather than creating images that declare what is "good" or "bad" for the Jews. They incorporate images for the purpose neither of refuting or supporting them, but commenting upon them.

Rhonda Lieberman, for example, created a work in 1994 entitled "Pushy/Cushy/Tushy (Sandra Bernhard triptych from the series "Purse Pictures)," a series of three beaded and lush fake Chanel shopping bags featuring images of the performance artist Sandra Bernhard.[41] Lieberman pays homage to this Jewish performance artist who herself consistently challenges singular forms of identity by associating her with shopping and designer labels through the bags. Her play with language, however, ties the associations of Jewishness and gender together more directly. The Yiddish word, *tushy,* an endearing diminutive for the buttocks, is rhymed with English words associated with stereotypes of Jews as powerful (*pushy*) and affluent (*cushy*). Celebrity, Jewishness, consumption, and women as consumers are linked through these three shopping bags. Bernhard appears as a Marilyn Monroe–like suburban woman watering her lawn on the Pushy bag. She floats on a pool looking glamorous and well-heeled on the Cushy bag, and on the Tushy bag her image is taken from the *Playboy* cover for which she posed as a "Playboy Bunny."

Bernhard explores her gender, sexuality, and Jewishness in her performance art. Her style outrages. She uses her body, her face, her voice, and her clothing to critique acceptable norms of American life. It is not difficult to draw a direct line from the vamping of comics like Milton Berle and Jack Benny to the sexual ambiguities and outrageously costumed statements of Bernhard. She too plays on Jew as outsider and loser in her work. As Jew and woman Bernhard addresses the same territory as Lieberman.[42] For Lieberman, Bernhard embodies cultural clichés and transcends them at the same time. Bernhard has come to represent an "in your face, JAPpy spokesmodel" who outrages by challenging norms of what is beautiful and what is acceptable for women. She transgresses seamless ideas of womanhood. Lacking a classically beautiful face, she puts herself in situations that normally belong only to "beautiful women"–the cover of *Playboy,* a lounge singer–and actively pursuing both men and

Rhonda Lieberman, "Pushy/Cushy/Tushy (Sandra Bernhard triptych from the series Purse Pictures)," 1994; glitter, glue, paper.
(Courtesy of Rhonda Lieberman)

women as sex partners. But she shows her own vulnerability to those rules while challenging them. As a self-identified Jewish performer, Bernhard breaks rules and becomes literally part of the fabric of Lieberman's work, which challenges fake and authentic expressions of beauty and culture.

In the same year, Rhonda Lieberman was commissioned by Barneys, an upscale New York department store, to create one of their Christmas windows. Once again juxtaposing celebrity, images from popular culture, and Jewish difference, she created "Barbra Bush," a fake, white Christmas tree festooned with six-pointed stars of David. Each star hangs on a gold chain over a tree branch decorated with identical images of Barbra Streisand wearing a tiara and holding her hands together as in Christian prayer.[43]

The iconoclastic bush starkly addresses Jews' discomfort with a holiday that does not belong to them, and to which they have accommodated throughout the century. The "Hanukkah bush," a "fake" celebration of a commercialized Christmas, like the "fake" Chanel bags, underlines Jewish marginality from the mainstream.[44]

With her bush, Lieberman inverted the incongruity of a 1991 work she created with Cary Leibowitz, "Chanel Hanukkah."[45] For this work they purchased a fake gold Chanel purse from a street vendor and created a Hanukia by placing nine lipsticks on top of it. Some of the lipsticks remain below the surface of their containers in order to create the illusion of lighted and unlighted candles.[46] To complete their assemblage they attached bags of Hanukkah candies to a heavy "fake" Chanel chain and decorated an inexpensive, mass-produced Hanukia with the Chanel trademark.

Leibowitz and Lieberman took the designer labels of affluence and beauty and linked them to the most Americanized and secularized holiday of the Jewish calendar, whose celebration is inseparable from an equally commercialized Christmas. Leibowitz's and Lieberman's work lays out their central themes in exploring American Jewish identity: difference, commercial culture, authenticity, and gender. They juxtapose each of these themes against visual symbols and objects that together position Jewishness in relation to American culture and to a milieu with which middle-class Jews are saturated.

Lieberman describes that world as "secularized, ethnically thick and coded as Jewish," but remarkably lacking in "overt content." The "cultural soil" of that world is paradoxically without much content for the "People of the Book," at the same time that it is highly self-conscious of its Jewishness and difference from the mainstream. That paradox is something Lieberman wants very much to capture rather than reduce. Her art asserts all of the poles of that Jewish experience, refusing to choose among them, condemn or praise some as against others.

In 1996, Norman Kleeblatt, curator of New York's Jewish Museum, exhibited some of this art in a controversial exhibit, "Too Jewish?

Challenging Traditional Identities." Lieberman and Leibowitz were both included in it. In the exhibition catalog he noted that the art aimed to be "confrontational and embarrassing."[47] In drawing on popular stereotypes of Jews in order to assert Jewish difference, the artists challenged the authority of the art world as well as the authority of the Jewish community. The exhibition flaunted Jewishness on the one hand, but also associated being a Jew with the popular culture, with consumption, and with women's display of self and affluence, ignoring any normative behaviors of Jewish life and observance.

The art was funny, shocking, and playful. It placed the subjectivity of the artist at the center of each work. Her or his synthesis of Jewishness and America was very much a work of personal identity that asserted difference from the larger society. For the artists, there is no art apart from their identities, in this case a Jewish identity often forged within and against middle-class values and norms, and irreducible to a flat set of markers.[48]

Stereotypes of American Jews in general, and American Jewish women in particular, become a terrain to explore in representing an identity imposed on and claimed by the artist. Humor and parody are central to this work because it is the medium through which these artists "talk back" to a dominant culture that marginalizes and rejects Jewishness. At the same time, many of the artists leave ambiguous their use of images powerfully associated with Jewish women. Celebrating Hanukkah in the medium of both inexpensive, mass-produced ritual objects, and "fake" expensive accessories remade as those objects, suggests more than the marginalization of Jews at Christmas. It also links Jewish women to affluence and consumption, perhaps hinting at a preoccupation with them.

Another artist in the exhibition explicitly took up the image of the Princess. Nurit Newman's installation, "Complex Princess," created in 1995, suspends gold crowns of various sizes and adorned with rhinestones, glitter, and pink tulle fabric from the ceiling over a floor covered in hot pink feathers. On the floor rests a television monitor running a tape of a woman engaging in compulsive behavior–playing with her shoes, and picking at her fingernail polish.[49]

Newman's crowns are made of matzo meal, which she molds and casts, transforming a humble, Jewish foodstuff used for cooking on Passover into the stuff of excess and suburban affluence. The assemblage, through the use of matzo meal, invites the viewer to fill in the missing word "Jewish" in reading the title of the piece. He or she is certainly helped in understanding these images of the princess as "Jewish" by the behaviors depicted on the monitor–empty, senseless gestures in part connected to appearance and adornment.

Like Lieberman and Leibowitz, Nurit Newman leaves ambiguous her appropriation of the JAP stereotype in creating her art. Perhaps commenting on the relationship between the Jewish Mother and the JAP (matzo meal versus crowns), or perhaps critical of the long-standing stereotype of the excessiveness of bored, unemployed Jewish women, she creates a work that draws on the well-known representation to explore issues of art and Jewish identity.

Writing about the "Too Jewish?" exhibition, critic Linda Nochlin argues, "It destroys or sends up Jewish stereotypes (for better or for worse) at the same time that it powerfully and wittily evokes the range and variety of modern Jewish identities."[50] These artists' commitment to explore Jewishness, gender, and in several cases sexuality, within the context of Jews as an American minority, finds in stereotypes a powerful representation of the complexities of identity.

In fact these art works use many of the "strategies" of the popular novels and television sketches that preceded them. In these works, there is nothing seamless about Jewishness. Its location in and close association with the middle class creates a jagged rather than holistic construction. The viewer and reader laugh at the juxtapositions of matzo meal and princesses, Vuitton purses and Jewishness, and Chanel bags and Jewish festivals. At the same time, the works' meanings are left obviously ambiguous. Are the Jewish women depicted as tragic dupes of the consumer society that has reduced them to seeking middle-class luxury? Are they protesting and contesting those values by flaunting their Jewishness and reminding their interlocutors of their separation from that world? As Nochlin asks, do they "send up" or dismember the stereotypes?

The "Too Jewish?" artists explore the issue of "fake" and "authentic" in their work, just as the novelists continually place their narrators in the problem of understanding what is "real" and what is "illusion." This lack of authenticity constitutes a response to being the object of stereotypes. Continuously made to represent a class, an attitude, and the failure to be the norm, the stereotypes of Jewish women are simultaneously flaunted, explored, and rejected in these works.

At the same time, the stereotypes become a powerful vehicle for claiming a sense of oneself as different from the majority society, a world in which Jews can easily "pass," but often feel and are perceived as different or feel betrayed by their Jewish bodies. The novels' narrators emphasized that position both in their persistent desire to create "Jewish" relationships, and to define themselves as Jews without any evidence of normative Jewish behavior. So too the "Too Jewish?" artists pursued their sense of difference from the larger society through their ironic use of products, labels, and secularized holidays. They use popular and commercial culture as a means for asserting their difference and their subjectivity. As Kleeblatt argues, they reject any traditional form of authority—religious or cultural—to assert their unique synthesis of Jewishness, gender, and sexuality. In addition, Lieberman comments that she refuses to "moralize" in her art, to select between "pro" and "con" associations with Jews. Rather, her art engages all positions. While she finds in the postwar culture of American Jewish suburban life a "surreal excess," she also locates a joyousness in that excess that is uniquely Jewish.

The "Too Jewish" identity art is far less taken up with issues of love and the reproduction of the family than the 1970s popular literature. In both cases, however, the works talk back to the ways Jewishness in general, and gender in particular, act to represent the experience of being a Jew in America. In commenting upon those images, these works assert the power of women's voices, as well as many men's, to explore and thus sever representations that have for decades intertwined realities of Jewishness and class, and Jewishness and gender in the making of the American Jew. These various expressive forms challenge the inevitability of those connections, and envision instead a Jewishness that does not depend upon the consuming woman as an icon because Jewishness is not defined primarily in terms of acculturation or membership in the middle class. Jewishness, instead, constitutes an identity from which an artist can question and critique the dominant culture.

Jewish gender stereotypes are marked by two central realities. They change and they stay the same. The themes of desire, excess, and longing to belong are as evident in a Barneys window display as they were in the demands and anxieties engendered by the Ghetto Girl. These themes, however, took shape in radically different environments. It is now New York's Upper East Side where Jews live, display themselves, and are displayed as representations of American culture. And anxiety is intertwined with critique, rejection, ambivalence, and parody. The great-grandchildren of those turn of the century immigrants do not simply negotiate their world through gender stereotypes, but also reformulate and comment on those stereotypes as part of the process of cultural negotiation. They no longer have to fight to become Americans; they must fight to keep some distance from a culture that continues to use Jewishness to reflect on its own troubled relationship to diversity, consumption, and success.

Jewish acculturation has not caused Jewish gender stereotypes to disappear. To the contrary; it has exacerbated them. Jews gained greater access to American life through class mobility. With their ability to become middle-class white Americans, in time there was no part of American life—its institutions, privileges, and families—Jews could not claim. Those opportunities created a new set of problems and anxieties.

Jews who want to maintain their distinctiveness worry about their ability to love and marry other Jews, who with increasing ease can find non-Jewish marriage partners. Jews' ability to become professionals continues to evoke anxieties about expectations for success and wealth. Jews' freedom to integrate fully into America causes constant concerns about whether or not other generations of Jews will replace them.

As Jews' place in America changed, the post–World War II stereotypes evolved from a suffocating, parochial mother to a whining, consuming, and withholding princess whose enslaving demands made her thoroughly undesirable. These representations of American Jewish womanhood encoded a profound anxiety about how Jews fit into American society and culture. In keeping Jews apart from the majority, the Mother endangered Jewish acculturation, while plunging Jews into the middle class and its desires, the Jewish American Princess tainted affluence. In both cases, these monster women emasculated Jewish men.

These images are not abstractions or cultural texts that only preoccupy scholars interested in their secret meanings. They found their way into the hearts of Jewish young men and women who, as I described at the outset, met one another at a workshop they attended, probably as much for its topic as for the chance of meeting someone with whom they might spend their lives. The slurs and stereotypes they offered about Jewish men and women–their demands, their whining, their inability to love, their hopeless self-absorption–were for them the product of their Jewishness and gender, and not of their generation, their class, or even their nation. It was being a Jewish woman or man, raised by a Jewish family, that created their most unattractive features.

What differentiated them from the mainstream–their Jewishness–and from one another–their genders–served as sources of conflict between them. These sources of difference served them, as they have every other generation of American Jews of this century, as a language with which to reckon the experience of being an American Jew. If difference might well be a source of pride for many Jews, in love relations it was at least symbolized as a source of conflict and pain. Jews continue to negotiate the experience of being a minority through the anxious images of private life, the intimacies that might be more satisfying if only they weren't "too Jewish."

One clue as to why these processes continue in an America that is more embracing of its white ethnics than any other time in the twentieth century might be found in the fact that acculturation has not prevented Americans from continuing to use Jews as symbols of excess. Indeed, one could well argue that antisemitic stereotypes flourished even as so many barriers to American life fell away. The presence of the images of mothers and princesses on television and film only underlined the absence of a private world in which Jews could be contentious with one another. To Americans in the 1980s the JAP was the Jew, just as in the 1950s the teenager spending excessively was the suburban Jewish adolescent.

In this same period Americans and American culture grappled with the meaning of diversity and pluralism. Increasingly, ethnic identity became masklike—a consumer item that like foreign food and clothing styles could be changed at will. Jewish humor, novels, and comedians could be integrated into the mainstream easily. Jews were seen as generically funny, anxious, and excessive, and Jewish women and men had special connections to those qualities. Excess was the purview of women.

When women stopped laughing, and Jewish women in particular rejected their representations as whining and excessive, the shallowness of the pluralism and the specificity of gender to the anxiety could no longer be denied. Jews made hateful jokes about one another not because familiarity bred contempt, but because they reflected a powerful range of fears about their lives as Jews and as Americans.

No longer perceived as a marginalized race having to look longingly at a middle-class America, Jews nevertheless continue to contend with the experience of their difference from the dominant culture. Even as the twentieth century draws to its close, cultural difference continues to be reckoned hierarchically in the United States. Jews, therefore, continue to create and recreate themselves at least in part in response to the American mirror in which they gaze to find themselves portrayed simultaneously as outsiders and powerful insiders, as excessive consumers and tight-fisted misers, as arbiters of upper-class taste and tacky marginals who believe that more is better.

When Jews look into the harsh mirror held up by the dominant culture their images are refracted in a fun house mirror reflection in distorting glass. For the entire century they have reshaped those accusations into a panoply of stereotypes that have set Jews of different classes, genders, and generations at odds with one another. The nation has forced them, like all minorities, to fight one another in their effort to join it. That Jews who are gay, women, or politically radical have found voices to reject these representations is a sign of promise that internalizing prejudice can be stopped. On the other hand, the astonishing persistence of Jewish gender stereotypes serves as a reminder that winning the fight to become Americans exacts a devastating price.

Appendix

A Note on the American Jewish Press as a

Source 1897–1930

In my research for this book I have followed Jews to learn where I might best locate their stereotypes. For the century's first decades, from 1900 to 1930, I found no source richer than the Jewish press. I was particularly interested in the English pages that appeared in the three major Yiddish dailies–the *Jewish Daily News,* the *Jewish Daily Forward,* and the *Day*–from 1897 to 1932. While historians of American Jewish life have used the press widely, virtually none of them distinguish between what is written in Yiddish and in English in those newspapers; scholars have tended to draw on both sources to make similar points. Since the editors of the newspapers included English pages to attract a different readership–Americanized and literate in English–I found these pages especially helpful for establishing the key themes and issues that occupied those readers most interested in acculturation.

Newspapers are a crucial source for much historical inquiry. However, like any source they cannot be taken at face value. The anguished letters and articles concerned with love and the economics of marriage were printed to lure readers in a competitive market for readership. The English pages clearly aimed to raise provocative topics. Articles that were published with bylines like "Lawyer" or "Doctor" one might well assume were written by journalists and not ordinary readers. On the other hand, both the Yiddish and English-language sections received and printed letters regularly. They featured essay contests and published contestants' entries, names, and addresses.

Even if some portion of the readers' correspondence was produced within the newspaper, it would have been impossible for a small number of writers to produce all of the steady stream of letters and responses to various essay contests. When the press exaggerated and dramatized some of these issues, they could only have done so with the knowledge that those issues appealed to their readership. The fact that the stereotypical views of unmarried Jewish women and men appeared across three newspapers of different political ideologies for more than thirty years also spoke to the persistence of these themes in the lives of the English language readers.

The purpose of this appendix is to provide an overview of the press sources I have used and information about them, as well as to indicate something about their orientations and the differences among them.

Regrettably no single work exists on the Yiddish press, nor even on particular newspapers.[1] Critical records that might reveal how editorial decisions were made no longer exist. Given those realities one can still account for some of the obvious limitations and advantages of the sources.

The first English pages appeared in 1897 in the *Jewish Daily News* (*Yiddishes Tageblatt*) which was published from 1885 to 1928, when it was absorbed by the *Morning Journal.* By the mid-1890s it had the highest circulation of all Yiddish papers. The *Jewish Daily News* was an Orthodox, politically conservative, Zionist newspaper, and it reflected American journalistic practices of the time—reporting on crime and violence as well as exaggerating and inventing news. One of the central features of the English page was the anonymous "Observer" column that for more than ten years addressed and debated issues about men and women and marriage. The *Jewish Daily News* lost its dominant position in the Yiddish press during this time period.

The *Jewish Daily Forward* published its first issue in April 1897, and within a decade became not only the most popular Yiddish newspaper, but a significant immigrant institution. Abraham Cahan, its visionary editor, introduced "The Bintel Brief" feature in 1906, and this advice format proved to be enormously popular and subsequently an important source for many historians on love and Americanization. The *Forward*'s English pages appeared for the first time in February 1923. It was called "Our English Page," and was part of the expanded Sunday format that included a variety of special features on the arts. It initially included a drama column and contributions attributed to "sons and daughters of our readers" concerning "the most interesting experience in my life." Cahan responded to the question, "Why an English page?" with the following reply: "We want to bring the American born children of our readers into closer touch with their parents." The *Forward* published a weekly English page through January 1931. By April 1926 it had expanded to four pages. The announcement of the expansion described three groups of readers for whom it was designed: American-born and bred young men and women engaged in various trades and occupation, Jewish public school, high school, and college boys and girls, and Yiddish speakers who read American dailies and magazines. The editor wrote, "The language of the American Jew is English, and he who would be understood by the American Jew must talk English." The number of English pages were reduced over time. There was no announcement explaining the cancellation of the English section, but it is clear that the Yiddish press could not draw an audience of English readers who were reading the English-language press.

The English pages included stories on politics, theater, books, and art. They systematically offered information on good occupations for young Jews and described a great many of them. They offered contests on "the ideal vacation," "the life of the stenographer," and other topics. And they included a great deal of material on dating, marriage, sex, and love. The English pages featured articles written for the newspaper by well-known Jewish and non-Jewish psychologists, philosophers, anthropologists, and educators, among them Alfred Adler and Franz Boas. These pages regularly printed many letters from readers as well.

The third paper that featured English pages was the *Day*, which was published from 1918 to 1953, when it too was absorbed by the *Morning Journal*. A Democratic, liberal Zionist, and eventually bourgeois Yiddish paper, it appealed to a readership about a decade younger than those of the other Yiddish dailies. They were most likely post-1910 immigrants. The *Day* had a "department store" quality; its writers represented a wide range of political outlooks. The *Day*'s English page appeared on a weekly basis from October 1923 until December 1932, and eventually expanded to two pages. The section included a mix of news, frequently about Zionism, on the upper half of the page, and articles about love, family, and work on the bottom half.

Two Newspapers in One:
Comparing the English and Yiddish Pages

I undertook a comparison of the 1924 Yiddish and English pages of the *Forward* to learn something about the contrasts in the content of both sections. I have included that analysis in this appendix because it is particularly relevant to the use of the press as a source for understanding the period. I sampled the Yiddish pages every other day for the month of May of that year. There were real differences in tone and subjects in the two sections. The Yiddish pages, of course, more extensively covered the news, domestic and international. They also were more substantially focused on crime and crimes of passion in particular. The advice column, "The Bintel Brief," featured the problems of married women and families more than the English pages did. Problems of "coarseness" in husbands (May 4, 1924) virtually never appeared in the English pages, which were more likely to address intergenerational struggles.

The Yiddish pages regularly translated articles from the American press on topics such as " Why Kings and Politicians Cannot Do without Wars," "Most Miners Are American Born," " Detective Writer Tells about His Work" (May 4, 1924), and "What Happens in the Kitchens of Restaurants in Rich Building" (May 12, 1924). It also included a woman's page that was devoted to issues about food for children.[2]

At the same time the Yiddish section included articles that were comparable to those found in the English pages. The May 10, 1924 issue of the paper reported in Yiddish on the American Jewish writer Edna Ferber's ideas about "American (Jewish) girls earlier and today." She emphasized the importance of work to today's young women. On May 12, 1924, Z. Hilelson reported on "interesting and good single men who are Cunning men." He described "the sport, the strict materialist, and, the exacting man." These men had problematic characters, and the article was written as a warning to unmarried "girls." In the same issue another article was devoted to women, money, and love.

Issues directed to the unmarried who were interested in love overlapped with the content of the English pages, which seem to be oriented to younger male readers with aspirations for white-collar jobs, and women readers who aspired to the middle class.

On the whole, the English pages of the press provided a rich vein of material about attitudes concerning marriage and dating that revealed powerful tensions between young Jewish women and men personified by one another as excessively consuming women and arrogant, indifferent, or economically driven men.

The Yiddish press reached its peak readership in 1916. The English pages of both the *Forward* and the *Day* came substantially after that time. In some measure they were intended to expand the readership and a variety of its features encouraged readers to participate as letter writers and contestants for cash prizes. Their efforts were limited by the power of Americanization that made the mastery of English essential to any aspiration for mobility. An English portion of the Yiddish press could not capture the loyalty and interest of its readers for long. In the period that these pages were published, however, they encouraged lively debates that were quite specific to its readers.

In addition to Yiddish dailies, I examined three other Yiddish language sources. The only Yiddish weekly, the *American (Der Ameri-*

kaner), offered an important mix of news and information about modern technology and Americanization.

Two Jewish women's magazines, the *Women's World* (*Froyen Velt*) that was published from 1913 to 1914, and the *Jewish Women's Home Journal* (*Froyen Zhurnal*) that appeared from 1922 to 1923, and which featured an English page, were particularly directed at women and mothers. The latter declared itself in its first issue of May 1922 "a true Yiddish American journal that will deal with all Jewish and American issues. The Froyen Zhurnal will help create the most important thing that has been missing from our lives, a bridge between mothers and children." Both magazines, but especially the *Froyen Zhurnal*, because it appeared in the 1920s, not only reflected the sentiments of women's magazines of the period, but were centrally taken up with issues of Americanization and generational tensions because women were so singularly associated with their Americanizing children.

English-Language Press Sources

The English-language Jewish press on which I drew for this book began in the 1870s and reached its crest of influence by the early 1900s, when these middle-class Jews were attempting to integrate East European immigrants.[3] This community-based press reported the full range of Jewish opinion, tended to adopt moderate positions, and primarily served the established Jewish population that belonged to synagogues and other Jewish fraternal and philanthropic organizations. Women's interests received substantial coverage in many of these publications, demonstrating that women were active readers of the press and participants in the community. The women's pages were an especially important source of stereotypes of East European Jewish women and the reactions of middle-class American Jews.

I surveyed a sample of the English-language press including San Francisco's *Jewish Journal* from 1928 to 1930,[4] Cleveland's *Jewish Independent* from 1920 to 1925,[5] New York's *American Jewish News* from 1918 to 1924, and the *American Jewish Chronicle* for 1918 and 1919,

St. Louis Modern View from 1918 to 1922, the *American Hebrew* from 1910 to 1924, and the *Philadelphia Exponent* from 1908 to 1915.[6]

It is impossible to generalize about the English-language Jewish community press. The *Independent*, for example, focused on community activities and news, while the *Jewish Journal* consistently reviewed the arts and culture as well as reporting news. Most of the Jewish press during the late teens and '20s included a women's page that focused on issues of family and often concerned the Americanization of immigrants. During the 1930s, as I suggest in chapter 4, virtually all of these features disappeared. The newspapers continued to print wedding notices and trips, but the interest in family and children vanished, paralleling the dominant cultural press of the time as well.

In sum, the Jewish press served as a critical source of the stereotypes generated by Jews during the twentieth century. In Yiddish and in English, the themes of conflict between parents and children and men and women have consistently appeared in the press of this period.

Notes

INTRODUCTION

1. This exercise was modeled on the work of Judith Weinstein Klein, who describes her "ethnotherapy" in *Jewish Identity and Self Esteem: Healing Wounds through Ethnotherapy* (New York: American Jewish Committee, 1980). Klein argued that expressions of gender stereotypes, always negative, are helpful to group members as a background for self-reflection. She wrote, "It is extremely revealing and cathartic for Jews to voice their stereotypes of Jewish men and women. The negative traits exposed provide the focus for much group interaction and self-scrutiny. Are the stereotypes deserved? Members wonder: 'Do I fit the stereotype of the over-intellectual, arrogant yet dependent, non-physical Jewish male?' 'Am I the smothering, achievement-oriented, demanding, nerve-wracking Jewish woman?'" (p. 39) Weinstein also found that ethnotherapy groups for a number of minorities, including Jews and African Americans, "almost never include positive valuation of the sexuality of the opposite sex. Men and women both end up feeling de-sexualized by the opposite sex group members" (p. 40).

Ellen Jaffe McClain describes a similar event that took place at a California Jewish Federation Council meeting in 1992. On this occasion men and women were asked to write down their associations for each gender. She said negative attributions ran three to one. *Embracing the Stranger: Intermarriage and the Future of the American Jewish Community* (New York: Basic Books, 1995), 53–54.

2. Rabbi Irwin Kula was kind enough to arrange for me to receive a tape of this session.

3. The Observer, *Jewish Daily News*, October 13, 1901, English Department.

4. *Jewish Daily News*, February 25, 1923, p. 3.

5. Thelma Kaplan, *Jewish Daily News*, July 17, 1927, English p. 4.

6. H. B., "Letter " *Day*, January 15, 1928, English Section.

7. See Judith Butler, *Excitable Speech: A Politics of the Performative* (New York and London: Routledge, 1997), 34, for a discussion of hate speech.

8. For a discussion of this process see Susan Glenn, *Daughters of the Shtetl: Life and Labor in the Immigrant Generation* (Ithaca: Cornell University Press, 1990) and Charlotte Baum, Paula Hyman, and Sonya Michel, *The Jewish Woman in America* (New York: Plume Books, 1975).

9. See, for example, Hutchins Hapgood, *The Spirit of the Ghetto,* ed. Moses Rischin. (Cambridge, Mass.: Harvard University Press, 1967); Mary Van Kleeck, *Artificial Flower Makers* (New York: Russell Sage Foundation, 1913).

10. Two excellent attempts to explore Jewish identity within American multiculturalism are David Biale, Michael Galchinsky, Susannah Heschel, eds., *Insider/ Outsider: American Jews and Multiculturalism* (Berkeley: University of California Press, 1998) and Jeffrey Rubin-Dorsky and Shelley Fischer Fiskin, eds., *People of the Book: Thirty Scholars Reflect on their Jewish Identity* (Madison: University of Wisconsin Press, 1996).

11. There is a growing literature on these economic relations. See particularly Baum et al., *Jewish Woman in America,* and Glenn, *Daughters of the Shtetl.*

12. If middle-class Jewish women entered the workforce, it was usually only before marriage and after childrearing.

13. See David Roediger, *The Wages of Whiteness: Race and the Making of the American Working Class* (London: Verso, 1991); Eric Lott, *Love and Theft : Blackface Minstrelsy and the American Working Class* (New York: Oxford University Press, 1993).

14. Michelle Wallace wrote with great insight about this dynamic in the African American community in *Black Macho and the Myth of the Superwoman* (London: Verso, 1990). bell hooks also reflected on these issues in *Black Looks: Race and Representation* (Boston: South End Press, 1992). Evelyn Beck has written about the ways in which the JAP image reflects classic antisemitic stereotypes in "From 'Kike' to 'JAP': How Misogyny, Anti-Semitism and Racism Construct the 'Jewish American Princess,'" ed. Margaret L. Anderson and Patricia Hill Collins, *Race, Class, and Gender: An Anthology* (Belmont, Calif.: Wadsworth Publishing Co., 1992).

15. Aviva Ben Ur's analysis of the Ladino press makes clear that these processes are in no way unique to Jews of East European descent. In the press, the prescriptive tone of articles and advice columns expressed anxiety about women's vulgar behavior and clothing, and fear of being judged as undesirable by Ashkenazic Jewish neighbors. "Ladino Press," *Jewish Women in America: An Historical Encyclopedia,* ed. Paula E. Hyman and Deborah Dash Moore (New York: Routledge, 1997), 780–85.

16. Laura Levitt's *Jews and Feminism: The Ambivalent Search for Home* (New York: Routledge, 1997) carefully and originally unpacks the concept of home and the place of marriage in it in her feminist analysis of American Jewish identity.

17. Sander L. Gilman, *Jewish Self Hatred: Anti-Semitism and the Secret Language of the Jews* (Baltimore and London: Johns Hopkins University Press, 1986), 2.

18. Daniel Boyarin's *Unheroic Conduct: The Rise of Heterosexuality and the Invention of the Jewish Man* (Berkeley: University of California Press, 1997) provides a powerful analysis of how Rabbinic Jewish culture has defined a masculinity in opposition to the one offered by the dominant culture. His work demonstrates a strategy used by Jews and Jewish men in particular that is different from the one described by Gilman.

19. Classical and contemporary works of American Jewish history focus on the ways Jews successfully accommodated to American society while consistently maintaining their ethnic, religious, and cultural distinctions. In the last two decades scholars have debated over their optimistic and pessimistic scenarios for the future of American Jewry as a distinct group within the United States. My point is not to enter that debate, nor to dispute the persistence of Jewishness in America. Scholars with the zeal to declare America hospitable or inhospitable to the persistence of an American Jewish culture have not examined the specificity of Jews' anxieties and their cultural consequences. Nor has that been these scholars' purpose. They have raised legitimate concerns about the conditions that create the viability of a minority. See Steven M. Cohen, *American Assimilation or Jewish Revival* (Bloomington: Indiana University Press, 1988) for one of the most thoughtful discussions of the debate.

20. Werner Sollors first coined the term *invention* in this context in his work *Beyond Ethnicity: Consent and Descent in American Culture* (London: Oxford University Press, 1986), but the idea has been widespread. My discussion of the concept is indebted to Kathleen Neil's Conzen et al., "The Invention of Ethnicity: A Perspective from the USA," *Journal of American Ethnic History* 12 (Fall 1992): 3–41.

21. For a fine example of this approach, see April Schultz, *Ethnicity on Parade: Inventing the Norwegian American through Celebration* (Amherst: University of Massachusetts Press, 1994).

22. No scholar has been more central in this work than Sander Gilman. See, for example, *The Jew's Body* (New York: Routledge, 1991). For a parallel effort in the study of American Jews in the early twentieth century, see Daniel Itzkovitz "Secret Temples," ed. Jonathan Boyarin and Daniel Boyarin, *Jews and Other Differences: The New Jewish Cultural Studies* (Minneapolis: University of Minnesota Press, 1997), 176–202. For another approach that places representation at the center of study, see Linda Nochlin and

Tamar Garb, *The Jew in the Text: Modernity and the Construction of Identity* (London: Thames and Hudson, 1993).

23. See Ella Shohat and Robert Stam, *Unthinking Eurocentrism: Multiculturalism and the Media* (London and New York: Routledge, 1994), 198–99, for a thoughtful discussion of stereotype analysis. See Judith Butler, *Excitable Speech: A Politics of the Performative* (New York and London: Routledge, 1997), 34–35, for a thoughtful discussion of hate speech as constitutive.

24. Ann Pellegrini raises this problem in her analysis of Gilman's work on the collapse of "Jew" with "the feminine" within Europe. This slur on Jewish masculinity, she notes, leaves no room for any understanding of the Jewish female. She locates the "female subject" in an analysis of notable Jewish women–Sarah Bernhardt and Freud's patient Dora–in "Whiteface Performances: 'Race,' Gender and Jewish Bodies," ed. Boyarin and Boyarin, *Jews and Other Differences*, 138–50, and her *Performance Anxieties: Staging Psychoanalysis, Staging Race* (New York: Routledge, 1997).

25. A parallel problem exists in the study of immigration. Donna Gabaccia's *From the Other Side: Women, Gender, and Immigrant Life in the U.S. 1820–1990* (Bloomington: Indiana University Press, 1994) attempts to address this problem. Sonya Michel also notes this problem in "Jews, Gender, American Cinema," ed. Lynn Davidman and Shelley Tenenbaum, *Feminist Perspectives on Jewish Studies* (New Haven: Yale University Press, 1994), 244–45.

26. See Elizabeth Ewen for an important attempt to place women at the center of immigration. *Immigrant Women in the Land of Dollars: Life and Culture on the Lower East Side, 1890–1925* (New York: Monthly Review Press, 1985). See John Higham's classic work on Americanization for the opposite approach: *Send These to Me: Immigrants in Urban America*, rev. ed. (Baltimore: John's Hopkins University Press, 1984).

27. In *Gender and Assimilation in Modern Jewish History: The Roles and Representations of Women* (Seattle: University of Washington Press, 1995) Paula Hyman has to some extent taken this approach in her seminal analysis of "the project of assimilation." Her comparative study of the effect of dominant cultural attitudes and policies toward Jews on Jewish men's understanding of Jewish women in France, Germany, and the United States engages this dynamic. Similarly, Naomi Seidman's analysis of the assertion of masculine control over language in the 1890s in the first settlement (Yishuv) of Israel suggests that language conflicts and gender ideologies were a product of Jewish men's response to antisemitism in Europe. Naomi Seidman, "Lawless Attachments, One-Night Stands: The Sexual Politics of the Hebrew-Yiddish Language War" ed. Boyarin and Boyarin, *Jews and Other Differences*, 279–305. These scholars are interested in the intersection of gender, representation, and Jewish cultures. Miriam

Peskowitz and Laura Levitt's *Judaism since Gender* (New York: Routledge, 1997) offers a more global attempt to integrate gender analysis within Jewish Studies.

28. Jonathan Sarna developed the notion of the internal melting pot. He argued that while a national melting pot never materialized, every group who came to the United States experienced the loss of a variety of indigenous markers and became a single group within the nation. "From Immigrants to Ethnics: Toward a New Theory of Ethnicization," *Ethnicity* 5 (March 1978): 370–78.

Chapter 1: Ghetto Girls and Jewish Immigrant Desire

1. During its heyday in the 1910s, the *Jewish Daily Forward* was the most widely circulated Yiddish paper and ethnic paper in the United States. See the appendix for a further discussion of the press. African American newspapers of this period also features black women on their covers to emphasize feminine beauty and accomplishment. See Paula Giddings, *When and Where I Enter: The Impact of Black Women on Race and Sex in America* (New York: William Morrow, 1984), 185.

2. *Jewish Daily Forward*, October 11, 1925, Art Section.

3. *Frank Leslie's Popular Monthly* 56 (May 1903), 58.

4. The Ghetto Girl was an English-language rather than Yiddish-language image. I found references to "her" as early as 1902 in the English-language page of the *Jewish Daily News*, Vol. 16, English Department.

5. The most famous stereotype of the Jewish woman was the stage presence in Europe and the United States of the "Belle Juive." She was an exotic, Oriental figure, often the subject of Western men's passions and longings. See Harley Erdman, *Staging the Jew: The Performance of an American Ethnicity, 1860–1920* (New Brunswick: Rutgers University Press, 1997), 40–62, for a helpful history of the character and her other persona as the Jewish hag, and Ellen Schiff, *From Stereotype to Metaphor: The Jew in Contemporary Drama* (Albany: State University of New York Press, 1982).

6. Naomi Cohen, *Encounter with Emancipation: The German Jews in the United States 1830–1912* (Philadelphia: Jewish Publication Society, 1984), 12.

7. John Higham, *Send These to Me: Immigrants in Urban America*, rev. ed. (Baltimore: Johns Hopkins University Press, 1984), 131.

8. The Progressive Movement is usually dated between 1898 and 1911. Their reformist concerns lasted throughout the 1920s as America's cities continued to confront overcrowding and the absorption of immigrants. The Progressive Movement varied from region to region and was sometimes a catalyst for social changes that involved no radical economic transformations. Its various faces certainly affected America's

Jewish immigrants, who were both supported and scorned by professionals with this point of view.

9. Hutchins Hapgood, *The Spirit of the Ghetto*, ed. Moses Rischin (Cambridge, Mass.: Harvard University Press, 1967), 72-75.

10. Cited in Robert Singerman, "The Jew as Racial Alien: The Genetic Component of American Antisemitism," ed. David Gerber, *Anti-Semitism in American History* (Urbana: University of Illinois Press, 1986), 109.

11. For a concise history of American efforts to restrict immigration see Higham, *Send These to Me*, 29-70.

12. Benjamin Ginsberg, *The Fatal Embrace: Jews and the State* (Chicago: University of Chicago Press, 1994), 75-87; Higham, *Send These to Me*, 95-116.

13. Cohen, *Encounter with Emancipation*, 32.

14. Ginsberg, *Fatal Embrace*, 79-81.

15. Ginsberg, *Fatal Embrace*, 81-87. Frederic Cople Jaher demonstrates that prior to this period, through the 1850s, fiction, drama, newspapers, and even guidebooks to New York employed classical Christian antisemitism. *A Scapegoat in the New Wilderness: The Origins and Rise of Anti-Semitism in America* (Cambridge, Mass.: Harvard University Press, 1994), 211-41. Michael Dobkowski, *The Tarnished Dream: The Basis of American Anti-Semitism* (Westport: Greenwood Press, 1979) provides evidence for this perspective as well.

16. Minnie Louis, "Mission Work among the Unenlightened Jews," Jewish Women's Congress, *Papers of the Jewish Women's Congress* (Philadelphia: Jewish Publication Society of America, 1894). Thanks to Barbara Kirshenblatt-Gimblet for this reference.

17. Marion Golde, "The Modern Ghetto Girl: Does She Lack Refinement?, Part I" *American Jewish News*, March 22, 1918, p. 11.

18. "Jewish College Students," *American Jewish Chronicle*, May 24, 1918, p. 58. A classic example of a similar point of view may be found in Walter Lippmann's work. See Ronald Steel, *Walter Lippmann and the American Century* (Boston: Little, Brown, 1980).

19. Naomi Cohen discusses this modeling in *Encounter with Emancipation*, 110-12.

20. Evyatar Friesel, "The Age of Optimism in American Judaism, 1900-1920," *A Bicentennial Festschrift for Jacob Rader Marcus*, ed. Bertram Wallace Korn (New York: Ktav Press, 1976), 131-54.

21. Anonymous, "East Side Fashions. They Keep Pace with Those of Fifth Avenue, and Perhaps Outshine Them a Little," Jacob Marcus, *American Jewish Women's Documents* (New York: Ktav Press, 1981), 497–501.

22. Golde, "Modern Ghetto Girl, Part I."

23. For a discussion of Jewish racial identity in the late nineteenth century, see Eric L. Goldstein, "Different Blood Flows in Our Veins: Race and Jewish Self-Definition in Late Nineteenth Century America," *American Jewish History* 85 (March 1997): 29–56. For a discussion of Jews, eugenics, and the Americanization movement in this period, see Robert Singerman, "The Jew as Racial Alien," ed. David Gerber, *Anti-Semitism in American History*, (Urbana: University of Illinois Press, 1986), 103–28.

24. Cited in Eli Lederhendler, "Guide for the Perplexed: Sex, Manners, and Mores for the Yiddish Reader in America," *Modern Judaism* 11 (1991): 333.

25. Rabbi Israel Levinthal, "Style," a sermon delivered December 26, 1916, 2–4. Israel Levinthal papers, Box 2, Ratner Center for American Jewish Experience, Jewish Theological Seminary.

26. Lillian Wald, *The House on Henry Street* (New York: H. Holt, 1915), 190.

27. Wald, *House on Henry Street*, 191.

28. Hilda Satt Polacheck's memoir of Chicago's Hull House from 1896 to 1912, *I Came A Stranger: The Story of a Hull House Girl*, ed. Dena J. Polacheck Epstein (Urbana: University of Illinois Press, 1991), provided a description of the Progressive ideal of fashion. What Polacheck admired about America's most eminent Progressive, Jane Addams, was her lack of interest in clothing. She described Miss Addams's clothing, telling the reader, "Compared with the (immigrant) women of the neighborhood, she was always well dressed. Compared with the wealthy women who came to the house, I would say that she dressed in simple, good taste. I know that she gave very little, if any thought to her clothes" (pp. 101–3).

In Hilda's eyes Miss Addams's restraint and seriousness were embodied in her indifference to clothing, which served as a powerful model for proper American femininity. Hilda's greatest wish was to emulate Miss Addams, who was in every way the opposite of Hilda's own mother and neighbors. Nor did Miss Addams emulate the looks of fashionable young women. Miss Addams lacked the desires that so visibly marked immigrants with their aspirations for Americanization. Hilda learned to fashion herself in the image of Progressive America, an Americanization practiced by a cadre of the wealthy and their children who foreswore wanting after achieving success. Hilda made sure, by her careful attention to models for Americanization, that she would not be confused with a Ghetto Girl.

29. By contrast, Margaret Sanger, who pioneered birth control for women, was quite critical of Progressives. In a Yiddish pamphlet in which she wrote about how to raise a modern American girl, she was impatient with those who stifled and inhibited young women's desire for self-adornment and self-expression. Lederhendler, "Guide for the Perplexed," 327.

30. Cohen, *Encounter with Emancipation,* discusses German Jews' strategies for expecting their behavior to be "at least as good as everybody else" (p. 110).

31. Viola Paradise, "The Jewish Immigrant Girl in Chicago," *Survey* 30 (September 16 1910): 704.

32. Jewish women did participate in prostitution and "White Slavery," as it was called. Ruth Rosen demonstrated that prostitution was one of several avenues for economic support open to women during the first decades of the twentieth century, along with factory work, marriage, and sales and secretarial work. Women were also occasionally prostitutes, depending on their economic needs. "Introduction," *The Mamie Papers,* ed. Ruth Rosen and Sue Davidson (Bloomington: Indiana University Press, 1977). But women often turned to prostitution as a form of support created by desperation. Rather than pursuing luxuries, women became prostitutes directly as a result of their husbands' desertion. See Reena Sigman Friedman, "'Send Me My Husband Who Is in New York City': Husband Desertion in the American Jewish Immigrant Community, 1900–1926," *Jewish Social Studies* 44 (1982): 7–8. Egal Feldman argues that immigrant women were often pitied as victims, but immigrant men were vilified as the organizers of white slavery, and anti-immigrant campaigns were openly waged on the premise that Italians and Jews were dangerous to the nation because of their "vile natures." "Prostitution, the Alien Woman and the Progressive Imagination, 1910–1915," *American Quarterly* 19 (1967): 192–206. Naomi Cohen also discusses the profound anxieties of German Jews about the Jewish problem of white slavery in *Encounter with Emancipation,* 32.

33. Jewish commentators publishing in Jewish newspapers were reluctant to write about sex and promiscuity. They might well have feared the judgments of others, or they might have hesitated to discuss sexuality because of religious concerns for "modesty" that prohibited public speech about sexual matters. In either case, Jewish publications avoided the conclusions that Viola Paradise advanced.

34. Nancy B. Sinkoff, "Educating for "Proper" Jewish Womanhood: A Caste Study in Domesticity and Vocational Training, 1897–1926," *American Jewish History* 77 1988): 572–96.

35. Kathy Peiss's important work on early twentieth-century urban working women's culture underlines the fact that women supplemented their wages by men's

gifts, often bought at the price of their consent to trade sexual favors. *Cheap Amusements: Working Women and Leisure Time in Turn-of-the-Century New York* (Philadelphia: Temple University Press, 1986).

36. *Il Progreso*, an Italian-language paper published in New York, also carried an English page during this period. Its first English-language page appeared in late 1928, and was a feature of the Sunday paper. Like the English-language page of the Yiddish press, it too was designed to attract young adult readers. It appeared to be more news-oriented than the English pages of the Yiddish press, and featured virtually nothing parallel to the Yiddish or English-language Jewish press about gender conflict. *Il Progreso* offered a regular series of success stories about people who rose from rags to riches. They were not exclusively stories about Italians, though the majority were. All of the people profiled were men, but women did appear occasionally because of their achievements. The photographs featured in the newspaper were of the rich and famous, not of ordinary women. Thanks to Rudolph Vecoli for directing me to *Il Progreso*.

37. Leo Robbins, "Trolly Car Girls with Rolls Royce Tastes," *Jewish Daily Forward*, May 13, 1923, p. 3.

38. Leopold Lazarus, "Do Our Eastsiders Know How to Dress?" *Jewish Daily Forward*, April 13, 1924, p. 3.

39. The 1910 U.S. census measured the number of earners in the nuclear family. The Yiddish-speaking household contained a higher mean number of earners in the nuclear family (1.7) than Italian and other East European households who immigrated at a similar time (1.4) and than households of native-born Americans (1.4). The Public Use Sample is a nationally representative sample of household and individual records from the 1910 census. A 1-in-250 sampling fraction was used, producing a total of 88,814 households. The sample selection was designed so that each household and each individual in the manuscript population had an equal probability for being selected. The sample is therefore self-weighted. Michael A. Strong et al., *User's Guide: Public Use Sample, 1910 U.S. Census of Population 1989*.

40. Susan Glenn, *Daughters of the Shtetl: Life and Labor in the Immigrant Generation* (Ithaca: Cornell University Press, 1990), 84. Glenn draws her information on wages from the "Report on Condition of Woman and Child Wage-Earners, Vol. I, Men's Ready Made Clothing Industry." Daughters and sons, rather than mothers, supplemented fathers' wages. Daughters also used their wages to bring family members from Europe. Elizabeth Ewen, *Immigrant Women in the Land of Dollars: Life and Culture on the Lower East Side 1890–1925* (New York: Monthly Review Press, 1985).

41. See Christine Stansell, *City of Women: Sex and Class in New York 1789–1860* (Urbana: University of Illinois Press, 1987), 76–78, for a discussion of these relations among New York working women in the eighteenth and nineteenth centuries. Critical

social commentary on factory girls began in the 1830s and expanded during the 1850s. These workers symbolized female self-assertion to many commentators of the time, as young Jewish women did in the beginning of the twentieth century. Unlike the more modest Jewish press, the dominant American press was concerned primarily with working women's immorality and prostitution, not poverty or working conditions. Her critics associated her with passion and vanity. As a foremother of young Jewish working women, the working women of the 1830s in the Bowery district of New York's East Side expressed their unique class and sex pride through their clothing. Their clothes were brightly colored and worn in combinations of colors that were anything but modest or subdued. The "Bowery gal" offered a complete contrast to the Victorian lady, and like her Jewish sisters who arrived fifty years later, she flaunted her style walking on public streets with her friends. Stansell, *City of Women*, 89–91, 115–17.

42. Zelda, "Just Between Ourselves Girls," *Jewish Daily News*, December 22, 1903, English Department.

43. Cited in Jacob Rader Marcus, *Jewish Women in America: A Documentary History* (Cincinnati: American Jewish Archives, 1981), 500. Lillian Wald commented on this same phenomenon in her memoir. She responded to a newspaper editorial on the stylish appearance of working women by asking a young woman how she afforded her clothing, and learned about her frugal and efficient purchases. She declared that the young woman was able "to show excellent discretion in the expenditure of income." *House on Henry Street*, 194–195.

44. Miriam Shomer Zunser, "The Ghetto Girl Again," *American Jewish News*, April 19, 1918, p. 15.

45. Golde, "Modern Ghetto Girl, Part I," p. 11.

46. Cited in Lederhendler, "Guide to the Perplexed," 327.

47. Mrs. Asch was born Matilda Spiro in Lodz, Poland, in approximately 1883. She was from an urban, cosmopolitan family. Personal communication, David Mazower. Clearly her class bias is revealed in her reaction to immigrant women.

48. Marion Golde, "The Modern Ghetto Girl: Does She Lack Refinement?, Part II," *American Jewish News*, March 29, 1918, p. 11.

49. For a recent biography of Fanny Hurst in the context of American Jewish women's history, see Joyce Antler, *The Journey Home: Jewish Women and the American Century* (New York: Free Press, 1997), 150–72. For a recent consideration of Fanny Hurst's writing in relationship to her family, see Janet Handler Burstein, *Writing Mothers, Writing Daughters: Tracing the Maternal in Stories by American Jewish Women* (Urbana: University of Illinois Press, 1996) 50–59.

50. Golde, "Modern Ghetto Girl, Part I," p. 11.

51. Golde, "Modern Ghetto Girl, Part I," p. 11. Fanny Hurst ultimately acknowledged the antisemitic nature of her remarks about East European Jews in her autobiography, *Anatomy of Me: A Wonderer in Search of Herself* (New York: Doubleday, 1958), 350. Janet Burstein brought this reflection of Hurst's to my attention.

52. As George Mosse noted in his work on nationalism and sexuality, both nationalism and ideas about "respectability" provided a sense of order and normality. Whatever threatened those categories also threatened order. Distinctions between men were crucial to that orderliness. *Nationalism and Sexuality: Middle-Class Morality and Sexual Norms in Modern Europe* (Madison: University of Wisconsin Press, 1985), 16.

53. T. J. Jackson Lears, "From Salvation to Self-Realization: Advertising and the Therapeutic Roots of the Consumer Culture, 1880–1930," *The Culture of Consumption: Critical Essays in American History 1880–1930*, ed. Richard Wrightman Fox and T. J. Jackson Lears (New York: Pantheon Books, 1983). Fox and Lears note in their Introduction what anxious pleasures consumption created for the Protestant native-born majority new to the developing class of managers and technicians (p. xi). Ironically, it was around consumption that Jewish newcomers and the native-born found common ground. What promised immigrants and their children access to the dominant culture constituted uncertainty and anxiety for the majority.

54. Cohen, *Encounter with Emancipation*, 112 and Higham, *Send These to Me*, 117–52.

55. "A School-Girl's Stratagem," *Harper's Bazaar* 13 (July 31, 1880), p. 490.

56. Rudolf Glanz, *The Jewish Woman in America: Two Female Immigrant Generations_1820–1929: The German Jewish Woman, Volume II* (New York: Ktav Press, 1976), 55; Cohen, *Encounter with Emancipation*, 112.

57. Cited in Glanz, *Jewish Woman in America*, 56. The anxiety over appearance in resorts was not a happenstance. The rise of "social discrimination" occurred through antisemitic policies restricting Jews' access to summer resorts, including ones they once frequented. Just six years before this article appeared, Joseph Seligman, a nationally prominent banker, was denied lodging at a Saratoga hotel. During the 1880s discrimination against Jews was open and increasing. Advertisements for summer lodging regularly excluded Jews and dogs. Higham, *Send These to Me*, 127–29.

58. Hasia Diner, *A Time for Gathering: The Second Migration 1820–1880* (Baltimore: Johns Hopkins University Press, 1990), 189–90.

59. Robert A. Woods and Albert J. Kennedy, eds., and abridged by Sam Bass Warner, *Zones of Emergence* (Cambridge, Mass.: Harvard University Press, 1962), 167, 173. Dobkowski, *The Tarnished Dream* discusses the continuing stereotype of the Jews as

Shylock, the miser and thief throughout the late nineteenth and early twentieth centuries in the United States.

60. Quoted in Higham, *Send These to Me*, 160–61.

61. "Foreign Criminals in New York," *North American Review* DCXXXIV (September 1908): 383. This accusation was the source of a major protest and Bingham ultimately recanted the extent of the accusation.

62. Kenneth L. Roberts, "Why Europe Leaves Home," cited in Dobkowski, *Tarnished Dream*, 102.

63. Arthur Goren, "The Jewish Press," *The Ethnic Press in the United States: A Historical Analysis and Handbook*, ed. Sally M. Miller (New York: Greenwood Press, 1987).

64. Julia Weber, "Have You a Pleasing Voice?" *American Jewish News*, July 26, 1918, p. 368.

65. Weber, "Have You a Pleasing Voice," p. 368. Sander Gilman's book, *The Jew's Body* (New York: Routledge, 1991) discusses the Jewish voice in the context of long standing anti-Jewish accusations of a secret Jewish language. From the Gospels' treatment of Jesus the Jew, through parodying of Jewish languages and accents, to the notion of Jews' special vocabulary, Gilman argues that accusations of sounding different are a way of creating the Jew as different and corrupt. The problem of the "voice" is particularly interesting in the United States, where it is not tied to accent or specific language, but to sound alone, the nasalized vowels.

66. The voice continued to haunt Jewish women throughout the first half of the century. Ruth Jacknow Markowitz's study of Jewish women enrolled at New York's public Hunter College recounted that women feared that they would not be certified for teaching because of their failure to speak English properly. All students were subjected to oral exams and the possibility of remedial courses to correct accented speech. *My Daughter the Teacher: Jewish Teachers in the New York City Schools* (New Brunswick: Rutgers University Press, 1993).

67. "Voice Influence," *Jewish Daily News*, Vol. 31 (1915), English Department.

68. Cited in Lederhendler, "Guide to the Perplexed," 333.

69. Golde, "Modern Ghetto Girl, Part II," p. 11.

70. "The City Business Girl Must Be Good-Looking," *Day*, February 23, 1929, English Section. This anxiety concerning dress and the workplace persisted. In Gertrude Stein's 1930 article, "Straight Talk to Girls Who Seek Office Jobs," she was at pains to note that she was not practicing religious discrimination, but "things that make it harder for Jewish girls to get satisfactory employment in New York City." Included among her five points is the inevitable critique of excessive clothes and makeup com-

bined with their failure to "ingratiate themselves." *Day*, March 30, 1930, English Section.

71. "City Business Girl."

72. Terry Selber, "As Many Employers See Our Taste in Clothes," *Day*, October 10, 1926, English Section. Jews' anxiety about women's behavior in the office was echoed in the dominant culture as well. Angel Kwolek-Follard argues that the office of this period blurred gender boundaries and called into question the ideal distinctions between private and public formerly associated with women and men. By defining some work as "female," the working woman could be made to conform to ideas about the biological inevitability of male and female roles. These issues were played out around women's clothing as well. Clothing styles were an aspect of women's office behavior that management consistently found offensive. Business educator and theorist Edward Kilduff in 1924 expressed it best: "The secretary should realize that a business employer silently criticizes the secretary who wears clothing more suited for social affairs than for office work. . . . Some women secretaries do not seem to realize that it is a business mistake to wear their 'party' clothes to the office, that it is not in keeping with the general scheme of a business office to be 'dressed up.'" This sort of admonition had been common from the time women began to work in offices. In one of the earliest advice books to prospective female office workers, Ruth Ashmore counseled women in 1898 to purchase sensible, dark clothing. Wearing fancy dress at work, she claimed, suggested to employers that a woman was more interested in parties and the social whirl than in earning a living. *Engendering Business: Men and Women in the Corporate Office 1870–1930* (Baltimore: Johns Hopkins University Press, 1994), 10–11, 43, 96, 174. The Jewish press reveals again that what was an American problem was made a Jewish problem specific to Jewish women.

73. M. S., "By Their Dress Shall You Know Them," *American Weekly Jewish News*, December 26, 1918, p. 704.

74. Ruth Schwartz Cowan, "The Industrial Revolution in the Home Household: Technology and Social Change in the Twentieth Century," *Material Culture Studies in America*, ed. Thomas J. Schlereth (Nashville: American Association for State and Local History, 1982), 222–36.

75. Susan Bordo writes perceptively about the place of the body in the act of self-policing in *Unbearable Weight: Feminism, Western Culture and the Body* (Berkeley: University of California Press, 1993).

76. David Levering Lewis describes a parallel situation for northern educated African Americans when southern African Americans moved north during the great migration. Classes in etiquette, focus on personal habits, and other efforts at "education" were all undertaken in larger measure to combat growing racism. Lewis argues

that the black Jewish alliance took shape in this period, aligning elite African Americans and Jews to protect their standing that fell because of migrations from Eastern Europe and the south. "Parallels and Divergences: Assimilation Strategies of Afro-Americans and Jewish Elites from 1910 to the Early 1930s," *Journal of American History* 31 (December 1984): 543–64.

77. Sander Gilman raises a parallel problem in the differentiation of German Jews from Eastern European Jews, which he also attributes to the notion of sounding "too Jewish." He argues that German Jews internalized a Western Christian concept of a secret Jewish language, thereby identifying with Western civilization against Eastern Jews. "Chicken Soup, Or the Penalties for Sounding Too Jewish," *Shofar* 89 (Winter 1991): 55–69.

78. Daniel Itzkovitz explores the issue of assimilable differences for Jews in "Secret Temples," *Jews and Other Differences: The New Jewish Cultural Studies*, ed. Jonathan Boyarin and Daniel Boyarin (Minneapolis, University of Minnesota Press, 1997), 197–202.

79. The Observer, *Jewish Daily News*, January 13, 1902, English Department.

80. The Observer, *Jewish Daily News*, September 24, 1901, English Department.

81. The Observer, *Jewish Daily News*, July 25, 1901, English Department.

82. Leo Robbins, "Boys Who Base Their Romance on Papa's Bank Account," *Jewish Daily Forward*, March 16, 1924, English page.

83. Rabbi Israel Levinthal's 1923 sermon at the Brooklyn Jewish Center synagogue was devoted to the flapper. He declared the flapper to be a term inclusive of men and women. He then condemned them in his sermon for their slavish attachment to fashion. "Flapperism in Civilization and Religion," March 9, 1923. Israel Levinthal papers, Ratner Center for the Study of Conservative Judaism in America, Jewish Theological Seminary, Box 2. For a discussion of the development of that synagogue and Levinthal's leadership, see Deborah Dash Moore, "A Synagogue Center Grows in Brooklyn," in Jack Wetheimer, ed. *The American Synagogue: A Sanctuary Transformed* (Hanover: Brandeis University Press, 1987), 297–326.

84. Cited in Marcus, *American Jewish Women's Documents*, 499.

85. Barbara Schreier notes that contemporary observers paid less attention to "male plumage" and that when they did their language was less condemning or beseeching. The Yiddish press seemed less sanguine about these men than other sources. *Becoming American Women: Clothing and the Jewish Immigrant Experience, 1880–1920* (Chicago: Chicago Historical Society, 1994), 9.

CHAPTER 2: MARRIAGE MAKING AMERICANS

1. Fanny Edelman, *The Mirror of Life: The Old Country and the New,* trans. Samuel Pasner (New York: Exposition Press, 1961 [originally, in Yiddish, 1948]), 22.

2. Edelman, *Mirror of Life,* 38.

3. Julius Drachsler, *Intermarriage in New York City: A Statistical Study of the Amalgamation of European Peoples* (Ph.D. Dissertation, Columbia University, 1921) found that Jewish marriage of this period was overwhelmingly endogamous. He also found evidence of intermarriage before 1915, as did Deanna L. Pagnini and S. Philip Morgan, "Intermarriage and Social Distance among U.S. Immigrants at the Turn of the Century,'" *American Journal of Sociology* 96 (September 1990): 424. Jewish men during this period were far more likely to intermarry than women.

4. Yezierska has been "recovered" as a writer in the last two decades. Despite her immense popularity in the early twentieth century, she was ultimately dismissed as too emotional, and ceased to be read or written about. Irving Howe, for example, in his popular *World of Our Fathers: The Journey of the East European Jews to America and the Life They Found and Made* (New York: Schocken Press, 1976), 269, described her novel *Hungry Hearts* as "overwrought, ungainly, yet touching in its defenselessness." But feminists have found tremendous value in understanding her dilemmas as a writer wishing to live on her own during a time when such autonomy was nearly impossible for a working woman. See Alice Kessler Harris, "Introduction," Anzia Yezierska, *Bread Givers: A Struggle Between a Father of the Old World and a Daughter of the New* (New York: Persea Books, 1975 [originally 1925]). Anzia Yezierska, "The Miracle," *How I Found America: Collected Stories* (New York: Persea Press, 1991, 5l.

5. Yezierska, "Miracle," 51.

6. Anzia Yezierska, reflecting her own atypical life, has Sara Reisel seek out "real" Americans. Her love, ultimately unreturned, is for a Protestant teacher. She fails to find the love or wealth the New World promised.

7. Yezierska, "How I Found America," 110.

8. Examples of works about women who were primarily concerned with education include Elizabeth Hasanovitz, *One of Them: Chapters from a Passionate Autobiography* (Boston: Houghton Mifflin, 1988); Sydney Stahl Weinberg, *World of Our Mothers: The Lives of Jewish Immigrant Women* (Chapel Hill: University of North Carolina Press, 1988); Susan Shavelson, "Language and Identity in the Autobiographies of Emma Goldman and Rokhl Kirsh Holtman" (unpublished manuscript); Charlotte Baum, Paula Hyman, and Sonya Michel, *The Jewish Woman in America* (New York: Dial Press, 1975).

9. Weinberg, *World of Our Mothers*, 208.

10. See David Biale, *Eros and the Jews: From Biblical Israel to Contemporary America* (New York: Basic Books, 1992) for a discussion of romantic love and Jews in this period in Europe.

11. Miriam Shomer Zunser, *Yesterday* (New York: Stackpole Sons, 1939), 77–78.

12. Biale, *Eros and the Jews*.

13. Nahma Sandrow, *Vagabond Stars: A World History of Yiddish Theater* (New York: Harper and Row, 1977), 48. However, after 1880, with growing antisemitism, Goldfadn, the primary author of these plays, wrote anti-Enlightenment works that reinforced the virtue of arranged marriage (p. 60).

14. Zunser, *Yesterday*, 85–86.

15. Arthur Goren's survey of the American Jewish press suggests that it was responsible for supporting an ethnic culture. He also demonstrates that "women's interests" received attention in the press. Love, however, concerned both men and women, and for immigrants, the newspaper "was the most accessible, authoritative source of information, guidance, and news." "The Jewish Press," in *The Ethnic Press in the United States: A Historical Analysis and Handbook* (New York: Greenwood Press, 1987), 216.

16. Isaac Metzker, *A Bintel Brief: Sixty Years of Letters from the Lower East Side to the Jewish Daily Forward* (New York: Ballantine Books, 1971), 102.

17. The German Jews, whose immigration preceded East European Jews by at least two decades, created no arenas for discussion of these matters in their fiction or journalism. Young German Jewish women brought a dowry to marriage, in contrast to young working Russian Jewish women, ensuring that the choice of a mate would remain a matter of parental control. See Rudolph Glanz, *The Jewish Woman in America: Two Female Immigrant Generations 1820–1829: The German Jewish Woman, Volume II* (New York: Ktav Press, 1976), 69–73.

18. Isaac Metzker has collected examples of letters from the "Bintel Brief" as well as describing its role in Jewish American life in *A Bintel Brief*.

19. George Wolfe translated both printed and unprinted letters received by the newspaper for his M.A. thesis at Graduate School for Jewish Social Work, *The "Bintel Brief" of the "Jewish Daily Forward" as an Immigrant Institution and a Research Source* (M.A. Thesis in the Graduate School for Jewish Social Work, Jewish Scientific Institute, 1933). Wolfe compared letters written in 1906 and 1927 to analyze how problems changed as immigrants Americanized. He also analyzed how the letter writers changed and the themes of the letters written. Wolfe interviewed Abraham Cahan, the editor, to learn about immigrant needs.

20. Wolfe, *"Bintel Brief,"* 373, letter 42.

21. Wolfe, *"Bintel Brief,"* 87, letter 71.

22. Wolfe, *"Bintel Brief,"* 93, letter 76.

23. Abraham Cahan, the editor of the *Forward* and well-known immigrant writer, was much taken up with issues of romance and love in his journalism and his fiction. Relations between the sexes were most radically modified by immigration, and according to historian Moses Rischin, presented Cahan a particular challenge. Moses Rischin ed., "Introduction," *Grandma Never Lived in America: The New Journalism of Abraham Cahan* (Bloomington: Indiana University Press, 1985). Cahan used the theme of love in his realist literature to critique much about immigrant life, including the treatment of women. See Susan Kress, "Women and Marriage in Abraham Cahan's Fiction," *Studies in American Jewish Literature*, Vol. 3 (Albany: State University of New York Press, 1983).

24. See Jenna Weissman Joselit, *The Wonders of America: Reinventing Jewish Culture, 1880–1950* (New York: Hill and Wang, 1994), 15–17, for a discussion of Yiddish works on etiquette in romance.

25. Young American Jews, immigrants and native-born, learned that in America, in contrast to their European families, there was little debate about freely chosen marriage and romantic love, as each had been the norm for almost a century. Parents stopped giving consent for marriage before the turn of the nineteenth century, and arranged marriages disappeared entirely. The gentry had a full knowledge of romantic love by the eighteenth century, given the magazines, fiction, and poetry they read. These publications indicate that their readers understood romantic love to be the basis of marriage. The close connection between love and marriage was firmly established by the early nineteenth century, a half-century prior to the first mass wave of Jewish immigration. See Karen Lystra, *Searching the Heart: Women, Men and Romantic Love in Nineteenth Century America* (New York: Oxford University Press, 1989); Sondra Herman, "Loving Courtship or the Marriage Market? The Ideal and its Critics 1871–1911," *American Quarterly* 25 (1973): 235–52.

26. Glanz, *German Jewish Woman*, 74–80.

27. Glanz, *German Jewish Woman*, 78.

28. Kate Simon, *Bronx Primitive: Portraits in a Childhood* (New York: Viking Press, 1968), 4, 44–45. In this sense Jews followed what was long held to be the classic pattern of American assimilation outlined in Ruby Jo Reeves Kennedy, "Single or Triple Melting-Pot? Intermarriage Trends in New Haven, 1870–1940," *American Journal of Sociology* 49 (1944): 331–39. She argued that in New Haven marriages were made between ethnic groups who shared a religion. Catholic ethnics married one another across ethnic lines, as did Protestants and Jews. Kennedy's work has been widely cited

and accepted as an explanation for American pluralism. Ceri Peach reanalyzed Kennedy's data and came to a different conclusion. He wrote, "Thus the cleavage of white society into Protestant, Catholic and Jewish national groups, which Kennedy foresaw as the American future, did not exist even in embryonic form at the beginning of the period for which she took her data and looked even more improbable in the final year for which she took her material." Peach instead discovered a pattern of overlapping and asymmetric choices of one group for another, rather than distinct, independent parcels of reciprocated interaction within "religious" divides. "Ethnic Segregation and Ethnic Intermarriage: A Re-Examination of Kennedy's Triple Melting Pot in New Haven, 1900–1950" *Ethnic Segregation in Cities*, ed. Ceri Peach et al. (Athens: University of Georgia Press, 1981), 207. Interested only in Catholic and Protestant marriage, he found that Italians and Poles did intermarry with one another, but the Irish did not. The Irish were far more geographically dispersed in the community, and hence the degree of segregation was more predictive than religion in determining marriage patterns. Peach *Ethnic Segregation*, 208–14.

On the other hand, Waters's and Lieberson's analysis of the 1980 census data did suggest that Catholics were likely to intermarry across "national origins." Stanley Lieberson and Mary C. Waters, *From Many Strands: Ethnic and Racial Groups in Contemporary America* (New York: Russell Sage Foundation, 1988), 235. Jews do, nevertheless, appear to follow the pattern predicted by Reeves initially by their endogamy, which was the dominant form of marriage until the early 1960s.

29. Elaine Tyler May, *Great Expectations: Marriage and Divorce in Post-Victorian America* (Chicago: University of Chicago Press, 1980), 49; Lystra, *Searching the Heart*, 42.

30. Jewish law opposes the marriage of a Jew to a non-Jew, and according to normative Judaism a Jew is the child of a Jewish mother. Intermarriage has been prohibited for centuries to maintain the solidarity of the Jewish people. With the rise of intermarriage many of these rules have changed for Reform Jews. In the 1990s the intermarriage rate for American Jews is about 50 percent.

31. Robert McCaa, "Ethnic Intermarriage and Gender in New York City," *Journal of Interdisciplinary History* 24, (Autumn 1993): 207–31.

32. Stanley Lieberson, *Ethnic Patterns in American Cities* (New York: Free Press, 1963).

33. Julius Drachsler grouped ethnics by the frequency of their in-marriages. Jews and "Colored" were the least likely to intermarry. He noted that the Northern, Northwestern, and Central European peoples tended to have the highest intermarriage. Italians, Irish, the Poles from Russia and Austria, the Slovaks, Greeks, and Finns were the "middle-ground." *Intermarriage in New York City*, 43–45.

34. At the same time he noted what subsequent historians have, that there were many more men than women of ethnic groups, and men were forced to choose between out-marriage and celibacy. Driven less by an ideology of "amalgamation" than a desire to marry, intermarriage was the cost of immigration. Drachsler, *Intermarriage in New York City*, 66–67.

35. Thomas Kessner, *The Golden Door: Italian and Jewish Immigrant Mobility in New York City 1880–1915* (New York: Oxford University Press, 1977), 30.

36. McCaa, "Ethnic Intermarriage and Gender," 216–24.

37. Jews were, of course, divided by class differences, and as noted in chapter 1, Western and East European Jews were also divided from one another. Many salient features differentiated Jews by forms of religious practice, politics, place of birth, and others, but Jews shared an ethnic and religious identity that did not give other differences the weight of intermarriage.

38. See Joselit, *The Wonders of America*, 48–55 for a discussion of Jewish anxiety about intermarriage during this period.

39. McCaa, "Ethnic Intermarriage and Gender," 208, 217, 226.

40. Doris Sommer uses the term *foundational fictions* in her analysis of literary themes in Latin American fiction. "Irresistible Romance: The Foundational Fictions of Latin America," *Nation and Narration*, ed. Homi K. Bhabha (London: Routledge, 1990), 71–98.

41. Werner Sollors, *Beyond Ethnicity: Consent and Descent in American Culture* (Oxford: Oxford University Press, 1986).

42. Joyce Flynn, "Melting Plots: Patterns of Racial and Ethnic Amalgamation in American Drama Before Eugene O'Neill.," *American Quarterly* 38 (1986): 417–38, also explores ethnic amalgamation in American theater, arguing that a range of works existed including "amalgamation" and "cosmopolitanism" which showed ethnics coexisting without merging into a single identity (pp. 428–29). Harley Erdman discusses stage performances concerning Jewish–Christian romances in *Staging the Jew: The Performance of an American Ethnicity, 1860–1920* (New Brunswick: Rutgers University Press, 1997), 118–57. A parallel to the love between ethnic opposites is marriages made across class lines. Herman, "Loving Courtship," 241, found frequent objection to romantic love merged with such marriages between 1871 and 1911. Nevertheless, the "Cinderella ideal" continued to appear in short stories and plays of the period. Writers took pains to demonstrate that Cinderella was not a fortune-hunter. For example, women's mass circulation magazines of the century's first decade often revealed at the end that the woman had a fortune, and it served as a reward for authentic love. Nan Enstad discovered similar themes in working-class dime novels. *Ladies of Labor, Girls*

of Adventure: Working Women, Popular Culture and Labor Politics at the Turn of the Twentieth Century (New York: Columbia University Press, in press).

43. Israel Zangwill, *The Melting Pot* (New York: Macmillan, 1916 [originally 1909].

44. A scholarly debate exists over how committed Zangwill was to complete amalgamation. For an analysis of *The Melting Pot* that challenges traditional readings, see Neil Larry Shumsky, "Zangwill's *The Melting Pot:* Ethnic Tensions on Stage," *American Quarterly* 27 (March 1975): 29–41.

45. This marriage and the response of New York's working women, including Jewish workers, is well described in Nan Enstad, *Ladies of Labor.*

46. The reaction of the Jewish press to the engagement and marriage is discussed in Stephen Birmingham, *The Rest of Us: America's Eastern European Jews* (Boston: Little Brown and Company, 1984), 50–69, and Joselit, *Wonders of America*, 45–47.

47. Miriam Shomer Zunser, "The Jewish Literary Scene in New York at the Beginning of the Century," *YIVO Annual of Jewish Social Science* 7 (1952): 293.

48. "The Fire Beneath the Melting Pot," (translated), *Yiddish Daily Courier* 1918.

49. See Karen Murphy, *Reconstructing the Nation: Race, Gender, and Restoration: The "Progressive Era"* (University of Minnesota Dissertation, American Studies, 1996).

50. Michael G. Corenthal, *Cohen on the Telephone: A History of Jewish Recorded Humor and Popular Music 1892–1942* (Milwaukee: Yesterday's Memories, 1984), 30.

51. Historian Lary May found in a random sample of plots of films produced between 1914 and 1958 that marriage and romance across ethnic lines reached the height of popularity in the mid-1920s. *The Big Tomorrow: Hollywood and the Politics of the American Way* (Chicago: University of Chicago Press, forthcoming). In 1918, fewer than 20 percent of the film plots featured this relationship, but by 1926 nearly 40 percent of films in the sample concerned marriage and romance across ethnic lines. By 1930, the theme had plummeted from popularity, appearing in less than 10 percent of the films in the sample. At the height of its subsequent popularity in 1950, interethnic marriage occurred in less than 20 percent of the films. Marriage in general was a popular theme at this time, but in 1926, when film plots centered on interethnic romance, it reached its peak. Films ending in marriage occurred in slightly more than 30 percent of the plots. Marriage as a happy ending reached its high point in 1918 (65 percent of the plots) and 1930 (55 percent of the plots). Interethnic romance was also far more popular than marriage and romance across class lines. In 1926 only 20 percent of the films' plots focused on cross-class love.

52. Mary V. Dearborn, *Pocahontas's Daughters: Gender and Ethnicity in American Culture* (New York: Oxford University Press, 1986), 104–5.

53. Kathleen Mari Fielder, "Fatal Attraction: Irish–Jewish Romance in Early Film and Drama," *Eire: A Journal of Irish Studies* 20 (1985): 6–18.

54. David Desser demonstrates that Jewish intermarriage features in a variety of films from 1908 to 1915 preceding the feature film era. Ninety percent of the films involve a Jewish woman and a non-Jewish man. He compares this theme to that of intermarriage between Asian Americans and whites. In both cases Desser argues that white male anxiety about ethnicity is alleviated by the sexual conquest of the ethnic other. "The Cinematic Melting Pot: Ethnicity, Jews and Psychoanalysis," *Unspeakable Images: Ethnicity and the American Cinema*, ed. Lester Friedman (Urbana: University of Illinois Press, 1991), 396.

55. Thomas Cripps, "The Movie Jew as an Image of Assimilation, 1903–1927," *Journal of Popular Film* 4 (1975): 190–207.

56. Why popular culture paired Jews with Irish and not either of them with Italians or Norwegians, for example, has not been the source of much speculation. John J. Appel offers one interpretation in his analysis of American caricature. He argues that the two are paired in a "Dionysian versus Apollonian cultural war. The Irish are portrayed as irrational in contrast to Jews' calculation and self-restraint. The Irish are thwarted by their own lack of control, but Jews' social mobility was cast as an attack on the status quo." "Jew in American Caricature: 1820–1914," *American Jewish History* 71 (September 1981): 115. Stephen Whitfield comments on the symbolic attraction of the Irish to Jews in *American Space Jewish Time: Essays in Modern Culture and Politics* (New York: North Castle Books, 1996), 154. He notes that Jews envied their language advantage in the United States.

57. *The Cohens and the Kellys*, Universal, 1926, Archive of the Museum of Modern Art.

58. Cripps, "Movie Jew as an Image of Assimilation," 201.

59. *Abie's Irish Rose*, Paramount, 1928, Archives of the Library of Congress.

60. One of the other few extant films from this genre, *Pleasure Before Business* (Columbia, 1927, Archives of the Library of Congress) uses the same visual and rhetorical cues of the other films. An attractive younger generation and a caricatured older generation make the intermarriage synonymous with Americanization. In this film, the Jewish daughter has a Jewish suitor who is exposed as a fortune-hunter. With her parents' approval she will wed a non-Jewish physician who is wealthy and generous. This film, like the others, emphasizes that the older, European generation cannot consume as effectively as the younger one.

61. Needless to say, these films and plays concerned only Americans of European descent, and not of different races. The envisioned society did not include toleration of

either cultural or racial diversity. Indeed, this very period was characterized by an anti-immigration hysteria, and many laws that eventually closed off immigration. Some of these laws advocated registering aliens and depriving them of many basic rights.

At the same time anti-miscegenation laws forbade the love of racial opposites. Blacks and whites, for example were not the subject of amalgamation drama in the nineteenth and twentieth centuries. Joyce Flynn argues that the mulatto, the personification of blacks on the American stage, was a figure of "powerful domestic tragedy" when love occurred, "Melting Pots," 198. For a discussion of anti-miscegenation laws, see Robert J. Sickels, *Race, Marriage and the Law* (Albuquerque: University of New Mexico Press, 1972). While such legislation was passed in the seventeenth century in the United States, in the 1920s, during this same period, these acts were particularly potent.

Interethnic love plots also rarely included marriages between the classes during this period. In short, the single dominant message of these romances was that America could be created by overcoming generational differences. Descendants of Europeans would become Americans by abandoning past loyalties. No radical transformation was otherwise required.

62. Michael Rogin's *Blackface White Noise: Jewish Immigrants in the Hollywood Melting Pot* (Berkeley: University of California Press, 1996), 78–79, explores the romance between Jew and Gentile in the 1927 *Jazz Singer*. He argues that blackface facilitates marriage between Jew and non-Jew rather than black and white. His attention to the intermarriage theme against racial polarization is useful, but it is best read in tandem with reviews by Lary May, *American Jewish History* 85 (March 1997): 115–19, and Hasia Diner, "Trading Faces," *Common Quest* 2 (Summer 1997): 40–44, who make clear that Rogin overlooks several important contexts for his analysis.

63. Rischin, "Introduction," *Grandma Never Lived in America*, xxxiii–xxxiv.

64. Abraham Cahan, in Rischin, "Introduction," *Grandma Never Lived in America*.

65. Cahan, "God Is Everywhere!" (originally published in 1902), in Rischin, *Grandma Never Lived in America*, 208.

66. Cahan, "God Is Everywhere!," 208.

67. Cahan, "God Is Everywhere!," 210.

68. Abraham Cahan, *The Rise of David Levinsky* (New York: Harper and Row, 1960, [originally 1917]).

69. Cahan's earlier novel *Yekl* offered yet another variation on these themes. The difficulty of integrating Old World marriage into the New World and the demands of each were played out in the lives of immigrants in New York (New York: Dover, 1970 [originally 1896]).

70. *Der Amerikaner* was aimed at a readership that was still "religious" but was committed to Americanization and mobility. *Der Amerikaner*'s masthead proclaimed it to be a national Jewish weekly devoted to "science, art, and literature." Articles on how electricity and other forms of technology worked, as well as serialized fiction and discussions of the Bible, demonstrated the extent of the paper's commitment to a contemporary American Jewish life.

71. The Torah, the first five books of the Bible, is read three times a week in synagogues. Each week is assigned a section of Torah called by the first name of the portion. The entire Torah is read annually.

72. Elbe was best known as a children's writer. Although the lexicons that provide entries for Elbe do not list *Der Amerikaner* as one of the venues for which he wrote, one can safely assume that he is the Lamed Baysnik to which the entries refer. The *Lexicon of Yiddish Literature* (New York, 1981 [originally 1956]), 227–28, suggests that he portrayed life during the first period of Jewish immigration. In his comic sketches he writes about the "graven materialism of the American Jewish environment." Even his children's stories "ridiculed Jews brought up in America." Both the uncommon pen name and the style of writing are found in these columns. His other pen name, Reb Leybele, clearly draws on his Yiddish name, Leibe. Biographical material is taken from *Biographical Dictionary of Modern Yiddish Literature* (1956) and from *Lexicon of the Yiddish Literature, Press and Philogy*, Vol. 1: *Presse un filogie*, ed. Z. Reyzin (Vilna, 1925). Thanks to Zachary Baker and Jocelyn Cohen for help with finding and translating this information.

73. Abraham Cahan's earliest forays as a Yiddish writer in the United States involved a similar use of a traditional Jewish form to reflect not on satire but on politics. In the *Arbeiter Zeitung* he wrote a weekly feature called "Sidra" (the section of the Bible read each week). He linked the passages to his analysis of the unjust treatment of workers. Prior to this 1890 publication he had used a similar formulation in a briefly lived 1896 newspaper. Cahan believed that this "folk religion" revealed an important connection between Judaism and socialism. Ronald Sanders, *The Downtown Jews: Portraits of an Immigrant Generation* (New York: Dover, 1969), 109, 111.

74. All quotations from *Der Amerikaner* are translated from the Yiddish by Nina Warnke.

75. Lamed Baysnik, *Der Amerikaner*, July 13, 1917, p. 21.

76. Lamed Baysnik, *Der Amerikaner*.

77. Lamed Baysnik, *Der Amerikaner*.

78. Fred Somkin, "Zion's Harp by the East River: Jewish-American Popular Songs in Columbus's Golden Land, 1890-1914," *Perspectives in American History* 2(1985): 187.

79. Somkin, "Zion's Harp by the East River," 218-19.

80. See Elaine Tyler May, *Barren in the Promised Land: Childless Americans and the Pursuit of Happiness* (New York: Basic Books, 1995) for a discussion of reproductive issues related to new marriages in the late nineteenth and early twentieth centuries.

81. Rose Cohen, *Out of the Shadow* (New York: George H. Doran Co., 1918), 74.

82. Lawrence J. Lipton, "The Ladies–God Bless 'Em!" *Jewish Daily Forward*, August 7, 1927, p. E3.

CHAPTER 3: CONSUMING LOVE

1. The Observer, *Jewish Daily News*, February 23, 1900, English Department.

2. Moses Rischin, *The Promised City: New York Jews 1870–1914* (Cambridge, Mass.: Harvard University Press, 1962), 93.

3. *Reports of the United States Immigration Commission.* Volume 1, "Abstracts of Reports of the Immigration Commission, 1907-1910," 1911, 117. This study designated Jews as a race called the Hebrews. Hebrews were distinguished as either Russian or "other." I have chosen to use the term Jew to deracialize the category.

4. Andrew Heinze, *Adapting to Abundance: Jewish Immigrants, Mass Consumption, and the Search for American Identity* (New York: Columbia University Press, 1990). *Reports of the United States Immigration Commission*, 117, 185, noted that only 18 percent of the Russian Jews occupied the five rooms these women longed for.

5. The Observer, *Jewish Daily News*, February 23, 1900, English Department.

6. The Observer, *Jewish Daily News*, February 23, 1900, English Department.

7. "Americanizing Jewish Alien Girls," *American Hebrew* 101 (October 12, 1917): 652-53.

8. A. Irma Cohen, "Judaism and the Modern Woman," *Jewish Woman* 4 (October 24, 1922): 11-14.

9. My discussion of the rise of the American middle class and its consciousness is indebted to the pioneering work of Stuart Blumin, *The Emergence of the Middle Class: Social Experience in the American City, 1760–1900* (Cambridge: Cambridge University Press, 1989).

10. Blumin, *Emergence of the Middle Class*, 186.

11. A thorough discussion of the development of consumer capitalism may be found in William Leach, *Land of Desire: Merchants, Power and the Rise of a New American Culture* (New York: Vintage Press, 1993).

12. Leach, *Land of Desire.*

13. Leach, *Land of Desire,* 4–7.

14. Leonard Kahn, *The Role of the Family in the Adjustment of the Jewish Immigrant in the United States* (M.A. Thesis, Political Science, Columbia University, 1930), 107.

15. The study is cited in Heinze, *Adapting to Abundance,* 34. Heinze effectively argues that credit made it possible for Jews to purchase consumer items and save money from their wages as well. His innovative study demonstrates that rather than afflicted by poverty, Jewish immigrants experienced substantial abundance in their consumption of goods and leisure. He argues that Jews were crucial pioneers in consumer capitalism as both producers and consumers and that women were crucial to this process as household managers.

16. The American novelists Henry James and Edith Wharton have both been associated with themes of love, women's consumption, and money among the rich and noveau riche. Edith Wharton's *The Custom of the Country* (New York: Penguin Books, 1987 [first published 1913]) is only one novel among many that takes up this theme.

17. The Observer, *Jewish Daily News,* October 13, 1901), English Department.

18. Peter Laipson has written about the emergence of bachelorhood as an alternative to matrimony. He writes, "In part, this ideological transformation was accomplished by positing male singleness as the unfortunate result of women's inordinate propensity for commercial consumption." "'Til Debt Do Us Part': Consumerism, Gender, and Bachelor Identity, 1870–1910," Paper presented at the American Studies Association meetings, November 1995, p. 4.

19. Nathan Zalowitz, "What Is the Matter with Our Jewish Girls?" *Jewish Daily Forward,* February 25, 1923, English page 3.

20. Zalowitz, "What Is the Matter with Our Jewish Girls?" "Mrs. de Puymter" is an upper-class name. Division Street is on New York's Lower East Side. The Grand Concourse is in the Bronx and was an address that represented real upward mobility from life in New York City outside of the ghetto.

21. Leon Kornbluth, *Jewish Daily Forward,* May 24, 1925), English page 3.

22. "I Married a Poor Girl," *Day,* October 24, 1926, English Section.

23. Lawrence J. Lipton, "The Ladies–God Bless 'Em!" *Jewish Daily Forward,* August 7, 1927, p. E3. The standard works on Yiddish theater do not mention the plots

that Lipton describes. It seems unlikely that he would have invented them given that his readers might well have been familiar with Yiddish theater. On the other hand, these English-speaking readers, at a time when silent and spoken film was quite popular, might not have been frequent theatergoers.

24. Anzia Yezierska, *Salome of the Tenements* (Urbana: University of Illinois Press, 1995 [originally 1923]), 42.

25. The Observer, *Jewish Daily News,* February 23, 1900, English Department.

26. Rischin, *The Promised City.*

27. H. B., "Letter to the Editor," *Day,* January 15, 1928, English Section.

28. Reflecting both the period–the late 1920s–and the increasing Americanization of Jewish youth, the *Forward* featured debates between men and women that concerned not only marriage, but dating as well. The "Great Ethel Controversy," for example, in 1925 concerned whether a woman could accept dinner from a man without being expected to be sexually intimate. "The Great Ethel Controversy Closes and Still they Come," October 25, 1925, English page. The article comments that most writers to the paper condemned Ethel's behavior. Another set of letters concerned what in the 1990s would be called sexual harassment. A woman wrote to the *Forward* about how she was treated by men in her office. Both stories brought a small number of responses. Both men and women who wrote seemed unsympathetic to women who wanted the freedom to work in offices and accept dinner from men, but who found sexual attention distressing. The women who wrote claimed that they were not troubled by men's attention. The men who wrote felt women were unreasonable (October 11, 1925, English page).

29. The Observer, *Jewish Daily News,* November 30, 1899, English Department.

30. "Fortune Hunters Need Not Apply," *Day,* March 18, 1927, English Section.

31. "I Can't Get Used to Jewish Men," *Day,* November 14, 1925, English Section.

32. The Observer, *Jewish Daily News,* January 8, 1900, English Department.

33. Nathaniel Zalowitz, "In Defense of Jewish Girls," *Jewish Daily Forward,* March 4, 1923, English Page 3.

34. The Observer, *Jewish Daily News,* November 21, 1899, English Department.

35. The Observer, *Jewish Daily News,* February 23, 1900, English Department.

36. Sarah Eisenstein noted that the dream of marriage, particularly to a romantic ideal, was the overwhelming ideal of working women's lives. *Give Us Bread But Give Us Roses: Working Women's Consciousness in the United States 1890 to the First World War* (London: Routledge and Kegan Paul, 1983), 124, 142. Alice Kessler-Harris, *Out to*

Work: A History of Wage Earning Women in the United States (New York: Oxford University Press, 1982), 113.

37. Kessler-Harris, *Out to Work.* Alice Kessler-Harris suggests that in this same turn-of-the-century period women of "better" classes did enter the workplace, but in jobs out of the reach of the vast majority of working women. With mass-produced clothing, canned food, and other examples of a changing household technology, women were freed from managing a large number of servants and household work. They sought meaningful work, pioneering in fields like social work, 112–14.

38. Ethel Taurog, "Pleasure Seekers," *Modern View* (December 23, 1927): 19.

39. Cohen, *Out of the Shadows,* 126. Certainly not all Jewish women sought only to marry and join the middle class. Women anarchists and union leaders are among the most public examples of Jewish women who chose a different path. Nor did marriage and upward mobility turn Jewish women away from concern for the working class and employed women. However, like the majority of women of their day, Jews did marry, and did aspire to middle-class life. On anarchism, see Naomi Shepherd, *Price Below Rubies: Jewish Women as Rebels and Radicals* (Cambridge, Mass.: Harvard University Press, 1993). On labor see Annelise Orlick, *Common Sense and a Little Fire: Women and Working Class Politics in the United States 1900–1965* (Chapel Hill: University of North Carolina Press, 1995).

40. Peter Filene, *Himself/Herself: Sex Roles in Modern America* (New York: Harcourt, Brace, Jovanovich, 1975), 241. Peter Filene describes the female labor force in 1910. One-fourth of the 1910 female jobholders were married and worked because of necessity. Another 15 percent lost their husbands through death and divorce. In 1930 one of every seven employed homemakers was the sole wage earner for the family (pp. 29, 137–38).

41. Marie Jastrow, *A Time to Remember: Growing Up In New York Before the Great War* (New York: W. W. Norton and Co., 1979), 78.

42. Lawrence B. Glickman, *A Living Wage: American Workers and the Making of Consumer Society* (Ithaca: Cornell University Press, 1997), 42, 48.

43. *Statistical Abstracts of the United States,* No. 53, 1931, Table 365. Department of Commerce, U.S. Government Printing Office Washington, D.C., 1931; Claudia Goldin, *Understanding the Gender Gap: An Economic History of American Women* (New York: Oxford University Press 1990), chaps. 2, 4, and 5. Goldin explains in detail how women workers from 1890 to 1930 were confined to a "short job ladder" based on the assumption that they would not work. Therefore, they had little opportunity to gain skills and expertise in their work. Wages in manufacturing and sales, the dominant occupations of Jews of this period, are the source of much of her data.

44. Jurgen Kocka, *White Collar Workers in America 1890–1940: A Social-Political History in International Perspective*, Maura Kealey, trans. (London: Sage Publications, 1980), 101; Margery Davies argues that the feminization of clerical work lay in both political and economic conditions that were not related to the job itself. The increased demand for clerical workers was met by women who were less costly than male labor, and women were more likely to be literate. *Women's Place Is at the Typewriter* (Philadelphia: Temple University Press, 1982), 59.

45. Susan Porter Benson, *Countercultures; Saleswomen, Managers, and Customers in American Department Stores, 1890–1940* (Urbana: University of Illinois Press, 1986), 183.

46. Sheila M. Rothman, *Women's Proper Place: A History of Changing Ideals 1870 to the Present* (New York, Basic Books, 1978), 55.

47. Lipton, "The Ladies," p. E3.

48. Orlick, *Common Sense and a Little Fire*, 36.

49. *Jewish Daily Forward*, June 7, 1925, English page 3. In fact the *Forward* never printed any replies to the contest.

50. From the Public Use Sample of the 1910 census. The Public Use Sample is a nationally representative sample of household and individual records from the 1910 census. A 1-in-250 sampling fraction was used, producing a total of 88,814 households. The sample selection was designed so that each household and each individual in the manuscript population had an equal probability for being selected. The sample is therefore self-weighted. Michael A. Strong et al., *User's Guide: Public Use Sample, 1910 U.S. Census of Population* (1989).

51. Most Yiddish-speaking women, the census category in which East European women fell, did not work because they came to the United States married or married shortly after arriving. These young working women in 1910 were likely not married and certainly were far more Americanized than their parents or married siblings.

52. Thomas Kessner and Betty Boyd Caroli argue that between 1880 and 1905 both Italian and Jewish women both moved up the occupational ladder in the United States. However, ethnicity was more significant than sex in determining which jobs young women took. Neither group had the access to white-collar classification that their brothers had, but Jewish women were more likely to be employed than Italians, and their occupational profiles were more like their brothers'. "New Immigrant Women at Work: Italians and Jews in New York City, 1880–1905," *Journal of Ethnic Studies* 5 (Winter 1978): 25.

53. The Public Use Sample of the 1910 Census revealed that different ethnic groups kept their children of different genders, aged 8–15, in school for different lengths of

time. Italians were more likely to keep their sons than their daughters in school (41 percent versus 46 percent). Yiddish speakers were more likely to keep their sons than their daughters in school, but they kept both in school at a higher proportion than other groups (58 percent versus 64 percent), even to a greater extent than the native-born, who kept about 40 percent of their children in school.

54. Yiddish speakers and their daughters, however, still lagged significantly behind in teaching, an occupation that required longer education and outstanding mastery of English. Jewish women eventually sought careers in education. In 1920, 26 percent of the new teachers in New York City were Jewish, and by 1930 Jewish women made up 44 percent of the new teachers. New York was particularly hospitable to Jewish women's ambitions for teaching during the interwar period. Teacher training was free. Married women were not required to leave their jobs, and other occupational opportunities, for example clerical work, were declining. During the 1920s, by contrast, New York's educational system was expanding dramatically. Ruth Jacknow Markowitz, *My Daughter, the Teacher: Jewish Teachers in the New York City Schools* (New Brunswick: Rutgers University Press, 1993), 2.

55. *Jewish Daily News,* February 23, 1900, English Department.

56. Thomas Kessner, *The Golden Door: Italian and Jewish Immigrant Mobility in New York City 1880–1915* (New York: Oxford University Press, 1977), 60.

57. Selma C. Berrol, "Education and Economic Mobility: The Jewish Experience in New York City, 1880-1928," *American Jewish Historical Quarterly* 65 (March 1976): 264.

58. Berrol, "Education and Economic Mobility," 262.

59. Deborah Dash Moore, *At Home in America: Second Generation New York Jews* (New York: Columbia University Press, 1981), 51.

60. Kocka, *White Collar Workers in America,* 44–47.

61. Stephen Thernstrom, *The Other Bostonians: Poverty and Progress in the American Metropolis 1880–1970* (Cambridge, Mass.: Harvard University Press, 1973), 142.

62. Kessner, *Golden Door,* 110.

63. Julia Weber, "Anomalous Tribe," *American Jewish News,* May 17, 1918, p. 15.

64. Celia Silbert, "The Regents' Girl," *American Jewish Chronicle,* September 15, 1916, pp. 590–91.

65. Jean Jaffe, "Gone Is the Poor Working Girl," *Day,* January 22, 1928, English Section.

66. George Wolfe, *The "Bintel Brief" of the "Jewish Daily Forward" as an Immigrant Institution and a Research Source.* (M.A. Thesis in the Graduate School for Jewish Social Work, Jewish Scientific Institute, 1933), 184.

67. Wolfe, *"Bintel Brief,"* 239. In Wolfe's Master's Thesis he estimated that nearly 19 percent of letters in 1906 and 13 percent of letters in 1907 received by the *Forward* concerned romance. The only category which received more letters was the generic "letters of opinion" in 1906.

68. "Constance," *Jewish Women's Home Journal* 2 (September 1923): 49.

69. "Marry a Yiddisher Boy," words by A. Seymour Brown and music by George Botsford (New York, Detroit: Jerome H. Remick and Co.)

70. Nina Kay, *American Hebrew,* April 12, 1929, pp. 793–99.

71. *Day,* November 14, 1925, English Section.

72. "Is the Jewish Beau Stingy," *Day,* June 2, 1929, English Section.

73. "Is the Jewish Beau Stingy."

74. These numbers are drawn from the public use sample of the 1920 census undertaken by the University of Minnesota.

75. Calvin Goldscheider, "Demography of Jewish Americans: Research Findings, Issues, and Challenges," *Understanding American Jewry,* ed. Marshall Sklare (New Brunswick: Transaction Books, 1982).

76. From the 1910 Public Use Sample.

77. From the 1920 Public Use Sample.

78. Constance, "Heart to Heart Talk," *Jewish Woman's Home Journal* 2 (August 1923): 43 received a letter from S. L., who described a non-Jewish sweetheart as "the Viking Lord." Zalowitz, "What Is the Matter with Our Jewish Girls?" described Gentile married women who worked in offices happily.

79. Margaret E. Sangster, "Marriage: A Question of Cash," *Cosmopolitan* 51 (September 1911): 459.

80. Glickman, *A Living Wage,* 48.

81. Lois Banner, *American Beauty* (New York: Knopf, 1983), 103.

82. See, for example, "Girls Reply to Their Critic," *Day,* May 22, 1932, English Department.

83. For example, see Nathaniel Zalowitz, "Why Should Levy Become Lee and Rabinowitz Robins," *Jewish Daily Forward,* March 7, 1926, English page; Jacob C. Rich, "Why I Changed My Name to Sound More American," *Jewish Daily Forward,* April 4, 1926, pp. 3, 10. In addition, articles on the topic that writers called "Jewish self-hate"

appeared in the English page throughout 1923. See for example, Leo Robbins, "Are You a Member of the Jewish Ku-Klux Klan?" June 24, 1923, English page.

84. Bertrand Russell, "British Philosopher Explains Why So Many Modern Marriages Are Thoroughgoing Failures," *Jewish Daily Forward*, January 19, 1930, p. 11; "Stenographer versus Factory," *Jewish Daily Forward*, May 20, 1923, p. 3; "Too Many Jewish Professionals?" *Jewish Daily Forward*, July 11, 1926, p. 3; "Sales Jobs Are Hard," *Jewish Daily Forward*, February 7, 1926, p. 3.

85. *Jewish Daily Forward*, October 19, 1930, English page.

86. "The Business of Being a Wife," *Jewish Daily Forward*, January 31, 1926, English page.

87. See chapter 4 for a discussion of some of these contests.

88. T. J. Jackson Lears, "From Salvation to Self-Realization: Advertising and the Therapeutic Culture, 1880–1930," *The Culture of Consumption: Critical Essays in American History, 1880–1980*, ed. Richard Fox and T. J. Jackson Lears (New York: Pantheon Books, 1983).

CHAPTER 4: FADING FEUDS

1. See, for example, Leonard Dinnerstein, *Anti-Semitism in America* (New York: Oxford University Press, 1994).

2. By 1945, only 11 percent surveyed replied that they would act against Jews, but the intensity of anger directed at them underlined the tenor of the times. These data are taken from Charles Stember, *Jews in the Mind of America* (New York: American Jewish Congress, 1966), 124–32.

3. Beth Wenger, *New York Jews and the Great Depression: Uncertain Promises* (New Haven: Yale University Press, 1996).

4. Judith Smith also makes this point in her comparative study of Italian and Jewish families during this period. *Family Connections: A History of Italian and Jewish Immigrant Lives in Providence, Rhode Island, 1900–1940* (Albany: State University of New York Press, 1985).

5. Wenger, *New York Jews and the Great Depression*, 71.

6. See Lizabeth Cohen, *Making a New Deal: Industrial Workers in Chicago, 1919–1939* (Cambridge: Cambridge University Press) for a discussion of this process for ethnics. Henry Feingold's *A Time for Searching: Entering the Mainstream 1920–1945* (Baltimore: Johns Hopkins University Press, 1992), 60, notes that what cemented Jews together by the 1920s was the American popular culture. His examples include music, dance, crossword puzzles, and sports. By the 1930s this process had advanced significantly.

7. Ewa Morawska, "Changing Images of the Old Country in the Development of Ethnic Identity among East European Immigrants, 1880s–1930s: A Comparison of Jewish and Slavic Representations," *YIVO Annual* 12 (1993): 313; Feingold, *Time for Searching,* 87.

8. See Morawska, "Changing Images of the Old Country."

9. A Yiddish culture continued to exist in the United States during this period, particularly in New York. Yiddish theaters continued to offer plays, and a Yiddish film industry in the United States and Europe flourished at the end of the decade. Yiddish literature continued to be published in the press and books. Though significant for their artistic value, these cultural works were not read or enjoyed by the majority of American Jews because Yiddish was in such rapid decline. The closing of immigration in 1924 essentially cut off the supply of Yiddish speakers coming to the United States, and the demand that those who wanted to succeed in the United States speak English in combination with the onus placed on immigrant behavior made it impossible for Yiddish to flourish for the majority of Jews. On Yiddish theater, see Nahama Sandrow, *Vagabond Theater: A World History of Yiddish Theater* (New York: Syracuse University Press, 1977), and on Yiddish film, see J. Hoberman, *A Bridge of Light: Yiddish Film Between Two Worlds* (New York: Museum of Modern Art, 1991). Feingold, *Time for Searching,* provides an overview of these processes as well (pp. 62–89).

10. Feingold, *Time for Searching,* 75. Nevertheless, Feingold points out that in 1927 there were still nine Yiddish dailies and a total of 111 Jewish periodicals in Yiddish, Hebrew, and English (p. 275).

11. In the archive of the 92d Street Young Men's Hebrew Association.

12. *News from the School of the Jewish* Woman 1 (November–December 1935).

13. For example, one student wrote about subway conversations when she tried to study for school. She described women who discussed dieting, their children as brats, and being chastened by an old friend who asked, "Are you still studying?" She concluded all that she had time to learn was that there are many types of women. The author, Edith Serenson, described herself as enrolled in Elementary Hebrew. "All in the Subway School," 1 (January 1936): 6.

14. See Deborah Dash Moore, "Trude Weiss-Rosmarin and the Jewish Spectator," *The "Other" New York Jewish Intellectuals,* ed. Carole S. Kessner (New York: New York University Press, 1994), 101–21 for a discussion of Weiss-Rosmarin and the school.

15. Dr. B. L. Wiseman, "The Clinic of Personal Problems," *Jewish Spectator* 1 (June 1936): 24.

16. Wiseman, "Clinic of Personal Problems."

17. I surveyed these three weekly newspapers for the years 1936 and 1942 because they had been sources that consistently included comments on family and women in the 1910s.

18. According to its masthead, the *American Hebrew* in fact absorbed six other newspapers, most from the Northeast, that clearly were unable to survive independently by the early 1930s.

19. Emil L. Smith, "Prize Letter," *Day*, February 26, 1928, English Department.

20. Nathan Morton Fibish, *Day*, March 4, 1928, English Department.

21. "Must I Be a Lawyer: The Younger Generation in Full Revolt against Commercialism of Professional Life," *Day*, August 1, 1926, English Department; "Impractical Son," "Choosing Your Own Calling," *Day*, June 16, 1929, English Department; "Practical Minded Parents and Artistic Ambitions," *Day*, January 5, 1930, English page.

22. E., "Why Are Parents So Sure They Know What Is Best?" *Day*, September 9, 1928, English Department.

23. B. Lit., "What's Wrong with These Parents?" *Day*, March 28, 1930, English Department.

24. Letter to the Editor, "Finds Too Many Unmarried Girls," *Day*, February 27, 1927, English page.

25. Sol Division, "Jobs the New Dowry?" *Day*, July 10, 1932, English Department.

26. Ted Solotaroff, "Introduction," *Writing Our Way Home: Contemporary Stories by American Jewish Writers*, ed. Ted Solotaroff and Nessa Rapoport (New York: Shocken Books, 1992), xxiv–xxv.

27. A discussion of American Jewish religious ideology in this period may be found in Arnold M. Eisen, *The Chosen People in America: A Study in Jewish Religious Ideology* (Bloomington: Indiana University Press, 1983). Overviews of American Jewish synagogues and religion during this period may be found in Wenger, *New York Jews and the Great Depression*, and Feingold, *Time for Searching*.

28. Robert Warshow, "Clifford Odets: Poet of the Jewish Middle Class," *The Immediate Experience: Movies, Comics, Theatre and Other Aspects of Popular Culture* (New York: Doubleday, 1964 [originally 1946]).

29. Donald Weber, "The Jewish American World of Gertrude Berg: The Goldbergs on Radio and Television 1930–1950," *Talking Back: Images of Jewish Women in American Popular Culture*, ed. Joyce Antler (Hanover: Brandeis University Press, 1997), 94.

30. Weber, "Gertrude Berg," 95.

31. Odets was part of the Group Theater whose first production appeared in 1931. It was one of a series of theaters that challenged Broadway's dominance of the Amer-

ican stage through works of social protest, and was a source of criticism and concern to mainstream critics. Judd Teller argues that *Awake and Sing*, along with several other plays produced by the Group Theater, developed themes that were directly descended from Yiddish theater. Like others who have written about Odets, he too argues that the playwright's use of language set him apart in his ability to capture Jewish American experience. *Strangers and Natives: The Evolution of the American Jew from 1921 to the Present* (New York: Delta Books, 1968), 139–47.

32. Henry W. Levy, "A New Playwright–Clifford Odets," *Exponent* 95 (March 1935): 1.

33. Alfred Kazin, *Starting Out in the Thirties* (Ithaca: Cornell University Press, 1962), 80–82.

34. Warshow, *Immediate Experience*, 24–25.

35. Warshow, *Immediate Experience*, 25.

36. Kazin, *Starting Out in the Thirties*, 81.

37. Jews both created and appeared in mass-media venues that did not conform to these family tales. When one thinks of the great performers of the period a long list of Jews comes to mind. The Marx Brothers, Eddie Cantor, Red Hot Mamas like Sophie Tucker, Fanny Brice, Jack Benny, and Milton Berle are among the most famous. They identified as Jews and were identified with and by Jews. Their humor and style defined Jewish entertainment. Their irreverence, often brilliantly political in the case of the Marx Brothers, came to define what is thought of as American and Jewish humor. Their use of language is also thought of as Jewish, and as popular entertainers were viewed by far more Jews than Odets ever reached. However, none of them worked in narrative genres that conspired to reproduce reality. No journalist ever asked a Marx brother or Jack Benny or Fanny Brice if they took their characters from Jewish life. Many of them drew on the experience of outsiderhood to challenge issues of race, femininity, and sexuality. Jews set on a life within the middle class appreciated both the critique that resonated with their experience of being outsiders and embraced other representations that helped to negotiate their passage as Jews. I associate that passage with constructions of the Jewish family. In particular, how Jews, rather than critics, respond to the work is what interests me.

38. Clifford Odets, *Awake and Sing*, *Awake and Singing: Seven Classic Plays from the American Jewish Repertoire*, ed. Ellen Schiff (New York: Mentor, 1995 [originally 1935]), 284.

39. For example, in the *Jazz Singer*, the 1927 talking film about the struggles between an Old World father and a New World son, most of the narrative occurred outside of the family. The family served as the setting solely for confrontation and irrec-

oncilable conflict. By the mid-1930s separation, alienation, and gentler experiences of business worries and generational struggle are enacted at home, where unfolding daily life revealed how Jews struggled with American life.

40. Literary critic Elisa New writes that Delmore Schwartz's tragicomedies of the '30s captured "the warfare of parents and children who have sacrificed their hold on a ritual culture in pursuit of American perks. In Schwartz's families, the culture of materialism is so ritualized, so artfully superimposed onto Jewish tradition, that the children prove their respect for the faith by *buying* the things their parents could not buy, by making the money their parents would have made." Her view of Schwartz's work brings him more in line with the writings of young Jews in the press than the representations of family by Berg and Odets. In all cases, this critical transition period is realized through that family rather than the couple. Elisa New, "Killing the Princess: The Offense of a Bad Defense," *Tikkun* (March/April 1988).

41. Wenger, *New York Jews and the Great Depression*, 49.

CHAPTER 5: STRANGERS IN PARADISE

1. Jack Wertheimer, *A People Divided: Judaism in Contemporary America* (New York: Basic Books, 1993), 3–4.

2. Edward Shapiro, *A Time for Healing: American Jewry since World War II* (Baltimore: Johns Hopkins University Press), 1992; Gerald Sorin, *Tradition Transformed: The Jewish Experience in America of an Uneasy Encounter* (New York: Simon and Schuster, 1989).

3. Gladys Rothbell also notes this contrast between pre- and post–World War II mothers. "The Jewish Mother: Social Construction of a Popular Image," *The Jewish Family: Myths and Reality,*. eds. Steven M. Cohen and Paula E. Hyman (London: Homes and Meier Publications, 1986).

4. Patricia Eren, *The Jew in American Cinema* (Bloomington: Indiana University Press, 1984).

5. Alice Payne Hackett, *Seventy Years of Best Sellers: 1895–1965* (New York: R. R. Bowker, 1967), 198.

6. Herman Wouk, *Marjorie Morningstar* (New York: Doubleday, 1955). Wouk's novel and Philip Roth's *Goodbye, Columbus* of the same era are discussed in chapter 7.

7. Lester D. Friedman, *Hollywood's Image of the Jew* (New York: Ungar Publishing Company, 1982), 331–38; *Marjorie Morningstar*, Beechwald, 1958.

8. Esther Romeyn and Jack Kugelmass, *Let There Be Laughter: Jewish Humor in America* (Chicago: Spertus Press, 1997), 52–54.

9. These images were widespread enough to have found their way into literature, and the popular novels only intensified the concerns. The most famous, *Portnoy's Complaint*, came considerably later than this important period of community building, however. I discuss some of these issues in chapter 7.

10. For a discussion of the evolution of the literary Jewish Mother in the United States, see Beverly Gray Bienstock, "The Changing Image of the American Jewish Mother," *Changing Images of the Family*, ed. Virginia Tufte and Barbara Myerhoff (New Haven: Yale University Press, 1979), 173–91. For a discussion of American values that produced the Jewish Mother, see Aviva Cantor, *Jewish Women Jewish Men: The Legacy of Patriarchy in Jewish Life* (New York: Harper Collins, 1995), 207–31.

11. Contemporary with this more mainstream humor was the far more radical and critical humor of another group of Jewish comics that included Lenny Bruce and Mort Sahl. Their humor was far less familial and focused against society. The more centrist ethnic comics seemed to direct their humor inward, and particularly at women.

12. Jack Carter, *The Ed Sullivan Show*, CBS, February 21, 1960. From the Jewish Video Archive of the Jewish Museum.

13. Harry Golden, *Only in America* (Cleveland: World Publishing Company, 1958 [originally 1944]), 44–45.

14. Hackett, *Seventy Years of Best Sellers*, 228.

15. "How to be a Jewish Son?" *David Susskind Show*, WNEW-TV, November 29, 1970. From the Jewish Video Archive of the Jewish Museum.

16. Dan Greenburg, *How to Be a Jewish Mother: A Very Lovely Training Manual* (Los Angeles: Price/Sloan/Stern Publishers, 1964), 16.

17. Greenburg insists initially in the book that you don't have to be Jewish or a mother to be a Jewish Mother. This comic formulation was to shape a similar genre of books about the Jewish American Princess in the 1960s.

18. Greenburg, *Jewish Mother*, 34–35. Other joke collections offered her equally naive comments about sex and reproduction. William Novak and Moshe Waldocks, eds., *Big Book of Jewish Humor* (New York: Harper and Row, 1981), 264.

19. *The Ed Sullivan Show*, CBS, February 2, 1960. From the Jewish Video Archive of the Jewish Museum.

20. Rothbell, "The Jewish Mother," 120.

21. Zena Smith Blau wrote "In Defense of the Jewish Mother" for *Midstream*, one of the era's major Jewish magazines. The article was cited often and reprinted in several collections. In it she carefully documents the fact that Jewish achievement is related to children's longer period of dependence on parents. Drawing on scholarly stud-

ies as well as insider wisdom about Jewish life, Blau makes a careful case for the health of the Jewish family. The defensiveness of the strategy suggests how effective this humor was in suggesting that Jewish Mothers and their children were, as Blau states it, "neurotic." This defensive strategy continued for several more decades as Jewish women responded to one or another accusation about them within the Jewish community. *Midstream* 13 (February 1967): 42–49.

22. Leon Feldman, "The Jewish College Student," *Jewish Spectator* 20 (December 1955): 15. Though a Jewish professional, the article was based on a paper presented at a regional sociological meeting.

23. Albert Gordon, *Jews in Suburbia* (Boston: Beacon Press, 1959), 204.

24. David Boroff, "Jewish Readers and Jewish Writers," *Congress Bi-Weekly* 27 (December 19, 1960): 3. Boroff includes among these works made popular by women Leon Uris's *Exodus* and the sentimental writing of Harry Golden.

25. "The 'Vanishing Jewish Father,'" *Jewish Digest* 12 (October 1966): 62–63.

26. Gordon, *Jews in Suburbia*, 60.

27. Gordon, *Jews in Suburbia*, 61.

28. Roland B. Gittelsohn, "Should We Intermarry?" *Modern Jewish Problems*, 4th ed. (New York: Union of American Hebrew Congregations, 1964), 83–83.

29. Samuel Irving Bellman, "Jewish Mother Syndrome," *Congress Bi-Weekly* 32 (December 27, 1965): 4.

30. Gordon, *Jews in Suburbia*, 63. This position was to be advanced decades later again by the historian Arthur Hertzberg, who laid the failure of American Judaism entirely at the feet of Jewish women. As immigrants they had usurped men's power either because of men's incompetence or desertion of their families, and their own sentimental Judaism led to a lack of emphasis on observance or religious education, and to the promotion of success. Hertzberg, *The Jews in America: Four Centuries of an Uneasy Encounter* (New York: Simon and Schuster, 1989), 196–209.

31. Marshall Sklare, *Conservative Judaism: An American Religious Movement* (New York: Schocken Books, 1972 [originally 1955]), 89.

32. Sklare, *Conservative Judaism*. He also noted that social class could not explain this abandonment of Jewish men's responsibilities. While wealthy Jewish men did belong to far more organizations than other men, they remained recreational organizations.

33. Herbert Gans, "The Origin and Growth of a Jewish Community in the Suburbs: A Study of the Jews of Park Forest," *The Jews: Social Patterns of an American Group*,

ed. Marshall Sklare (Glencoe: Free Press, 1958), 217, 233. Thanks to Steven M. Cohen for a helpful conversation on this issue.

34. For example, the difference between the religious knowledge and abilities of young Jewish mothers and fathers was simply not what its experts asserted. Unquestionably, Jewish women had fewer years of formal Jewish education than their male peers; that was the norm of the Jewish religious system. Yet, the children of immigrants who settled in the suburbs, on the whole, were probably the least Jewish-educated of any generation in Jewish history, and men's educational advantages would have been slight. For example, Lucy S. Davidowicz noted in *On Equal Terms: Jews in America 1881–1981* (New York: Holt, Rinehart, Winston, 1982), that during the 1930s three-quarters of American Jewish parents neglected to give their children any Jewish education and that a national decline in religious beliefs and attendance at religious services was most marked among young Jews (pp. 97–99). At the same time, as I explained in chapters 3 and 4, immigrant Jewish families usually had multiple earners, which eroded the dominance of the father. With the economic downturn of the Depression, multiple earners again became the norm, as Beth Wenger describes in *New York Jews and the Great Depression: Uncertain Promise* (New Haven: Yale University Press, 1997), as does Judith E. Smith, *Family Connections: A History of Italian and Jewish Immigrants Lives in Providence Rhode Island, 1900–1940* (Albany: State University of New York Press, 1985).

35. Feldman, "Jewish College Student," 12.

36. Stuart Rosenberg, *The Real Jewish World: A Rabbi's Second Thoughts* (New York: Philosophical Library, 1984), 85–86.

37. Philip Wylie, *Generation of Vipers*, 2d ed. (New York: Holt, Rinehart and Winston, 1960 [originally 1955]).

38. Wylie, *Generation of Vipers*, 194.

39. In 1965 Irving Bellman commented that "what Philip Wylie . . . had to labor so hard to do during the second World War, as far as mother-baiting is concerned, the Jewish writers and entertainers have been able to accomplish with seemingly little effort and vastly greater success, at least for the Jewish audience." Irving Bellman, "The Jewish Mother Syndrome," 3. I suggest that it might have been the reverse direction.

40. Sidney Goldstein and Calvin Goldscheider, *Jewish Americans: Three Generations in a Jewish Community* (Englewood Cliffs: Prentice-Hall, 1968), 49.

41. Deborah Dash Moore, *To the Golden Cities: Pursuing the American Jewish Dream in Miami and LA* (New York: Free Press, 1994), 27.

42. Gerhard Lenski, *The Religious Factor: A Sociological Study of Religion's Impact on Politics, Economics, and Family Life* (New York: Doubleday, 1961), 72–73.

43. For a discussion of this process and its contribution to Jews' acculturation as "white," see Karen Brodkin Sacks, "How Did Jews Become White Folks?" *Race*, ed. Steven Gregory and Roger Sanjek (New Brunswick: Rutgers University Press, 1994).

44. See chapter 4.

45. Benjamin R. Epstein and Arnold Forester, "*Some of My Best Friends . . .*" (New York: Farrar, Straus and Cudahy, 1962), 97. Albert Gordon's survey of 388 suburban-ite Jews yields a virtually identical percentage. About two-thirds of his respondents experienced "no anti-Jewish feelings," and about one-third "some" (*Jews in Suburbia,* 167).

46. Leonard Dinnerstein compares some surveys that measured antisemitism in the 1940s, 1950s, and 1960s. He argues that antisemitism persists, but not to the degree that Americans embraced it in the 1930s and 1940s. *Anti-Semitism in America* (New York: Oxford University Press, 1994), 128–73.

47. Gertrude Selznick and Stephen Steinberg, *The Tenacity of Prejudice: Anti-Semitism in Contemporary America* (New York: Harper and Row, 1969), 170–71, 184.

48. Gordon, *Jews in Suburbia,* 172.

49. Judith R. Kramer and Seymour Leventman, in their late 1950s study *Children of the Gilded Ghetto: Conflict Resolutions of Three Generations of American Jews* (New Haven: Yale University Press, 1961), state that "friendship with Gentiles is becoming increasingly acceptable to some (though not all) North City Jews," though they show evidence of continuing rebuff (pp. 53–54).

50. Cited in Gordon, *Jews in Suburbia,* 170.

51. See Sacks, "How Jews Became White Folks," for a thorough discussion of occupational mobility and its contributions to the construction of a white identity for Jews.

52. Albert Gordon, for example, reported that in his survey of suburbanites nationally, 63 percent said that "there is no anti-Jewish feeling in the suburbs in which they reside." Though he reported that the Anti-Defamation League of Detroit discovered that 57 percent of the realtors admitted to practicing some form of discrimination against Jews in the housing market, Gordon noted that housing conditions had improved for Jews but that the lack of equality was still a matter of grave concern. Gordon, *Jews in Suburbia,* 167–68.

53. Kramer and Leventman, *Children of the Gilded Ghetto,* 194.

54. Marshall Sklare with Joseph Greenblum, *Jewish Identity on the Suburban Frontier: A Study of Group Survival in the Open Society,* 2d ed. (Chicago: University of Chicago Press, 1979 [originally 1967]), 322.

55. Gordon, *Jews in Suburbia*, 178–79.

56. Benjamin Ringer, *The Edge of Friendliness: A Study of Jewish-Gentile Relationships* (New York: Basic Books, 1967).

57. J. R. Seeley, R. A. Sim, E. W. Loosley, *Crestwood Heights: A Study of the Culture of Suburban Life* (New York John Wiley and Sons,: 1956), 307–8. This Canadian study is described by the sociologists to concern a North American suburb. They find the community deeply influenced by the United States as well as England. They also commented that the only unusual feature of the suburb was the presence of a significant minority of Jews. They commented that their informant was correct, that the high school had a majority of Jewish students because Christian parents removed their children, leaving Jews to become the dominant group.

58. Donald Katz, *Home Fires: An Intimate Portrait of One Middle-Class Family in Postwar America* (New York: Harper Collins, 1992), 99.

59. Ringer, *Edge of Friendliness*, 71–73.

60. Kramer and Leventman, *Children of the Gilded Ghetto*, 120; Abraham Fleischman, an employee of the Jewish Welfare Board, also commented on this transformation in 1953. He wrote that the nature of Jewish social activities had changed dramatically in the suburbs from their urban lives. They were drawn into groups like service organizations, and for that matter synagogues, that paralleled the lives of their non-Jewish neighbors.

He too attributed this change to the desire for status. "The Urban Jew Goes Suburban," *Reconstructionist* 19 (March 6, 1953): 23.

61. Lenski, *Religious Factor*, 201.

62. Barbara Ehrenreich argued that accusations of permissiveness preoccupied experts on American childrearing for most of the century. Permissiveness was clearly linked to consumption in the suburbs. Having was related to relaxing authority. But as she also noted consumption was not yet highly differentiated and what one owned was not usually distinct from what others had. Accusations against Jewish consumption were often, then, attacks on consuming itself. *Fear of Falling* (New York: Pantheon, 1989), 38.

63. Vivian Gornick, "Twice an Outsider: On Being Jewish and a Woman," *Tikkun* 4 (March/April 1989): 31.

64. Gornick, "Twice An Outsider," 31.

65. Double consciousness is a concept introduced by W. E. B. Du Bois in *Souls of Black Folk* (New York: Signet, 1995 [originally 1903]) in which he explored how the African American lives in a double reality of his own experience and being constructed by others.

66. Calvin Trillin, *Remembering Denny* (New York: Farrar, Straus, Giroux, 1994). Trillin learned that the year previously *Life* had covered a father-daughter weekend at Wellesley that had featured two families who were perceived to be Jewish. The college felt that it quickly became labeled a "Jewish school," and the publicity did more harm than good. Yale made sure to guard against repeating the mistake (pp. 83–84).

67. "Hadassah Arms," *People of the Book: Thirty Scholars Reflect on their Jewish Identity*, ed. Jeffrey Rubin-Dorsky and Shelley Fisher Fishkin (Madison: University of Wisconsin Press, 1996), 156–57.

68. Papers of Lois Greene in the Greene Family papers, 1910–1980. Box 3. American Jewish Historical Society.

69. Papers of Lois Greene.

70. Greene Family papers, Box 3, Presidential speech, p. 4. The Flushing Jewish Center was founded in 1936 and the Greene family joined in 1941.

71. Joan Jacobs Brumberg examined a sample of the diaries of Jewish adolescent girls. She learned that Jewish girls began to keep diaries in great numbers during the 1950s. She suggests that ethnic adolescent girls keep diaries only when they reach the middle class. Prior to World War II, adolescent diarists tended to be well-educated white Protestant girls. "The 'Me' of Me: Voices of Jewish Girls in Adolescent Diaries of the 1920s and 1950s," *Talking Back: Images of Jewish Women in American Popular Culture*, ed. Joyce Antler (Hanover: Brandeis University Press, 1997), 53–54.

72. Lois Greene diary, January 5, 1946. Greene Family papers, Box 3. It is clear from this entry that Lois did not observe the Jewish dietary laws because of mixing milk and meat and eating nonkosher meat.

73. Lois Greene diary, January 4, 1946.

74. Lois Greene diary, January 21, 1946.

75. Lois Greene diary, March 16, 1946.

76. Lois Greene diary, February 3, 1946.

77. Lois Greene diary, November 20, 1946.

78. Lois Greene diary, December 17, 1946.

79. Lois Greene diary, April 16, 1946.

80. Lois Greene diary, April 17, 1946.

81. Greene Family papers, 1910–1980. Box 3. American Jewish Historical Society.

82. John Slawson, "Social Discrimination: The Last Barrier" (New York: The American Jewish Committee, 1955), 6.

83. Paula Hyman has an important analysis of the Jewish Mother and this period in *Gender and Assimilation in Modern Jewish History: The Roles and Representation of Women* (Seattle: University of Washington Press, 1995), 158–61. Her earlier analysis was included in Charlotte Baum, Paula Hyman, and Sonya Michel, *The Jewish Woman in America* (New York: Plume Books, 1975), 235–61.

84. Charles Angoff commented favorably on the television program in a 1954 issue of the Jewish journal, the *Reconstructionist*. While unwilling to call it "art," he claimed that Gertrude Berg, its star and writer, captured American Jewish life well (December 24, 1954, 19–20). For a discussion of Berg in the context of the 1950s and Jewish women, see Joyce Antler, *The Journey Home: Jewish Women and the American Century* (New York: Free Press, 1997), 233–38. For an exceptionally insightful analysis of the Goldbergs as a response to immigrant shame within popular culture, see Donald Weber, "The Jewish American World of Gertrude Berg: The Goldbergs on Radio and Television 1930–1950," *Talking Back* ed. Joyce Antler, 85–99.

85. Gertrude Berg, *The Rise of the Goldbergs* (New York: Barse and Co., 1931), 16.

86. Berg, *Rise of the Goldbergs*, 22–23.

87. "Rosie's Nose," *The Goldbergs*, 1955. Syndicated, Guild Films Production from the Jewish Video Archive of the Jewish Museum.

88. Barry Chiswick, "The Occupational Attainment of American Jewry, 1890–1990: A Preliminary Report" (unpublished manuscript). The GSS was conducted by the National Opinion Research Center, and was a sample survey conducted yearly since 1972. The data cited here were drawn from 1972 to 1987 and are centered on 1980. Participants were asked their religious preference currently and at age sixteen. Chiswick's sample consists of 150 adult Jewish men.

89. Chiswick, "Occupational Attainment," 14.

90. While 59 percent of Jewish males were employed as workers in 1900, that number fell to 19 percent by 1957. Jews used their earnings to launch their own or their sons' careers as small proprietors and managers, and to a lesser degree as salespeople and professionals. Because Jews lived in cities, and because of ongoing discriminatory hiring practices in some fields, they engaged in a limited number of occupations. At the same time, these occupational choices changed as Jewish men continued to set their sights on economic mobility. Eli E. Cohen, "Economic Status and Occupational Structure" *American Jewish Yearbook* 51 (Philadelphia: Jewish Publication Society, 1950), 53–70. See also Ben B. Seligman, "The American Jew: Some Demographic Features, *American Jewish Yearbook* 51, 3–52; Sidney Goldstein, "American Jewry, 1970: A Demographic Profile" *American Jewish Yearbook* 72 (Philadelphia: Jewish Publication Society, 1971), 3–88. In the 1950s, sociologist Nathan Glazer argued that

Jews capitalized on economic advantages in the 1930s based on higher education and self-employment to maximize the economic opportunities available from 1940 to 1955. "The American Jew and the Attainment of Middle Class Rank: Some Trends and Explanations," *The Jews:* Marshal Sklare, ed., 139–40.

91. Kramer and Leventman, *Children of the Gilded Ghetto,* 18–19.

92. George Lipsitz has written on the role consumption plays in the transition from radio to television for a variety of programs that crossed both media. "The Meaning of Memory: Family, Class, and Ethnicity in Early Network Television," *Time Passages: Collective Memory and American Popular Culture* (Minneapolis: University of Minnesota Press, 1990).

93. Vance Packard, *American Social Classes in the 1950s: Selection from Vance Packard's The Status Seekers,* Daniel Horowitz, ed. (Boston: Bedford Books, 1995 [originally 1959]), 153–54.

94. Gans, "Origin and Growth of a Jewish Community," 231.

95. This point is well documented in Baum, Hyman, and Michel, *Jewish Woman in America,* 235–61.

96. Jewish American women were quite politically and philanthropically active during this period, as they always have been. That they were portrayed only as consumers or frivolous is largely in keeping with the attempt to contain only a portion of their identity. See Joanne Meyerowitz, "Beyond the Feminist Mystique: A Reassessment of Post-War Mass Culture, 1946–1958," *Journal of American History* 79 (March 1993), for a discussion of the complexity of women's representation in mass culture during this period.

97. Goldstein and Goldscheider, *Jewish Americans,* 69, found in their Rhode Island study that Jewish males exceeded females by only 0.3 years of education. Their level of education is highly correlated with generation status.

98. Peter Filene, *Him/Her Self: Sex Roles in Modern America* (New York: Harcourt, Brace, Jovanovich, 1974), 241.

99. This view of suburban life is indebted to the important scholarship of Elaine Tyler May, *Homeward Bound: The American Family in the Cold War* (New York: Basic Books, 1988) and Barbara Ehrenreich, *The Hearts of Men: American Dreams and the Flight From Commitment* (New York: Anchor, 1983).

100. Ehrenreich, *Hearts of Men,* 34.

101. For a particularly thoughtful overview of a historical and cultural understanding of the 1950s, see Lary May, "Introduction," *Recasting America: Culture and Politics in the Age of Cold War* (Chicago: University of Chicago Press, 1989).

102. See Lizabeth Cohen, *Making a New Deal: Industrial Workers in Chicago, 1919–1939* (Cambridge: Cambridge University Press) for an analysis of the forces leading to these coalitions and how they shaped national politics through the New Deal.

CHAPTER 6: THE JEWISH AMERICAN PRINCESS

1. "Make Me A Match: A *Moment* Interview," *Moment* 10 (October 1985): 47.

2. Ze'ev Chafets, *Members of the Tribe: On the Road in Jewish America* (New York: Bantam Books, 1988), 205–6.

3. Susan Schnur, "When a JAP Is not a Yuppie: Blazes of Truth," *Lilith*, 17 (1987): 10–11.

4. The Phil Donahue television show devoted one program in 1988 to the princess, including a Black American Princess and an Italian American Princess along with a JAP and the editor of *Lilith*. Women in the audience were convinced that Jewish American Princesses existed, and most were critical of them. One of the guests identified herself as one. Transcript 01128, Multimedia Entertainment.

5. Letter to the Editor, *Moment* 8 (May 1983): 3.

6. See for example, Jeffrey Salkin, "Shylock in Drag?: JAP Jokes and Other Modern Vulgarities," *Moment* 8 (March 1983): 38–39; Evelyn Torton Beck, "JAP Baiting is Serious," *Gesher: Bridge: Feminist Newsletter of New Jewish Agenda* 2 (January 1988): 4; Ruth Atkin and Adrienne Rich, "'J.A.P.'-Slapping: The Politics of Scapegoating," *Gesher: Bridge* 2 (January 1, 1988): 4.

7. "'JAP'-Baiting on Campus," *Lilith* (Fall 1987).

8. Judith Allen Rubenstein, "The Graffiti Wars," *Lilith* (Fall 1997): 8–9.

9. The B'nai B'rith began to circulate information about the antisemitism of the JAP stereotype through their National Student Secretariat and their Anti-Defamation League Civil Rights Counsel. The American Jewish Committee created a task force on "JAP Baiting on American College Campuses" (reported in *American Jewish World*, May 7, 1993, p. 16). The American Jewish Committee distributed "JAP Jokes: Hateful Humor" by Mimi Alperin in 1988 as well. Mainstream Jewish magazines also began to publish condemning articles, e.g. Pamela Nadel, "Second Thoughts on the Jewish American Princess," *Midstream* (February 1986): 28–31.

10. Cindi Leve, "Viewpoint," *Glamour* (April 1992); Debra Kent, *Seventeen* (April 1990), 90–93.

11. Feminist writer and activist Letty Cottin Pogrebin commented in 1991 that the JAP stereotype had faded from film "because we've done such a good job consciousness-raising–not because it's gone from the culture." *The Northern California Jewish Bulletin*, July 26, 1991, 26.

12. It may be too soon to write the epitaph of the Jewish Mother. Several television situation comedies that featured Jewish men in the 1990s did once again take up the Jewish Mother as cultural icon. Cultural critics include *Seinfeld, Mad about You,* and *Family Album.* See John J. O'Connor, "This Jewish Mom Dominates TV, Too," *New York Times,* October 14, 1993.

13. Scholars have also participated in interpreting the Jewish American Princess as a phenomenon of ethnic humor. Allen Dundes argues in the "J.A.P. and the J.A.M. in American Jokelore," *Journal of American Folklore* 98 (1985): 456–75. In seeking to understand whether or not the stereotypes are true, he places them in the context of the period that this "joke cycle" originated. Dundes concludes that it amounts to a rejection of traditional norms and expectations for all women, including Jewish women. Women present themselves as "all take and no give." They want the support of parents and spouse and none of the responsibility. While Dundes's pursuit of the historical context of the cycle is useful, his fairly literal reading of women's demands leaves out the complexity of their Jewishness and the intergender tensions. Evelyn Torton Beck, "From 'Kike' to 'JAP': How Misogyny, Anti-Semitism and Racism Construct the 'Jewish American Princess,'" *Race, Class and Gender: An Anthology,* Margaret L. Anderson and Patricia Hill Collins, ed. (Belmont, Calif.: Wadsworth Publishing Company, 1992) examines how the JAP reflects classic antisemitic stereotypes. Esther Romeyn and Jack Kugelmass address the JAP through the two handbooks that are drawn on the model of *The Official Preppy Handbook* of the era. They argue that the handbooks "patrol ethnic borders" and present JAPs as possessing "insurmountable cultural boundaries to non-Jews." They argue that such handbooks, about Mothers or JAPs, support the uniqueness of Jewishness in the face of the reality of Jewish acculturation. Whether it is legitimate to isolate one form of humor from all other forms and declare it of a different order is an assertion that it would not be appropriate to ask an exhibition catalog to defend. On the other hand, the borders on which it is constructed assert difference in two directions. The "How To" books that they cite frequently assert that one does not have to share the gender or ethnicity of the JAP or Mother, placing them at the center of the acculturating liberal consensus of the vaunted cultural pluralism of the period. Perhaps more to the point, the "uniqueness" of the JAP is built on her exaggeration of class features that protect no culture as clearly as the assimilatory dominant culture. As they point out, she is pictured in pursuit of a Jewish, professional husband, but the humor is less built on endogamy than class. Precisely because JAP humor and stereotypes are widely diffused into American Jewish life, the extent to which Jews report their anxiety about the Prince and Princess reflects the stereotypes' association with a Jewishness that creates not a patrolable boundary, but an insurmountable divide. *Let There Be Laughter: Jewish Humor in America* (Chicago: Spertus Press, 1997), 76–77. Janice L. Booker, *The Jewish American Princess and Other Myths: The Many*

Faces of Self-Hatred is not a work of scholarship, but it draws on scholarly sources to claim that the JAP image is self-hating, along with a wide range of phenomena such as criticisms of Israel. Remarkably, it blames Jewish feminists among others for the use of the JAP image (New York: Shapolsky Publishers, 1991). The earliest analysis of the JAP, drawing on literary, cultural, and social scientific sources, is Charlotte Baum, Paula Hyman, and Sonya Michel, *The Jewish Woman in America* (New York: Plume, 1975), 235–61.

14. J. Allen, *500 Great Jewish Jokes* (New York: Signet, 1990), 21.

15. In the Jewish Video Archives of the Jewish Museum, New York. The Radner sequence is undated on a compilation of Jewish-oriented material drawn from *Saturday Night Live*. She appeared on *Saturday Night Live* between 1975 and 1980, and in 1978 introduced her Rhonda Weiss character. See chapter 7 for a fuller discussion of Radner's work as the JAP.

16. Wendy Wasserstein, *The Sisters Rosenzweig* (New York: Harcourt, Brace and Co., 1993).

17. Sequoia, *JAP Handbook* (New York: Plume, 1982) 8, 11. She uses the term "JAP" to describe either a male or female, that is, a prince or a princess.

18. The classic antisemitic stereotypes of European Jewish women focus on her as "exotic" or highly sexualized, or sexually victimized by brutal Cossacks. This New World inversion, within Jewish American culture, is particularly striking. See Susan Weidman Schneider, *Jewish and Female: Choices and Changes in Our Life Today* (New York: Simon and Schuster, 1984), 297–98; Harley Erdman, *Staging the Jew: The Performance of an American Ethnicity, 1860–1920* (New Brunswick: Rutgers University Press, 1997). Some of the most famous Jewish actresses, such as Sarah Bernhardt (though ultimately a convert to Catholicism) embodied that sexuality.

19. Verbal communication, Jay Broadbar, 1994.

20. This joke is taken from the cut of an album "jokes," performed by Two Live Jews in 1991. At the height of charges of obscenity against the Rap group Two Live Crew, these men used a rap format to create a parody of both the group and the attack on their music. Their joke cut drew on familiar Jewish jokes. Thanks to Daniel May for the recording.

21. Included in an article by Susan W. Schneider, "In a Coma! I Thought She Was Jewish: Some Truths and Some Speculations about Jewish Women and Sex," *Lilith* (Spring–Summer 1979): 5.

22. Jokes from Joan Rivers, "What Becomes a Semi-Legend Most?" N. D., Geffen Productions, and Noble Works cards.

23. Anna Sequoia and Patty Brown, *The Official J.A.P. Paper Doll Book* (New York: New American Library, 1983).

24. Julie Baumgold, "The Persistence of the Jewish American Princess," *New York* 4 (March 22, 1971): 26.

25. Baumgold, "Jewish American Princess," 26.

26. Leslie Tonner, "The Truth about Being a Jewish Princess," *Cosmopolitan* (September 1976): 212.

27. Leslie Tonner, *Nothing but the Best: The Luck of the Jewish Princess* (New York: Coward, McCann and Geoghegan, 1975), xi–xii.

28. Tonner, *Nothing but the Best*, 49–51, 87, 98, 101–5, 108–12.

29. Sequoia, *JAP Handbook*, 8.

30. William Vogeler, "O. C. Judge Pulled from Case for 'Princess' Remark." *Los Angeles Daily Journal*, January 11, 1987, p. 1.

31. See Shirley Frondorf, *The Death of a Jewish Princess: The True Story of a Victim on Trial* (New York: Villard Press, 1988); Elisa New, "Killing the Princess: The Offense of a Bad Defense," *Tikkun* (March/April 1988). The book and New's review counterpose different interpretations of the Steinbergs.

32. Baumgold, "Jewish American Princess," 26.

32. Sequoia, *JAP Handbook*, 10.

34. Dan Greenburg, *How to Be a Jewish Mother: A Very Lovely Training Manual* (Los Angeles: Price/Sloan/Stern Publishers, 1965).

35. Sequoia, *JAP Handbook*, 20, 21.

36. "A School-Girl's Stratagem," *Harper's Bazaar* 13 (July 31, 1880): 490.

37. Sander Gilman argues that, in contrast with Germany where Jews personified difference, in the United States their difference was one among many and complicated the experience of difference. *Jewish Self-Hatred: Anti-Semitism and the Hidden Language of the Jews.* (Baltimore: Johns Hopkins University Press, 1986), 316.

38. See Phyllis Pease Chock, "The Landscape of Enchantment: Redaction in a Theory of Ethnicity," *Cultural Anthropology* 4 (May 1989): 163–81 for a discussion of how American ethnicity is theorized in terms of difference and the marketplace.

39. Baumgold, "Jewish American Princess," 26.

40. Sequoia, *JAP Handbook*, 12.

41. "The Jewish American Princess: Archetype or Stereotype," *Jewish Frontier* (March 1984): 12–13.

42. See Riv-Ellen Prell, "Why Jewish Princesses Don't Sweat: Desire and Consumption in Post War American Jewish Culture," *People of the Body: Jews and Judaism From An Embodied Perspective,* ed. Howard Eilbgerg-Schwartz (New York: State University of New York Press, 1992), 329–60.

43. Nora Ephron, *Heartburn* (New York: Knopf, 1983).

44. Zena Smith Blau entitled an article about the greater likelihood of Jewish boys to be encouraged over Jewish girls, "The Jewish Prince: Some Continuities in Traditional and Contemporary Life." Her evocation of the notion of Prince in the late 1970s was clearly a defensive response to the JAP stereotype as it was articulated particularly by Jewish novelists. *Contemporary Jewry* 3 (Spring 1977): 55–71.

45. Daniel Boyarin, *Unheroic Conduct: The Rise of Heterosexuality and the Invention of the Jewish Man* (Berkeley: University of California Press, 1997); Sander Gilman, *The Jew's Body* (New York: Routledge Press, 1991).

46. See Mary Douglas for the classic analysis of category ambiguity, *Purity and Danger* (London: Routledge and Kegan Paul, 1966).

47. See Sara Evans, *Born for Liberty: A History of Women in America* (New York: Free Press 1989).

48. Barry Kosmin, et al., *Highlights of the CJF 1990 National Jewish Population Survey* (New York: Council of Jewish Federations).

49. See Sylvia Barack Fishman, *A Breath of Life: Feminism in the American Jewish Community* (New York: Free Press, 1993) for a discussion of the impact of Jewish feminism on American Jewish life.

50. See Beth S. Wenger, "The Politics of Women's Ordination: Jewish Law, Institutional Power, and the Debate over Women in the Rabbinate," *Tradition Renewed: A History of JTS,* vol. II, ed. Jack Wertheimer (New York: The Jewish Theological Seminary of America, 1997), 483–523; Jack Wertheimer, *A People Divided: Judaism in Contemporary America* (New York: Basic Books, 1993), 15–150; Paula Hyman, "Ezrat Nashim and the Emergence of a New Jewish Feminism," *The Americanization of the Jews,* eds. Robert M. Sletzer and Norman J. Cohen (New York: New York University Press, 1995).

51. See, for example, Schneider, *Jewish and Female;* Letty Pogrebin, *Deborah, Golda and Me: Being Female and Jewish in America* (New York: Crown Publishers, 1991). Not surprisingly, Nora Gold's study of Canadian Jewish women demonstrated that those who considered themselves feminists were far more critical of the term "JAP" than nonfeminists. "Canadian Jewish Women and Their Experience of Antisemitism and Sexism: Results from Phase One." Halbert Centre for Canadian Studies at Hebrew University, Occasional Paper 21.

52. Sidney Goldstein, "American Jewry, 1970: A Demographic Profile," *American Jewish Yearbook* 72 (1971), 3–88.

53. Chapter 5 details differences between generations of Jewish men in terms of professionalization.

54. Marshall Sklare with Joseph Greenblum, *Jewish Identity on the Suburban Frontier: A Study of Group Survival in the Open Society,* 2d ed. (Chicago: University of Chicago Press. 1979 [originally 1967]), 25–26.

55. Judith R. Kramer and Seymour Leventman, *Children of the Gilded Ghetto: Conflict Resolutions of Three Generations of American Jews* (New Haven: Yale University Press, 1961).

56. See Elaine Tyler May, *Homeward Bound: American Families in the Cold War Era* (New York: Basic Books, 1989) for a discussion of suburban consumption.

57. Barbara Ehrenreich, *Fear of Falling: The Inner Life of the Middle Class* (New York: Pantheon Books, 1989); Sherry Ortner, "Reading America: Preliminary Notes on Class and Culture," *Recapturing Anthropology: Working in the Present,* ed. Richard G. Fox (New Mexico: School of American Research Press, 1991), 163–90.

58. *Private Benjamin,* 1980, Warner Bros.

59. *Crossing Delancey,* 1988, Warner Bros.

60. *Dirty Dancing,* 1987, Vestron Films. See Sonya Michel, "Jews, Gender, American Cinema," *Feminist Perspectives on Jewish Studies,* ed. Lynn Davidman and Shelly Tenenbaum (New Haven: Yale University Press, 1994) for an insightful discussion of *Dirty Dancing.* I believe that Michel "overreads" the patriarchal perspective of the film by not noting that the relationship will end in the summer and that the young woman will go onto her own college life and class advantages.

61. *Baby It's You,* 1982, Paramount Home Video.

62. Susan Faludi, *Backlash: The Undeclared War Against American Women* (New York: Doubleday, 1991).

63. Moshe Hartman and Harriet Hartman, *Gender Equality and American Jews* (Albany: State University of New York Press, 1996), 39, 42.

64. Hartman and Hartman, *Gender Equality and American Jews,* 50, 63, 65, 66, 87, 97, 101, 114, 234–35.

65. The 1957 data is derived from Sidney Goldstein, "American Jewry, 1970: A Demographic Profile." *American Jewish Yearbook* 72 (Philadelphia: Jewish Publication Society, 1970), 3–52. The 1990 data is derived from Sidney Goldstein, "Profile of American Jewry: Insights from the 1990 National Jewish Population Survey," *American Jewish Yearbook* 92 (Philadelphia: Jewish Publication Society, 1992), 77–176, and Barry

Chiswick, "Working and Family Life: The Experiences of Jewish Women in America" (unpublished manuscript).

66. Hartman and Hartman, *Gender Equality and American Jews*, 137. They argue, following "human capital theory," that men's human capital is raised because of support provided to them by family. These men marry later.

67. Hartman and Hartman, *Gender Equality and American Jews*, 118, 120, 142.

68. Hartman and Hartman, *Gender Equality and American Jews*, 194.

69. Sylvia Barack Fishman discusses the impact of these changes on several arenas of Jewish women's lives including religion and voluntary organizations. *A Breath of Life*.

70. In 1998, the *Wall Street Journal* featured a story on a new Girl Scout badge, "Fashion Adventure Program," which requires shopping at the Limited Too, its corporate sponsor. Consumption as American and Jewish are clearly joined in the JAP image. "Seeking Adventure, Girl Scouts Hike to the Mall," August 17, 1998, B1–B3. Thanks to Lucy and Mark Fischer for showing me this article.

71. Philip Wylie, *Generation of Vipers*, 2d ed. (New York: Holt, Rinehart and Winston, 1960, [originally 1955], 49.

72. Wylie, *Generation of Vipers*, 52.

73. Sander Gilman develops the notion of Jews' secret language in *Jewish Self-Hatred*, 18. Gilman notes in a variety of cultures and contexts that the Jews' secret language differentiates them and shows their incomplete and inadequate acculturation that often threatens members of the dominant culture. That the language of consumption should turn out to be the "secret language" of American Jews is consistent with their mode of acculturation and the dangers of consumption long held by a number of American thinkers.

CHAPTER 7: TALKING BACK THROUGH COUNTER-REPRESENTATION

1. The tradition of Jewish women comediennes and singers who challenge middle-class propriety and modesty stretches back from Fanny Brice and Sophie Tucker beginning in the 1910s and 1920s throughout the century. They include such figures as Belle Barth, Totie Fields, Joan Rivers, and Bette Midler, among others. Similarly, outspoken political activists from Emma Goldman to Bella Abzug have been consistently associated with challenging norms as Jewish women.

2. Philip Roth, *Portnoy's Complaint* (New York: Random House, 1969).

3. For a discussion of Jewish feminism see notes 49 and 50, chapter 6.

4. Anthropologist Keith Basso discussed the danger of reproducing stereotypes in social interaction in *Portraits of the Whiteman: Linguistic Play and Culture among the Western Apache* (Cambridge: Cambridge University Press, 1997).

5. Sander Gilman, *Jewish Self-Hatred: Anti-Semitism and the Hidden Language of the Jews* (Baltimore: Johns Hopkins University Press, 1989).

6. I analyzed these novels in "Cinderellas Who (Almost) Never Become Princesses: Subversive Representations of Jewish Women in Post War Popular Novels," *Talking Back: Images of Jewish Women in American Popular Culture*, ed. Joyce Antler (Hanover: Brandeis University Press, 1997), 123–38.

7. The classic work of this genre of sexual liberation, coming of age, and Jewishness is Erica Jong's *Fear of Flying* (New York: Holt, Rinehart and Winston, 1973). Jong's protagonist is, however, married, and that creates different tensions and issues for the character. Alix Kate Shulman's *Memoirs of an Ex Prom Queen: A Novel* (New York: Knopf, 1972) also deployed these themes with a married protagonist.

8. These novels, then, might well be read as a comic social realism created by middle-class feminists describing newly liberated sexuality and the challenge of a variety of new freedoms. One reviewer for *Booklist*, for example, characterized *The Girl That He Marries* as "another of those acutely observed and insistently comic novels in the tradition of Jong, Parent, and Drexler" 72 (May 1976): 1242. Another reviewer for *Publishers Weekly* described the book as "very much for the same market that loved *Fear of Flying*, this tackles virtually every aspect of the sexual encounter scene and proves that getting what you think you want isn't always the answer" "Forecasts" (May 1976): 55. While these mainstream press reviewers recognize the Jewish types that populate the novels—Jewish Mothers and Jewish Princesses chiefly—they place the novels within a comic feminist genre.

9. Ann Barr Snitow argued in her article about women novelists writing from 1969 to 1979 that they have been reluctant to write about sex. When they began to do so it was within the realist genre. She asserted that women writers, to a far greater extent than men, linked sexuality to social reality. "The Front Line: Notes on Sex in Novels by Women 1969–1979," *Signs: A Journal of Women, Culture and Society* 5 (Summer 1980): 702–18. It is striking the extent to which these eight novels fit into Snitow's model. They are largely works of realism, and in their location of these women's experience of sex within inter- and intra-personal relations they nicely illustrate her point.

10. Susan Lukas, *Fat Emily* (New York: Stein and Day, 1974).

11. Louise Rose Blecher, *The Launching of Barbara Fabrikant* (New York: David McKay, 1974).

12. Blecher, *Barbara Fabrikant*, 37.

13. Gail Parent, *Sheila Levine Is Dead and Living in New York* (New York: G. P. Putnam's Sons, 1972).

14. Marie Brenner, *Tell Me Everything* (New York: Dutton, 1976).

15. Brenner, *Tell Me Everything*, 29. In the eighth novel that I do not mention in this text–Sandra Harmon, *A Girl Like Me* (New York: Dutton, 1975)–the character, who is the product of the working class, overcomes her physical differences through plastic surgery, but among wealthy women realizes that she can never be as thin as they are, and cannot play tennis or exhibit other skills that would mark her as wealthy. She bitterly learned that she might please an affluent lover, but she did not belong in his world.

16. Blecher, *Barbara Fabrikant*, 11.

17. Myrna Blythe, *Cousin Suzanne* (New York: Mason/Charter, 1975).

18. Blythe, *Cousin Suzanne*, 36–37.

19. Mikhal Bakhtin, *Rabelais and His World*, trans. Helen Tsivolsky (Cambridge, Mass.: MIT Press, 1968), 321, 318. He examined the "grotesque body" to demonstrate changing ideas about the body in European novels from the Renaissance to later periods when fat, gluttony, and pleasure were rendered unacceptable.

20. Feminist scholarship, particularly in media studies, has offered a sophisticated analysis of how the camera constructs women in twentieth-century United States culture. The extent to which women can see as well as be seen is raised by this scholarship as well. These novels predate that scholarship, but share with it a consciousness of women as objects rather than subjects. The device of the gaze in these works, including the camera, appears to heighten self-consciousness and distance the narrator from herself. The gaze often incorporates the point of view of the other, the source of love. In this sense these novels are like other forms of media that feminist scholars examined in film and television criticism. See Teresa De Lauretis, *Alice Doesn't: Feminism, Semiotics, Cinema* (Bloomington: Indiana University Press, 1984). For an analysis of the gaze and race see bell hooks, *Black Looks: Race and Representation* (Boston: South End Press, 1992).

21. Parent, *Shelia Levine*, 49–50.

22. Lukas, *Fat Emily*.

23. Gail Parent, *David Meyer Is a Mother* (New York: Harper and Row, 1976).

24. Rhoda Lerman, *The Girl That He Marries* (New York: Holt, Rinehart and Winston, 1976), 127–28.

25. Herman Wouk's *Marjorie Morningstar* (New York: Doubleday and Company, 1955) and Philip Roth's Brenda Patimkin of *Goodbye Columbus* (Boston: Houghton Mif-

flin, 1989 [originally 1959]), have been the subject of Jewish feminist critiques for decades now, first and foremost in Charlotte Baum, Paula Hyman, and Sonya Michel, *The Jewish Woman in America* (New York: Plume, 1975).

26. *Marjorie Morningstar*, 1959, Beechwald. *Goodbye, Columbus*, 1969, Paramount Pictures.

27. Wouk, *Marjorie Morningstar*, 429–30. New Rochelle is a New York suburb.

28. Wouk's book was the top selling work of fiction that year. In her analysis of the best-selling books, Elizabeth Long argues that *Marjorie Morningstar* can be read as tragedy. Children go astray because of an overly rapid climb up the social ladder by parents. The children are left placeless. For Long, the book signals the beginning of a more "complex understanding of social mobility" which is apparent in themes of best-sellers by the end of the 1950's. Elizabeth Long, The American Dream and the Popular Novel (New York: Routledge and Kegan Paul, 1989), 90. Despite its popularity, *Marjorie Morningstar* did receive criticism from the Jewish press. Herman Wouk's own observance of orthodox Judaism did not spare him from some critics who were appalled by the lack of positive Jewish characters in the novel. See, for example, Allen G. Field, "The Strange Case of Mr. Wouk," *Jewish Spectator* 21 (January 1956): 28–30. On the other hand, Marie Syrkin's review of American Jewish literature written in the early 1960s noted that what was remarkable about Marjorie was her role as "a representative American character rather than as a quaint, sinister or romantic alien figure." Marjorie's world replicated the non-Jewish world. "Jewish Awareness in American Literature," *The American Jew: A Reappraisal,* ed. Oscar I. Janowsky (Philadelphia: The Jewish Publication Society of America, 1964), 211–34. *Time* magazine made a similar point in its 1955 article on Herman Wouk. The cover featured Wouk against an artist's rendition of Marjorie (September 1955: p. 48).

29. Wouk self-consciously gave Noel an anglicized version of the Yiddish cultural "type," the *Luftsmensch* or "airman" who cannot support his family or make a steady living.

30. Roth's choice of a poor African American child as the only one "freed" from the demands of American culture with whom Neil can identify is certainly worthy of note. Typical identification between white men and black men often turns on power and sexuality. Roth seemed to create the opposite connection.

31. Barbara Ehrenreich suggests that this was a perspective articulated in *Playboy* and other publications during this period. Women were blamed for their economic dependence on men at a time when only men were expected to work. See Barbara Ehrenreich, *The Hearts of Men: American Men and the Flight from Commitment* (New York: Anchor Books, 1983).

32. Wouk, *Marjorie Morningstar*, 172. Paul Cowan's *An Orphan in History: Retrieving a Jewish Legacy* describes his own anxiety about the Shirley in terms of his reluctance to be involved with Jewish women (New York: Doubleday, 1982, pp. 110-13).

33. Both stories associate Judaism with the mother, her membership in Jewish organizations and her concern for her daughter's endogamous marriage. Mrs. Patimkin is portrayed as particularly vacuous. When Neil mentions Martin Buber she can only think to ask what his denomination is. These novels grew in tandem with the comic Jewish Mother explored in Riv-Ellen Prell, "Rage and Representation: Jewish Gender Stereotypes in American Jewish Culture" *Uncertain Terms: Negotiating Gender in American Culture*, eds. Faye Ginsberg and Anna Lownhaupt Tsing (Boston: Beacon Press, 1990), 248-68, and G. Rothbell, "The Jewish Mother: Social Construction of a Popular Image," *The Jewish Family: Myths and Realities*, eds. Steven Cohen and Paula Hyman (New York: Holmes and Meier, 1986), 118-30. Sons, then, refuse both fathers and mothers through their daughters.

34. *Saturday Night Live* appeared on television just a year following the premier of *Rhoda* (played by Valerie Harper), a television series on CBS featuring a Jewish woman character. Rhoda had been a character on the Mary Tyler Moore series. She was the "loser" foil to Mary Tyler Moore's always upbeat personality. However, she was the comic to Moore's straight woman. Rhoda, a hard-working, low-paid window dresser, was anything but a Jewish American Princess. She, like the characters of the popular novels who appeared when she was on the Mary Tyler Moore show, personified the "loser" with anxieties about attractiveness. The presence of Radner and Miner as Jewish characters in popular television venues marks this period as one often characterized as dominated by resurgent (white) ethnicity. At the same time, the tiny number of "types" for Jewish women characters speaks not only to the limits of television, but to the cultural limits on the representations of American Jewish women. See Joyce Antler, "Epilogue: Jewish Women on Television, Too Jewish or Not Enough?" *Talking Back: Images of Jewish Women in American Popular Culture*, ed. Joyce Antler (Hanover: Brandeis University Press, 1997), 242-52.

35. *Saturday Night Live*, First Five Years. From the collection of the Jewish Video Archive, the Jewish Museum of New York City.

36. *Saturday Night Live*, First Five Years. From the collection of the Jewish Video Archive, the Jewish Museum of New York City.

37. In chapter 6 I discussed another famous Rhonda Weiss sketch, a commercial for "Jewess Jeans." In this work, the character also lampoons consumption and its "Jewishness."

38. Doug Hill and Jeff Weingrad, *Saturday Night: A Backstage History of Saturday Night Live* (New York: Vintage Books, 1987), 263.

39. Frank Rich used the terms *acts of provocation* to describe the works of art exhibited at the Jewish Museum's 1996 exhibit, "Too Jewish: Challenging Traditional Identities." "The Too Jewish Question," *New York Times*, March 16, 1996, p. 21.

40. For two thoughtful discussions of Jews and multiculturalism see "Introduction: The Dialectic of Jewish Enlightenment," *Insider/Outsider: American Jews and Multiculturalism*, eds., David Bial, Michael Galchinsky, and Susannah Heschel (Berkeley: University of California Press, 1998), and "Introduction: Multiculturalism, Jews, and Democracy: Situating the Discussion," *The Narrow Bridge: Jewish Views on Multiculturalism*, ed. Marla Brettschneider (New Brunswick: Rutgers University Press, 1996).

41. Lieberman's work is included in the catalog *Too Jewish? Challenging Traditional Identities*, ed. Norman L. Kleeblatt (New Brunswick: Rutgers University Press, 1996), 23. For a particularly insightful discussion of Sandra Bernhard see Ann Pellegrini, "You Make Me Feel (Mighty Real): Sandra Bernhard's Whiteface," *Performance Anxieties: Staging Psychoanalysis Staging Race* (New York: Routledge, 1997), 49–66.

42. Thanks to Deborah Appleman for a helpful conversation about Sandra Bernhard.

43. This window was designed when George Bush was President of the United States, thus it was also an irreverent play on the First Lady's name. Kleeblatt, *Too Jewish?*, 142.

44. Rhonda Lieberman explored some of these same themes in two witty essays on a character she calls Jewish Barbie. She creates the rocky road adventures of Jewish Barbie, who was separated from the famous Barbie at their creation. Lieberman details Jewish Barbie's inability to make contact with the "real" Barbie, who rebuffs her and her life path as student, model, embattled daughter, and finally mystic. Lieberman draws on many of the same themes in these essays that one sees in her art. "Je M'Appelle Barbie," *Artforum International* (March 1995): 21–22. "Goys and Dolls," *Artforum International* (April 1995): 21–22.

45. Kleeblatt, *Too Jewish?*, 141.

46. Jews light a candle for each of the eight nights commemorated on the festival.

47. Kleeblatt, *Too Jewish?*, x.

48. The exhibit featured many works of gay artists, some of which reflected on a gay Jewish identity.

49. Kleeblatt, *Too Jewish?*, 144.

50. Linda Nochlin, "Forward: The Couturier and the Hasid," *Too Jewish?*. ed. Norman Kleeblatt, xvii-xx.

APPENDIX

1. In addition to my own reading of the press I have drawn on the following secondary sources to illumine the Yiddish press: Irving Howe, *World of Our Fathers: The Journey of the East European Jews to America and the Life They Found and Made* (New York: Touchstone, 1976), 522-24; Jud L. Teller, *Strangers and Natives: The Evolution of the American Jew from 1921 to the Present* (New York: Delta, 1968), 19-60; Ronald Sanders, *The Downtown Jews: Portraits of an Immigrant Generation* (New York: Dover, 1987 [originally 1969]), 97-125, 148-80; Mordecai Soltes, *The Yiddish Press: An Americanizing Agency* (New York: Teachers College, Columbia University, 1924); Moses Rischin, *The Promised City: New York's Jews, 1870-1914* (Cambridge, Mass.: Harvard University Press, 1962).

2. An analysis of the *Forward's* woman's page in 1919 may be found in Maxine S. Seller, "Defining Socialist Womanhood: The Women's Page of the *Jewish Daily Forward* in 1919," *American Jewish History* 76 (1987): 416-38.

3. Arthur Goren, "The Jewish Press," *The Ethnic Press in the United States: An Historical Analysis and Handbook*, ed. Sally Miller (New York: Greenwood Press, 1987), 202-28. Goren's article also discusses the Yiddish press.

4. Its entire run was from 1928 to 1932.

5. Its entire run was from 1906 to 1963.

6. An analysis of the content of the *American Hebrew* in the late nineteenth and early twentieth centuries may be found in Yedhezkel Wsyzkowsi, "The American Hebrew: An Exercise in Ambivalence," *American Jewish History* 76 (1987): 341-53.

Acknowledgments

In the seven years of research and writing this book I have been deeply touched by the generosity of many colleagues, friends, and institutions, and it is a great pleasure to be able to acknowledge them.

The research for this book was supported in several ways by the University of Minnesota, my academic home. A Bush sabbatical supplement, a McKnight summer award, research funding from the Graduate School, teaching leaves from the College of Liberal Arts, and summer support from the Graduate School provided essential assistance. A Sol Center Research grant from the Program in Jewish Studies was a further source of funding. My research at the American Jewish Archive was supported by a Rapoport Fellowship in American Jewish Studies for research and writing. The Lucius Littauer Foundation provided me a grant in the final year to complete my work.

One of the great pleasures of this process has been working with a number of graduate students who served as my research assistants. I am first indebted to Matt Sobek of the University of Minnesota's Department of History who helped me to analyze data from 1910 U.S. Census Bureau Public Use Sample, and who did early runs on the 1920 census in a project just underway in 1996. Matt's patience and clarity were remarkable, and I appreciated his willingness to educate me.

I was helped with a variety of research tasks by Mary Ann Dickar, Jason Loviglio, Alex Lubin, Julia Mickenberg, Karen Murphy, and Steve Waksman. Rachel Buff thoroughly reviewed a wide number of sources, produced bibliographies, and talked with me at great length about issues of ethnicity, race, and gender. These conversations were a rewarding and important part of this process. Finally, Jonathan Munby spent a year carefully reviewing the *Forward*'s English pages, tracking down the plots of 1920s silent films, and analyzing Jewish research on occupations and wages with such intelligence and enthusaism that I felt very fortunate to work with him. Long after he was heading up his own American Studies program in England, I benefited from charts and thoughtful comments and observations that he had carefully produced.

I am particularly indebted to the libraries and archives where I worked and the archivists and librarians who helped me there. The New York Public Library's Jewish Division is testimony to a public commitment to knowledge. Its range and depth of sources were crucial to my work. YIVO's library was also a wonderful resource for me. I am deeply grateful to Zachary Baker, who found me very interesting sources, answered many questions in person and online, and always directed me to the people could help me most. At the Ratner Center for the Study of Conservative Judaism archive at the Jewish Theological Seminary, I was helped by its director, Professor Jack Wertheimer, and its archivist, Julie Miller, who directed me to sermons that were useful. I appreciated Ellen Smith's help at the Jewish Historical Society, where I found useful material as well. The Jewish Video Archive of the Jewish Museum provided a treasury of wonderful material. Finally, the American Jewish Archive and the libraries of Hebrew Union College–Jewish Institute of Religion were also a remarkable source. the Archive's former director, Abraham Peck, and archivist, Kevin Proffitt, were generous with their time and assistance. The month that I spent there at the beginning of the project was immensely helpful.

I appreciated the opportunity to work with Susan Worst at Beacon Press. I missed her presence in the final stage of the book's completion, but that in no way diminished the importance of her role. Thanks to Amy Caldwell who edited the final manuscript and dealt with the last stages of publication.

I have relied on many colleagues for help with this project, particularly because it required me to work with historical sources for the first time. I would especially like to acknowledge Jonathan Sarna's help for the last several years. Before I met him he was kind enough to write to me at length about the American Jewish Archive just as he left Hebrew Union College to move to a new position at Brandeis University. Over the years he has answered more questions than I wish to remember, and even when he did not agree with some of my leaps and interpretations, he has remained always ready to respond to yet another question.

I have presented portions of this work in a variety of settings. I want to particularly thank colleagues in Jewish Studies at the University of Washington, the Center for Judaic Studies at the University of Pennsylvania, a Melton Center conference at Hebrew University in Jerusalem, a Hebrew Union College conference, the Mayan Research Network, the Comparative Women's History Workshop at the University of Minnesota, and at the American Studies Association and the Association for Jewish Studies, for hard questions and lively debate.

The following colleagues have read various chapters and portions of this book, and all of them, fully engaged in their own projects and lives, took the time to reflect thoughtfully and helpfully on my work. I am very appreciative of the efforts of Isa Aron, Joyce Antler, Lee Bernstein, David Biale, Ann Braude, Rachel Buff, Janet Burstein, Lisa Collins, Steven Cohen, Maria Damon, Nan Enstad, Lila Foldes, Amy Kaminsky, Barbara Kirshenblatt-Gimblett, Jason Loviglio, Carol Miller, Deborah Dash Moore, David Noble, Cheri Register, David Roediger, Jeffrey Rubin-Dorsky, Naomi Scheman, Howard Schwartz, Judy Smith, Beth Wenger, and Stephen Whitfield.

I was very fortunate to have the entire manuscript read by Sara Evans, Steven Foldes, Laura Levitt, Lary May, Elaine Tyler May, and Miriam Peskowitz. Their comments were all exceptionally helpful and clarifying, and imagined directions for this work that I hope I will realize at some point in the future. I was unable to accomplish all that each of them hoped for this book, but the process of writing was enriched for me by their responses and their own scholarship.

I would also like to thank family and friends for their care and concern over the years of working on this book. My many research visits to New York were made all the more wonderful by the friends who shared their homes, meals, and time with me. Barbara Noble and Elizabeth and Kate McNamara, Faye Ginsburg and Fred and Samantha Myers, and especially Marge Goldwater were always the high points of each visit.

Howard Schwartz believed in this book long before I did. In a panel we organized together about the intersection of Jewish Studies and Anthropology for the American Anthropological Association I tried out these ideas for the first time. For years we discussed and debated the role of gender and culture in Jewish life. Though the subjects of our work were separated by seventeen centuries, we never failed to find common cause and sometimes conflict over a wide range of ideas. This collegial friendship has been one of my life's blessings.

I have probably spent hundreds of hours discussing issues about Jewish men and women in novels, films, and in people's lives with my friend Sylvia Kaplan. The conversations were reward enough, but in addition much of what we have discussed has formed the backdrop to this work.

Isa Aron has been an extraordinary friend to me for nearly twenty-five years. Her willingness to read my work no matter what the demands on her time has always touched me deeply. But more importantly, she remains one of my most important models of a person of great balance in all areas of her life, and my life has been so much the richer for all that we have shared and that she has taught me.

My debt to Sara Evans and Elaine Tyler May is difficult to express. They have read many, many versions of this book. In person over coffee, and electronically while Elaine was in Ireland for a Fulbright professorship, and when Sara has been in various locations, they have always had new suggestions, and offered endless support. I have relied on them very heavily to help teach me how to think a little more like an historian, and they have been enthusiastic and generous in this task. Our friendship for more than two decades has allowed us to weave together our scholarship, teaching, families, and life changes in ways that I have always understood to be a special gift.

My extended family has been a loving context for my life. My father Samuel Prell, my brother Joel Prell, and my cousin Marian Weissman have given to me so generously in so many ways. My in-laws George and Valerie Foldes have been a very important part of my life, and their ongoing interest in this project meant more to me than they would have guessed.

My daughters Lila and Livia Foldes have grown from children to young women over the course of this project. During my first year of research, spent partially at the American Jewish Archive, I photocopied 1920s fashions and interesting headlines for them from the Anglo-Jewish press. Over the last few months, as fourteen- and nineteen-year-olds, they have read various portions of the book, offered opinions on phrases and illustrations, and cheered me on whenever my spirits flagged. Their love, sardonic senses of humor, and considerable demands on my time are all very much a part of this work. Their unique and wonderful lives never cease to fill me with awe.

This project, as with every other in my life, is inseparable from my relationship to my husband, Steven Foldes. For many years he has been a wonderful respondent to the issues I tried to puzzle out in this book. His questions were always incisive and led to clearer thinking. In the last months of the project he did double duty by reading the book from end to end after his own long work days. He edited, cajoled, redrafted tables, and asked me to think again about what I had been sure was already sufficient. How he manages to do all of this with unfailing love and extraordinary kindness has remained a mystery and a blessing for me for nearly thirty years.

Index